W9-BQT-174

THE
BOOK
OF
SIGNS

31 UNDENIABLE PROPHECIES
OF THE APOCALYPSE

STUDY GUIDE | THIRTY-ONE LESSONS

DR. DAVID JEREMIAH

W Publishing Group

AN IMPRINT OF THOMAS NELSON

To Makiah, Love Mom
Covid Pandemic 2020 - ?

Published in Nashville, Tennessee, by W Publishing Group, an imprint of Thomas Nelson. W Publishing Group and Thomas Nelson are registered trademarks of HarperCollins Christian Publishing, Inc.

Published in association with Yates & Yates, www.yates2.com.

All Scripture quotations, unless otherwise noted, are taken from the New King James Version. Copyright © 1982 by Thomas Nelson. Used by permission. All rights reserved.

Scripture quotations marked CEV are taken from the Contemporary English Version. Copyright © 1995 American Bible Society. Used by permission. All rights reserved.

Scripture quotations marked NASB are taken from the New American Standard Bible®, Copyright © 1960, 1962, 1963, 1968, 1971, 1972, 1973, 1975, 1977, 1995 by The Lockman Foundation. Used by permission.

Scripture quotations marked NIV are taken from The Holy Bible, New International Version®, NIV® Copyright © 1973, 1978, 1984, 2011 by Biblica, Inc.® Used by permission. All rights reserved worldwide.

Thomas Nelson titles may be purchased in bulk for educational, business, fundraising, or sales promotional use. For information, please email SpecialMarkets@ThomasNelson.com.

ISBN 978-0-310-10972-3

Printed in the United States of America

HB 08.13.2020

Contents

PART 4: TRIBULATION SIGNS

PART 5: END SIGNS

How to Use This Study Guide

The purpose of this study guide is to reinforce Dr. David Jeremiah's dynamic, in-depth teaching and to aid you in applying biblical truth to your daily life. This study guide is designed to be used in conjunction with *The Book of Signs* by Dr. David Jeremiah, but it may also be used by itself for personal or group study.

STRUCTURE OF THE LESSONS

Each lesson is based on the corresponding chapter in *The Book of Signs* and focuses on specific passages in the Bible. Each lesson is composed of the following elements:

- **Outline:** The outline at the beginning of the lesson gives a clear, concise picture of the topic being studied and will provide a helpful framework for you as you go through Dr. Jeremiah's teaching or read the book.

- **Overview:** The overview summarizes Dr. Jeremiah's teaching on the passage being studied in the lesson. You should refer to the Scripture passages in your own Bible as you study the overview. Unless otherwise indicated, Scripture verses quoted are taken from the New King James Version.

- **Application:** This section contains a variety of individual and group discussion questions designed to help you dig deeper into the lesson and the Scriptures and to apply the lesson to your daily life. For Bible study groups or Sunday school classes, these questions will provide a springboard for group discussion and interaction.

- **Did You Know?** This section presents a fascinating fact, historical note, or insight that adds a point of interest to the preceding lesson.

PERSONAL STUDY

The lessons in this study guide were created to help you gain fresh insights into God's Word and develop new perspectives on topics you may have previously studied. Each lesson is designed to challenge your thinking and help you grow in your knowledge of Christ. During your study, it is our prayer that you will discover how biblical truth affects every aspect of your life and your relationship with Christ will be strengthened.

When you commit to completing this study guide, try to set apart a time, daily or weekly, to read through the lessons without distraction. Have your Bible nearby when you read the study guide, so you're ready to look up verses if you need to. If you want to use a notebook to write down your thoughts, be sure to have that handy as well. Take your time to think through and answer the questions. If you plan on reading the study guide with a small group, be sure to read ahead and be prepared to take part in the weekly discussions.

GROUP STUDY

The lessons in this study guide are suitable for Sunday school classes, small-group studies, elective Bible studies, or home Bible study groups. Each person in the group should have his or her own study guide. You may wish to complete the study guide lesson as homework prior to the meeting of the group and then use the meeting time to discuss the lesson. If you are a group leader, refer to the guide at the back of this book for additional instructions on how to set up and lead your group time.

FOR CONTINUING STUDY

For a complete listing of Dr. Jeremiah's materials for personal and group study, call 1-800-947-1993, go online to www.DavidJeremiah.org, or write to Turning Point, P.O. Box 3838, San Diego, CA 92163.

Dr. Jeremiah's *Turning Point* program is currently heard or viewed around the world on radio, television, and the Internet in English. Momento Decisivo, the Spanish translation of Dr. Jeremiah's messages, can be heard on radio in every Spanish speaking country in the world. The television broadcast is also broadcast by satellite throughout the Middle East with Arabic subtitles.

Contact Turning Point for radio and television program times and stations in your area, or visit our website at www.DavidJeremiah.org/stationlocator.

Note: This edition of *The Book of Signs Study Guide* is published by
Thomas Nelson and may differ slightly in content and format from
the editions published by Turning Point Ministries.

THE BOOK OF SIGNS

Imagine driving on a busy freeway in a large metropolitan area that is unknown to you. You've never been there before, and you are hopelessly lost. Now consider navigating those roadways without any signs—no indications of exits, street or city indicators, detours, or any other pertinent information. What a harrowing situation to be in!

We often take the placement and prevalence of signs for granted. Whether offered as information, invitation, or warning, each sign we encounter along a road is designed to help us move from where we are to where we want to be. In a similar manner, God has providentially placed a number of critical signs along the highway of human history. We often think of these signs as prophecies, and we have been made aware of them through the prophetic vehicle of God's Word.

However, it can be distressing and confusing to ascertain the true meaning behind all of these prophetic signs. That is why we have compiled this unique study guide called *The Book of Signs—31 Undeniable Prophecies of the Apocalypse*. The purpose of this study guide is to help you understand and discover your place in the great pattern of prophetic events foretold by God's prophets, written out in Scripture, and confirmed in the headlines of the day.

The thirty-one undeniable prophecies of the apocalypse can be thought of as a play that is told in five acts. Our story begins in act one with an examination of five nations and regions that will play important roles as the final events of the age emerge—specifically Israel, Europe, Russia, Babylon, and America. Scripture heralds the regathering of the Jewish people to their homeland as a precursor of the end times. This was materialized in 1948, and Israel will continue to play a grand part in this unfolding drama. The consolidation of power in Europe is an essential prelude to the coming of the Antichrist. The prophet Ezekiel speaks of a day when Russia will lead an alliance of nations to attack Israel. Babylon will rise once again as the rebuilt commercial capital of the world. And although America is not specifically mentioned in the Bible, it will play a pivotal role in many prophecies in regard to its alliances and its power.

As the story of the end-time events continues to unfold, we encounter several cultural signs in act two of what is to come—signs that are beginning to appear all around us even today. Daniel, Ezekiel, and Paul all warned that materialism would be a sign of the end times, and it can be easily asserted that materialism has become a virtue in our current culture. Immorality is also a sign of the times—is there any aspect of our society that has not been corrupted by moral decay? The rise of radical Islam will set the stage for the coming events found in Ezekiel 38–39. Spiritual warfare and Christian persecution will only increase and intensify as the end of the present age approaches. And, finally, there is a cultural threat that is ashamedly at hand— apathetic Christians who don't care about the signs of the times

In our third act of this saga, the story shifts upward as we begin to examine the heavenly signs of the end. This starts with the Rapture of the Church, as described by the apostle Paul in 1 Thessalonians 4:16. But that is only the beginning. The Rapture will immediately encompass the resurrection of dead believers and the transformation of living believers. At that point, Jesus will escort all of them to heaven. There in heaven, all the saints will experience the Judgment Seat of Christ, where rewards for faithful service will be handed out. After that, a praise and worship celebration unlike anything ever witnessed on earth will commence.

Following that heavenly scene, our play comes to the fourth act—the Tribulation. This is a seven-year period during which unspeakable horrors will be unleashed upon the world. The Tribulation features some of the most infamous characters in all of Scripture, including Satan, the Antichrist, and the False Prophet. Many martyrs will die in the name of Christ during this time, but even in the midst of this tragedy, heroes—such as the two witnesses and the 144,000—will shine like stars in a world of darkness. Everything will culminate in the Battle of Armageddon. By this time, the Dragon has appeared, and the mark of the Beast will have made its way around the world. As the rebellious nations of the world are gathered in full strength to destroy God's children once and for all, King Jesus returns in all of His glory.

This leads us to the last act in this cosmic drama. When Jesus returns on the clouds and forever defeats the enemies of God at the Battle of Armageddon, it sets into a Millennium of unprecedented peace on the earth. After that time, all the spiritually dead will stand before God at the Great White Throne Judgment. Then, the entire universe will be transformed by God's grace as a new heaven and a new earth emerge, forever establishing God's everlasting kingdom. When the final act ends and the curtain closes, eternity begins.

In the pages that follow, we will discover together what Scripture reveals about the signs of the times and the signs of God's prophetic plan—all the way to Paradise regained. Seeing these signs played out in the news, on television, and even in our own lives can create despair, anxiety, and confusion. But I am confident that understanding the signs presented in these five acts will help you live with confidence, hope, and a renewed sense of purpose.

The end times may be near, but as Christians, our future is secure and certain. Although we live in a chaotic world, we can be confident and at peace—for God is the author and sustainer of history—and the return of the Prince of Peace may be closer than we think.

PART I

INTERNATIONAL
SIGNS

Israel

GENESIS 12:1-3

In this lesson we discover why the nation of Israel is a sign to the world.

In the world of geo-eco-politics, it is not often that promises are kept over time. But a promise God made to Abraham more than 4,000 years ago is still in force. It is shaping our world today and will shape it even further as we approach the end of the age. God's promises are forever.

OUTLINE

I. An Unconditional Covenant

II. A Personal Covenant

III. A National Covenant

IV. A Territorial Covenant

V. A Reciprocal Covenant

VI. A Universal Covenant

VII. An Eternal Covenant

OVERVIEW

Most Israeli Jews, and many Jews living outside Israel, know someone who has been a victim of Palestinian terrorism in the Jewish homeland. Living with the prospect of death or injury due to Palestinian terrorism is a daily reality for Jews in Israel.

"Palestinians" is a generic term used to refer to Arabs who occupied the land of Palestine prior to 1948 and who were displaced when Israel was made a nation. Palestinians resent that displacement; they want their land back, and they want Israel to be erased from the map. They want Jews either to be killed or to leave their land and live elsewhere in the world. Acts of terrorism are their ongoing effort to attack Israel's right to exist.

Israel is a tiny, 9,000-square-mile island in a five-million-square-mile sea of Arab nations that surround her. Her status as a legally reformed nation has resulted in a constant state of vigilance against attacks. Thousands of Israelis have been killed by Palestinian (Islamic) terrorists, and thousands of Palestinians have died as a result of Israel's response to terror attacks. It is an ongoing conflict.

In recent years, Palestinians have gained the sympathy of the world because Israel has built settlements on two percent of West Bank (Arab) land to create a buffer zone against Palestinian attacks and to create civil order in an otherwise chaotic region. But Israel has never been the aggressor in Arab-Israeli conflicts. Israel has been willing to find a two-state solution, making concessions to the Palestinians, but her offers are always rejected because they include Israel's right to exist as a nation.

Israel is fighting for her very existence. The subtitle of an article by *World* magazine editor Marvin Olasky succinctly summarizes Israel's dilemma: "Slammed If You Do, Dead If You Don't." When Israel takes the tough but necessary measures to defend herself, she is slammed by world censure. If she fails to take those measures, she is attacked by hostile neighbors. In that article, Olasky filed this explanation of the impossible situation in which Israel finds herself today:

> The Holocaust's 6 million murders led to the creation of the Israeli state in 1948 and the willingness of Jews to fight for it against enormous odds. . . . The hardened men and women who founded the state of Israel and fought to defend it in the 1950s, 1960s, and 1970s, became known for saying, "Never again." Never again would they make it easy for mass killers. Never again would they go down without a fight.
>
> For several decades, non-Jewish Americans and Europeans understood that resolve. But then a generation grew up that did not know Adolf [Hitler]. Those without visceral awareness of the background saw Israelis not as victims trying to survive but as overlords

12

acting unjustly to poor Palestinians. Manipulators took the opportunity to re-package the old anti-Semitism as sympathy for an oppressed third-world population.[1]

Oppression and opposition to Jews is nothing new in world history. The descendants of Abraham were enslaved in Egypt for 400 years, then the ten northern tribes were captured by the Assyrians in 722 BC and the two southern tribes by the Babylonians in 586 BC. (Granted, these captivities were due to the Jews' sins.) Then Rome crushed the Jews in AD 70, dispersing them into the world where they lived for 1,878 years until the United Nations declared them a nation again in 1948. During the dispersion—the diaspora—more than six million Jews were exterminated by Hitler in the 1940s.

Only one factor can explain why the Jews still exist as a people and a nation: the promises of God. As God said through the prophet Ezekiel, He has preserved the Jews for His own name's sake: "'The nations shall know that I am the LORD,' says the Lord God, 'when I am hallowed *in you* before their eyes'" (Ezekiel 36:23, emphasis added). And through Isaiah God reminded the Jews that many of her hardships were discipline for her sins (Isaiah 40:2).

But discipline looks to a more righteous future. Why does God have a future for the Jews? Because of promises made to them in times past. The Jews represent a conundrum illustrated by the saying, "How odd of God, to choose the Jews."

It does seem odd from a human perspective. But there are two reasons God has preserved Israel as a nation: (1) because of a promise made to Abraham and (2) because of God's faithfulness to His Word. As we will see, nothing can cause God to break His promises to His people.

The promise made to Abraham began in Genesis 12:1–3 and was reaffirmed several times to Abraham as well as his son Isaac and grandson Jacob. Their descendants would be the inheritors of the promise God made to Abraham. Genesis 12:1–3 is a cornerstone, a foundational block of Scripture on which a right understanding of the Bible rests. To disregard the promises God made to the father of the Jewish people is to be confused about biblical eschatology.

There are seven features of God's promise (God's covenant) in Genesis 12:1–3 that serve as mileposts in the journey from Genesis to Revelation.

An Unconditional Covenant

When God says "I will" (five times in Genesis 12:1–3), that signifies an unconditional covenant. God is not asking Abraham to reciprocate; He is stating what He Himself will do for Abraham and his descendants. God confirmed the unconditional nature of this covenant in a unique ceremony in Genesis 15.

That ceremony was a common one in the ancient Near East. Sacrificial animals were cut in two and the parties to a covenant would walk between the pieces. They were saying, "May what happened to these animals happen to me if I break this covenant." But when God and Abraham conducted this ceremony, *God alone* walked between the pieces, taking full responsibility for the keeping of the covenant. This wasn't an agreement between equals; this was God promising to do something for Abraham and his descendants.

Paul Wilkinson notes that God alone signed and sealed the covenant, "since only He passed through the animal pieces. The inference drawn from Ancient Near Eastern custom is that in so doing, God invoked a curse upon Himself, should He ever break His promise."[2]

A Personal Covenant

God's promise to Abraham was personal: "I will bless you and make your name great" (Genesis 12:2). The personal pronouns "you" and "your" are used eleven times in verses 1–3. The promises have universal implications, but they began as personal promises to Abraham.

God directed Abraham to leave his home in Mesopotamia and settle in the rich and abundant land of Canaan (Exodus 3:8, 17; 13:5; 33:3). He prospered greatly and became wealthy with herds and servants (Genesis 14:14). The land of Canaan was promised to Abraham and his seed, a place where all his descendants could prosper as Abraham had done.

Abraham was revered in his own day as a powerful leader (Genesis 14:1–17) and is a pivotal figure in three world religions today: Judaism, Islam, and Christianity. The personal promise of the land to Abraham's descendants through Isaac and Jacob was never rescinded and remains in force today.

A National Covenant

Part of the promise to Abraham was that God would make a great nation from his descendants (Genesis 12:2). In spite of the millions of Jews who have been killed through the centuries, the Jews are indeed a great nation. Professor Amnon Rubinstein gives us an impressive summary of Israel's national achievements:

> Minute in size, not much bigger than a sliver of Mediterranean coastline, [Israel] has withstood continuing Arab onslaughts, wars, boycott and terrorism; it has turned itself from a poor, rural country, to an industrial and post-industrial powerhouse . . .

it has reduced social, educational and health gaps between . . . Arabs and Jews. Some of its achievements are unprecedented.[3]

A Territorial Covenant

Land—a homeland—was part of God's promise to Abraham (Genesis 12:1): "To your descendants I have given this land, from the river of Egypt to the great river, the River Euphrates" (Genesis 15:18). From the Mediterranean coast on the west to the Euphrates River on the east; from Kadesh in the south (Ezekiel 48:28) to Hamath in the north (Ezekiel 48:1), Abraham was promised a huge grant of land—all of modern Israel, Lebanon, the West Bank of Jordan, and large parts of Syria, Iraq, and Saudi Arabia.

Because Israel has never occupied all that land, many scholars believe the promise of land should be spiritualized to refer to heaven instead of a literal homeland. But couldn't that promise have been made and fulfilled back in Abraham's previous homeland of Mesopotamia? Why travel all the way to Canaan to make a promise about heaven? No, this was a promise about literal land that will one day be fulfilled.

The promise was also reiterated to Abraham's son Isaac (Genesis 26:2–5), to Isaac's son Jacob (Genesis 28:13; 35:12), and to Jacob's descendants (Exodus 33:1–3). The land in this promise is the most important block of real estate in the world. As such, it will be the most hotly contested land in the world until Christ returns. Israel has been removed from the land three times (the Egyptian sojourn, the Assyrian and Babylonian captivities, and the diaspora), but today she is back in the land. God has kept His promise to Abraham and his descendants.

The Old Testament is replete with God's promises, made through His prophets, about the land belonging to Israel forever: Jeremiah 32:37, 41; Ezekiel 11:17; 20:42; 34:13; 37:21, 25; 39:28; Amos 9:14–15. Taking these promises at face value is important. The last line of Amos 9:15, for example, says: "'And no longer shall they be pulled up from the land I have given them,' says the LORD your God." This could not apply to previous occupations of the land since the Jews were removed. But the day is coming when they will never again be "pulled up from the land."

When the United Nations created a homeland for the Jews in 1948, they carved off a portion of what had historically been Israel's land—part of Judea and Samaria, now called the West Bank—and gave it to Palestinians. But when these same Palestinians and others attacked Israel in 1967 in the famous Six-Day War, Israel won that West Bank territory back. They didn't take it by aggression. They won it while defending themselves from attack—land that had been given to Abraham by God thousands of years earlier!

God cares for this land, His gift to Abraham (Deuteronomy 11:12). Israel regaining the central part of her homeland in 1948 is a sign for all who know biblical prophecy. It is an indication that we are moving into the period prior to the Second Coming of Israel's King.

A Reciprocal Covenant

God's promise to protect and bless Abraham had a corollary—a promise to bless those who bless Abraham and his descendants: "I will bless those who bless you, and I will curse him who curses you" (Genesis 12:3). It's very simple: Nations that bless Israel will be blessed; nations that curse Israel will be cursed.

The prophet Zechariah warned the nations that came against Israel: "For he who touches [Israel] touches the apple of His eye" (Zechariah 2:8). And he warns nations of the future the same way (Zechariah 9:8). The pages of history (and the Old Testament) are littered with the decline of nations that came against Israel. In ancient times, powerful peoples like Egypt, Midian, Moab, Babylon, and Greece were ruined as a result of raising their hand against Israel.

In the modern era, Communist Russia was dissolved, and Nazi Germany was crushed. Perhaps the most dramatic example of God's protection was the aforementioned Six-Day War in 1967. The United Arab Republic, along with the Egyptian, Syrian, and Jordanian armies, attacked Israel from three directions. Although hopelessly outnumbered, Israel defeated all these nations and captured vast amounts of land including the Sinai Peninsula, the Golan Heights, the Gaza Strip, and the West Bank.

The most foolish thing any modern nation could do is to stand against Israel in its foreign policy.

A Universal Covenant

The universality of the covenant with Abraham reveals its most important purpose: "And in you [Abraham] all the families of the earth shall be blessed" (Genesis 12:3). The purpose of God's promise to Abraham was not to exclude the rest of humanity from God's blessing, but to ultimately include them! Abraham's descendants would be the rich repository of the knowledge of God that all humanity needs.

For example, almost all the writers of the Bible were Jewish. And most importantly, Jesus was a Jew—a descendant of Abraham, Isaac, and Jacob. Through "the blessing of Abraham" came a blessing for the Gentiles (the rest of humanity) in the person of Christ (Galatians 3:14). Finally, the land of Israel and city of Jerusalem exist because of the promises to Abraham being fulfilled through his descendants. It is to that land and city which the King of kings and Lord of lords will one day return to judge the world and establish His kingdom on earth. The entire human race has been blessed by the promises of God to Abraham.

An Eternal Covenant

God's promise to Abraham came in three stages: initiated in Genesis 12:1-3, formalized in Genesis 15:1-21, and amplified in Genesis 17:1-18. In Genesis 17, Abraham is nearly 100 years old, and God comes to him to affirm that the covenant is an "everlasting covenant" and the land of Canaan will be his descendants' "everlasting possession" (Genesis 17:7-8). That promise was affirmed graphically through the prophet Jeremiah: as long as the heavens and the foundations of the earth remain, so will God's faithfulness to Israel (Jeremiah 31:35-37; see also Psalm 105:8-9).

Particularly striking was the vision given to Ezekiel—dry bones (of Israel) coming back to life (Ezekiel 37:1-12). The dry bones represent the scattered nation of Israel being brought back to life and reunited to inherit the blessings of Abraham's covenant. That is what we are seeing

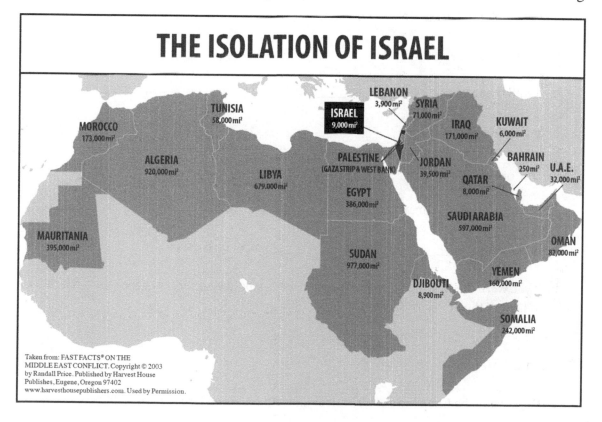

THE ISOLATION OF ISRAEL

Taken from: FAST FACTS® ON THE MIDDLE EAST CONFLICT. Copyright © 2003 by Randall Price. Published by Harvest House Publishes, Eugene, Oregon 97402 www.harvesthousepublishers.com. Used by Permission.

today! But rebuilding the "bones" of the nation is not enough. Israel has not been made totally spiritually alive yet. But Ezekiel saw the breath (Spirit) of God coming into the resurrected physical bodies (Ezekiel 37:8–10), and that will happen (Zechariah 12:10; Romans 11:27–28).

Two prophecies are yet to be fulfilled: Israel needs to inhabit all the land promised to her, and she needs to turn to her Messiah, Jesus Christ. But those will be fulfilled in God's time. Israel is indeed a sign to the world that God keeps His promises and the end of the age is approaching.

APPLICATION

Personal Questions

1. Identify each of the components of God's covenant promise to Abraham in Genesis 12:2–3.

   a. I will make you a _____ _____.

   b. I will _____ you.

   c. [I will] make your _____ _____.

   d. You shall be a _____.

   e. I will _____ those who _____ you.

   f. I will _____ him who _____ you.

   g. In you all the _____ of the _____ shall be blessed.

   h. If you were the leader of a nation on earth, what would your foreign policy toward Israel be in light of the promise of verse 3?

2. Read Ezekiel 36:22–23.

   a. What would be God's purpose in redeeming and restoring Israel (verse 22)?

b. What had Israel (in Ezekiel's day) done to God's "holy name" (verses 22–23)?

c. What does the phrase "in you" in verse 23 say about Israel's restoration?

d. How does "in you" make the restoration of Israel a sign to the world about God (verse 23)?

e. How has the world responded to Israel's restoration to her homeland? Is the world seeing the sign?

f. When the nations gather against Israel at the end of the age, how will they finally understand the sign that is Israel (Ezekiel 39:1–8)?

Group Questions

1. Read Genesis 12:1–2. Discuss what the word "if" addressed to Abraham signifies.

   a. What does that say about conditions Abraham must fulfill?

   b. How many times does God say "I will"?

   c. Who is taking responsibility for the fulfillment of these promises?

   d. How is Deuteronomy 28:1 different from Genesis 12:1–3? What does "if you . . . God will" suggest about this covenant? Is it conditional or unconditional?

   e. How does the conditional nature of this covenant justify the Assyrian and Babylonian captivities? What could Israel have done to avoid those unpleasant experiences?

   f. Is Jesus' promise in John 15:7 conditional or unconditional? If conditional, what are the conditions? What is the promise?

2. In Deuteronomy 7:6–8, how might God's words to Israel also be applied to God's election of you to salvation in Christ (Ephesians 1:4–6)?

DID YOU KNOW?

The term "diaspor" comes from the Greek word *diaspora*, a dispersion or scattering. While it can refer to the scattering of any ethnic or racial group from their homeland, "the diaspora" most frequently refers to the scattering of Jews from Judea. The Greek *diaspora* is used three times in the New Testament to refer to Jews living outside Judea as a result of the Assyrian and Babylonian captivities or persecution (John 7:35; James 1:1; 1 Peter 1:1). Many Jews who had believed in Jesus were driven from Jerusalem (Acts 8:1), and all Jews were scattered from the city when Roman armies destroyed it in AD 70. Though many Jews still live outside Israel, a return from the diaspora began in the first half of the twentieth century and continues today.

Notes

1. Marvin Olasky, "Israel at Age 67: Slammed If You Do, Dead If You Don't," *World*, April 21, 2015, http://www.worldmag.com/2015/04/israel_at_age_67_slammed_if_you_do_dead_if_you_don_t.
2. Paul R. Wilkinson, *Understanding Christian Zionism: Israel's Place in the Purposes of God* (Bend, OR: The Berean Call, 2013), 21.
3. Amnon Rubinstein, "Peace Won't Be Instant, but Can't Be Dropped," *JWeekly*, May 9, 2003, http://www.jweekly.com/article/full/19844 peace-won-t-be-instant-but-dream-can-t-be-dropped/.

Europe

DANIEL 2:31–45

In this lesson we track the modern revival of the ancient Roman Empire.

The last great empire on earth, impacting the most people, was the Roman Empire (27 BC-AD 395). Since then, some leaders have tried and failed to rule the world. But the day is coming when a revived one-world empire will become the stage for the coming Antichrist.

OUTLINE

I. **The Revelation of the Dream**

II. **The Interpretation of the Dream**
   A. The Kingdom of Gold: Babylon
   B. The Kingdom of Silver: Medo-Persia
   C. The Kingdom of Bronze: Greece
   D. The Kingdom of Iron: Rome
   E. The Kingdom of Iron/Clay: The Revived Roman Empire

III. **The Implication of the Dream**
   A. The Consolidation of World Powers
   B. The Coming of One World Leader
   C. The Condition for the Treaty with Israel

OVERVIEW

More than 2,500 years ago a prophet of God stood in front of the most powerful ruler in the world and delivered a panoramic overview of world history—from his own time until the Second Coming of Israel's Messiah, Jesus Christ. Daniel was the prophet, and Nebuchadnezzar was the Babylonian king.

Daniel's prophetic presentations were based on two dreams. One was a dream of Nebuchadnezzar that Daniel interpreted (Daniel 2), and the other was Daniel's own dream (Daniel 7). Both dreams had the same ultimate purpose: to communicate to the people of God the program of God for elevating His kingdom over all the kingdoms of earth.

The ten northern tribes of Israel had been taken captive by Assyria in 722 BC, and the two southern tribes of Judah were taken captive by Babylon in stages in the late sixth century BC. So it was easy for them to wonder: *Is God finished with Israel? Do His chosen people have a future? Are God's promises made to Abraham still valid?* Daniel's interpretations of the two dreams provided answers to those questions.

Nebuchadnezzar's dream was terrifying to him—so much so that he couldn't remember the content of the dream the next morning. When he threatened to kill all his wise men because they couldn't tell him his dream or its meaning, Daniel intervened and said he would reveal the king's dream and its meaning. Daniel and his three friends prayed to God for understanding, and it was revealed to him (Daniel 2:17–23).

It is the interpretation of Nebuchadnezzar's dream that we will study in this lesson (Daniel 2:31–45).

The Revelation of the Dream

The dream Nebuchadnezzar had was of an enormous statue that had five distinct sections (verses 31–33):

- Head of gold
- Breast and arms of silver
- Belly and thighs of bronze
- Legs of iron
- Feet of a mixture of iron and clay

The four metals—gold, silver, bronze, and iron—represented four distinct empires that would rule the world prior to the establishment of the kingdom of God under the rule of Christ.

The Interpretation of the Dream

The dream is all about kingdoms (the word "kingdom" appears nine times in verses 37–44). A kingdom is the domain of a king; it represents the right to rule. In his prayer of thanks to God for revealing the dream of the king, Daniel said, "[God] removes kings and raises up kings" (verse 21). So God is the one who establishes kings and their kingdoms on earth. For all the posturing of men in elections and appointments, it is God who makes the ultimate decisions.

The Kingdom of Gold: Babylon

The first kingdom is Nebuchadnezzar's kingdom: "You are this head of gold" (verse 38). Nebuchadnezzar's kingdom began in 606 BC and lasted seventy years. Babylon was "dripping" with gold in terms of its wealth and was known in the ancient world as "the golden kingdom."

The Kingdom of Silver: Medo-Persia

The kingdom that followed Nebuchadnezzar's would be "inferior" (verse 39) to Babylon. It was Medo-Persia, represented by silver in the statue in Nebuchadnezzar's dream.

When Nebuchadnezzar's grandson, Belshazzar, was king in Babylon, he hosted a banquet in which the God of Israel was mocked. A hand appeared on the wall writing out the fate of Babylon: "Your kingdom has been divided, and given to the Medes and Persians" (Daniel 5:28). That very night the Medes and Persians invaded Babylon and took over the realm. The two arms on the statue in Nebuchadnezzar's dream represented the Medes and the Persians.

The Kingdom of Bronze: Greece

In verse 39, the third successive kingdom is mentioned—a kingdom of bronze "which shall rule over all the earth."

Greece was the kingdom of Philip of Macedon and his more famous son, Alexander the Great. Alexander extended the Greek Empire over the known world: Macedonia, Asia Minor, the Middle East, North Africa, and Mesopotamia. It is said that he wept on one occasion because there were no more worlds for him to conquer.

The Kingdom of Iron: Rome

The fourth kingdom is noted in verse 40—a kingdom that "shall be as strong as iron, inasmuch as iron breaks in pieces and shatters everything." This fourth kingdom—the Roman Empire—conquered Greece and became the most dominant and influential kingdom in world history.

Rome assumed power in the Mediterranean world fifty years before the birth of Christ and ruled Palestine through His ministry and throughout the expansion of the Church in the

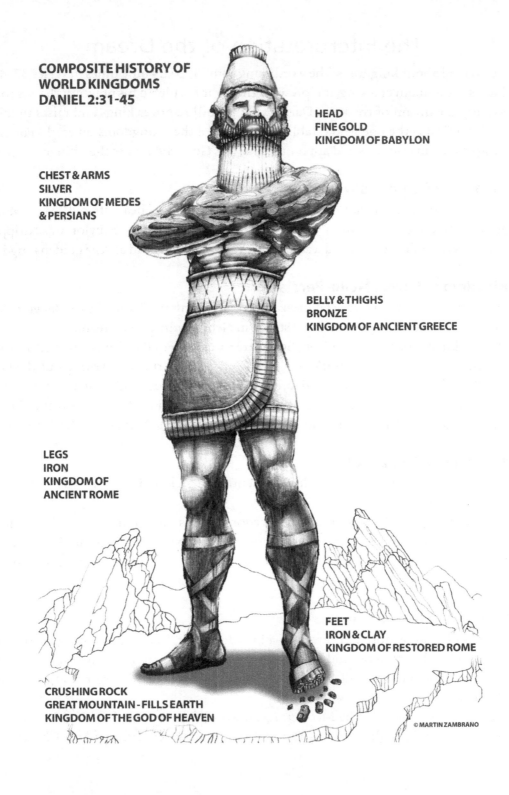

COMPOSITE HISTORY OF
WORLD KINGDOMS
DANIEL 2:31-45

HEAD
FINE GOLD
KINGDOM OF BABYLON

CHEST & ARMS
SILVER
KINGDOM OF MEDES
& PERSIANS

BELLY & THIGHS
BRONZE
KINGDOM OF ANCIENT GREECE

LEGS
IRON
KINGDOM OF
ANCIENT ROME

FEET
IRON & CLAY
KINGDOM OF RESTORED ROME

CRUSHING ROCK
GREAT MOUNTAIN - FILLS EARTH
KINGDOM OF THE GOD OF HEAVEN

© MARTIN ZAMBRANO

apostolic era. The Roman influence spread farther than any previous kingdom, throughout Europe and the British Isles—crushing all opponents with a heel of iron.

The Kingdom of Iron/Clay: The Revived Roman Empire

The four kingdoms succeeded each other just as Nebuchadnezzar's dream predicted, one after the other. But the final aspect of the Roman Empire—the mixture of iron and clay—is the most important for us since it is still in the future (verse 41).

The ten toes on the feet of the statue represent ten divisions, or sections. Those divisions did not exist during the original days of the Roman Empire, so they remain for the future. And verse 44 says that at the time of this revived version of the Roman Empire, "the God of heaven will set up a kingdom which shall never be destroyed." God's kingdom will "break in pieces and consume all these kingdoms, and it shall stand forever." That is the Millennial Kingdom of Jesus Christ, which He will establish when He returns.

The original Roman Empire was not suddenly destroyed—it simply dissolved over a long period of time. So it will have to be reconstituted in a ten-fold form in the future in order for Daniel's prophecy about it being destroyed to come to pass. The process of a ten-fold Roman Empire being rebuilt is already under way. In 1946, in the aftermath of World War II, Winston Churchill said, "We must build a kind of United States of Europe."[1] In 1948 a conference was held in Brussels, Belgium, where the foundation for the European Economic Community was laid. In 1957 the Treaty of Rome was signed, which brought six European nations together into what was called the Common Market. In 1973 England, Ireland, and Denmark joined, and in 1981 Greece joined, bringing the total number of nations to ten.

Some prophecy students thought that signaled the revived Roman Empire, but the text of Daniel refers to ten leaders, or powers, not necessarily ten nations. In 1986 Spain and Portugal were added and the European Economic Community adopted the goal of a political, unified Europe. In 1992 the economic borders between European nations were removed, making commerce and travel between member nations as seamless as traveling between states in America.

In 1995 Austria, Finland, and Sweden joined, and in 2002 the Euro currency was introduced. By 2013, thirteen additional nations had joined the European Union, expanding the total European Union population to more than 400 million—larger than the United States (326 million).

So there is now an economic and political union covering the same geographic area as the former Roman Empire—only much larger and stronger than before. This power needed to be in place before God's kingdom would appear and destroy it, making way for the Millennial Kingdom of Christ to be established.

The feet of the statue were iron and clay. Iron represents strength, but clay represents the more subjective will of the people involved. It is a portent of the volatility of mixing power with people from so many different national and cultural backgrounds as has happened in the unified Europe of today.

The Implication of the Dream

So what does the dream mean in practical terms? How can we expect Nebuchadnezzar's dream to be played out in the future?

The Consolidation of World Powers

In the days of the original Roman Empire there was one ruling power in the Western world: Rome. That has not been true since the dissolution of that empire. Hitler, Stalin, and others have tried but failed. But before Christ returns, world power will again be consolidated in one man. In the dream Daniel had (Daniel 7), which paralleled the dream of Nebuchadnezzar, Daniel was shown that "the ten horns are ten kings who shall arise from this kingdom. And another shall rise after them; he shall be different from the first ones, and shall subdue three kings" (verse 24).

When I first began to teach on prophecy many years ago, I wondered how one man could ever rule the world. As I have watched the confederation of European states come together in my lifetime, I now see that such an event is entirely possible. The "global village" that now exists through technology, communication, and commerce means that one individual's influence can be immediately transferred around the world. And to see nations who used to be enemies in Europe and the Mediterranean now joined together for purposes of commerce and protection—it suggests the possibility of one man rising to prominence over those unified nations. If world conditions—war, oil or food shortages, natural disasters—ever cause people to become desperate enough to give their allegiance to one leader, he could easily become the ruler of a majority of the world's population.

The Coming of One World Leader

The individual whom Daniel saw in his dream spoke "pompous words against the Most High" and "[persecuted] the saints of the Most High." He will "change times and law" and "the saints shall be given into his hand for a time and times and half a time" (verse 25).

We refer to this individual as the Antichrist. He will rise up as the leader of the revived Roman Empire and in opposition to the God of heaven and His people. In order for him to come on the world scene, there must be a confederation of states for him to lead, and that is exactly what is now in place in the union of European nations. Decades ago, such a platform did not exist. But it is in place today—and the future leader of this revived empire may be alive in the world today.

Paul-Henri Spaak, the first president of the UN General Assembly, first president of the European Parliament, and one-time secretary general of NATO, is credited with making this stunning statement: "We do not need another committee. We have too many already. What we want is a man of sufficient stature to hold the allegiance of all people and to lift us out of the economic morass into which we are sinking. Send us such a man and, be he god or devil, we will receive him."[2]

While we may not be able to envision the circumstances in the future that would cause hundreds of millions of people to submit themselves to a "devil" of a man, the Scriptures say it will happen. The idea of interpreting Scripture on the basis of what we can or cannot imagine is a faulty idea. We must read what the Bible says about the future and then look for its fulfillment regardless of how implausible it may sound. Because the coming Great Tribulation is going to create a situation like nothing the world has even seen, we have to imagine the reality of people doing things to save themselves that they might otherwise never have done. And that includes submitting to a one-world ruler who promises to deliver them from the judgments of God.

The Condition for the Treaty with Israel

Daniel 9:26–27 tells us that "the prince who is to come" (the Antichrist) will "confirm a covenant" (treaty) with Israel for "one week" (seven years). So the leader of the revived Roman Empire is going to establish a peace treaty with Israel for a period of seven years. That doesn't sound good—and it definitely will turn out not to be.

I'm sure you are aware of how much effort has been made in recent years to bring Jews and Arabs to the peace table. Multiple United States presidents have made strong efforts toward that end. So it is not out of the question that the world's most significant ruler would be able to broker a peace agreement of some kind with Israel. Israel has even been willing to give up part of the land that is hers in order to achieve some sort of peace with her Arab neighbors.

However, the Antichrist's treaty will not last: "But in the middle of the week [the seven years] he shall bring an end to sacrifice and offering. And on the wing of abominations shall be one who makes desolate" (verse 27). The treaty will have allowed Israel to carry out her religious life under the banner of peace for three and one-half years. But the Antichrist will then break that treaty, signaling the countdown to Armageddon.

The way the stage is being set for these developments to play out, any objective observer would have to admit that the prophetic clock is ticking. Paul's words in Romans 13:11 are as true today as when he wrote them: "Now it is high time to awake out of sleep; for now our salvation is nearer than when we first believed." For us that means that the coming of Jesus is nearer today than it was for Paul; nearer today than when we were first saved; nearer today than it was yesterday. We may not know the day or the hour, but judging from Jesus' admonitions to judge the signs of the times, we ought to be able to know the season. And the signs certainly seem to indicate that we are nearing, or in, the season of His return.

Think of the things that have happened in the last 100 years. Israel was re-established as a nation in 1948. There is in place a revived community of nations resembling the old Roman Empire. The Arab nations control most of the world's petroleum, which equals influence and power in the world's economy. Is it not true that we have entered a different season? I believe it is the season of the Lord's return.

So the question is, *Are you ready for this season?* God's plans and purposes wait for no man. We need to either be in step with God's timetable or be left behind. The way to get in step with Him is to make sure you have committed your life to the Lord Jesus Christ, receiving forgiveness for your sins and the assurance of eternal life. If Christ returns today, will you be ready?

APPLICATION

Personal Questions

Read Luke 19:11–12, 15.

a. What was the context of this parable? What were the people around Christ thinking (verse 11)?

b. Analyze verse 12. Where did the nobleman have to go to receive his kingdom? Where did he go after receiving it?

c. If a kingdom is geographical (a territory of a certain size), how did he bring the kingdom back with him? Therefore, what does it mean to "receive a kingdom"?

d. Who does the nobleman represent in the parable?

e. Describe Christ's going away to receive a kingdom, from whom He received it, and His return having received the right to rule.

f. With regard to the Antichrist, who ultimately will allow him to have authority and rulership over men (Daniel 2:21)?

g. But directly, who will give him authority and power to rule on earth (1 John 5:19)?

h. Who will win the final contest for the right to rule (Revelation 19:19–21)?

Group Questions

1. Read Daniel 2 and discuss the following questions:

   a. What do you learn about Daniel's approach to the problem he faced in Daniel 2 (verse 18)?

   b. How did God respond to Daniel's humble approach (verse 19)?

   c. How did Daniel respond to God's favor (verses 20–23)?

   d. What distinction between man's ability and God's did Daniel draw in verses 27–28?

   e. Who got the glory from Daniel's interpretation (verses 30, 47)?

2. Regarding the statue in Nebuchadnezzar's dream, how did Daniel explain the mixture of clay and iron in the feet (Daniel 2:42–43)?

   How do you interpret "partly strong and partly fragile" in verse 42?

3. As a group, discuss if you are ready for the arrival of the kingdom that will "stand forever" (Daniel 2:44).

DID YOU KNOW?

The European Union (EU) at present has twenty-seven member states with a combined population of more than 400 million citizens. The EU generates more than twenty percent of the world's gross domestic product. This union has a standardized system of laws covering commerce, travel, agriculture, and all affairs of the member nations. Twenty-four languages are spoken in the twenty-seven states, with the motto "United in Diversity." There are currently ten currencies in use, with the Euro being the most dominant.

Notes
1. Quoted in William R. Clark, *Petrodollar Warfare: Oil, Iraq and the Future of the Dollar* (Gabriola Island, Canada: New Society Publishers, 2005), 198; see also W. S. Churchill, *Collected Essays of Winston Churchill, Vol. II* (London, UK: Library of Imperial History, 1976), 176–186.
2. Paul-Henri Spaak, "Amazing United Nations Quotes," http://www.fdrs.org/united_nations_quotes.html.

Russia

EZEKIEL 38–39

In this lesson we discover what the future holds for Russia.

After World War II, the world had two superpowers: the United States and the Soviet Union. When the Soviet Union collapsed in 1991, Russia took a backseat in world affairs. But Russia is back, inserting herself in world affairs. Ezekiel saw her rise and coming demise centuries ago.

OUTLINE

I. The Russian Aggression
   A. The Language Argument
   B. The Location Argument

II. The Russian Alliance
   A. The Commander of the Alliance
   B. The Countries in the Alliance

III. The Russian Attack
   A. Why Will Russia and Her Allies Attack Israel?
   B. Where Will the Russian Invasion Occur?
   C. When Will the Russian Invasion Occur?

IV. **The Russian Annihilation**
   A. Monumental Convulsions
   B. Military Confusion
   C. Major Contagion
   D. Multiple Calamities

V. **The Russian Aftermath**
   A. The Birds and the Beasts
   B. The Burnings
   C. The Burials

OVERVIEW

One of the biggest news stories of 2014 was the Russian invasion and annexation of Crimea, a peninsula on the southern coast of the republic of Ukraine. Crimea has a centuries-old connection to Russia, and Russia wanted it back. So they took it. There was marginal opposition from Ukraine who was trying to manage internal turmoil of its own. The international community objected, but nobody opposed Russia. And Crimea is now back in Russian hands. This was a blatant display of Russian power by its president Vladimir Putin.

Since the annexation of Crimea, Putin has also led Russia to sell air defense systems to Israel's chief enemy, Iran, and has come to the defense of Syrian president Bashir al-Assad with air strikes against rebels seeking to topple the dictator. Putin's intervention in Syria was ostensibly to suppress ISIS forces, but it soon became apparent Russia was there in support of long-time ally Assad.

No one who knows the history of Vladimir Putin, the hardline KGB operative who rose to become president of Russia, is surprised at his aggressive geo-political moves. The dissolution of the Soviet Union in 1991 was a rebuke and an embarrassment to Soviets like Putin. Most analysts believe Putin's recent aggression has one goal: to return the former Soviet Union, if not to its former Communist political structure, at least to its role as a superpower on the world stage.

The Cold War (1947–1991) was won by the United States as signaled by the dissolution of the Union of Soviet Socialist Republics. Sensing a lack of American will on the international stage in recent years, Russia is testing all observers as it moves to center stage in world politics.

What does the future hold for Russia? Putin obviously wants to be recognized as the leader of a world power, and he should not be taken lightly. In fact, we can say with biblical certainty that Russia will move into a pivotal place of power in the Last Days. The prophet Ezekiel gives us a detailed picture of Russia's rise and ultimate demise.

The Russian Aggression

Ezekiel 38–39 describes the future invasion of Israel by Russia and a coalition of mostly Islamic nations. The prophecy begins with ten proper names (Ezekiel 38:1-6). The first, Gog (verse 2), is the name of a man, followed by the names of nine nations that will form an end-times alliance with Gog against Israel: Magog, Rosh, Meshech, Tubal, Persia, Ethiopia, Libya, Gomer, and Togarmah (verses 2 6). We find Russia at the head of the alliance. Ezekiel's two-chapter prophecy is the most detailed prophecy of war in the entire Bible.

"Russia" as a name doesn't appear in the Bible. But the name "Rosh" in Ezekiel's list refers to the nation ruled by the leader of the coalition. There are two strong reasons for believing Rosh refers to Russia.

The Language Argument

Rosh occurs in Ezekiel 38:2–3 and 39:1. It is a Hebrew word that means "head, top, or summit." It's easy to note the phonetic similarity between Rosh and Russia. The great Hebrew lexicographer Wilhelm Gesenius wrote that "Rosh" is "undoubtedly the Russians, who are mentioned by the Byzantine writers of the tenth century, under the name *the Ros*."[1]

The Location Argument

Ezekiel, along with ancient Jewish rabbis, saw Jerusalem as the center of the earth (literally, the "navel" of the earth—see "midst" in Ezekiel 5:5). This means that Jerusalem was the center of the compass. In Scripture, north means north of Jerusalem, south means south of Jerusalem, and so forth.

Both Daniel and Ezekiel saw the ruler who would lead an attack against Israel in the latter days as coming from "the North" (Daniel 11:5–35) or "far north" (Ezekiel 38:6, 15). If one draws an arrow due north starting from Jerusalem, the arrow stops in modern Russia. Russia alone occupies the giant land mass to the "far north" of Jerusalem.

The Russian Alliance

If Russia is the leader of the alliance that makes war against Israel, who are the other nations?

The Commander of the Alliance

Gog is "the prince of Rosh, Meshech, and Tubal" (Ezekiel 38:2). Several times in these chapters Gog (high or supreme) is spoken to as if to a person. Gog may be a title, like "President" or "Pharaoh," rather than a name. Gog is from the land of Magog, but he also rules Rosh, Meshech, and Tubal (Ezekiel 38:3). Gog is commanded by God to "be a guard" for these other nations (verse 7). "Guard" suggests that Gog is the commander and protector of the members of the alliance.

The Countries in the Alliance

Along with Rosh, these nations or lands are also listed by Ezekiel.

Magog

Gog is from the land of Magog (verse 2). Magog was a grandson of Noah (Genesis 10:2), and many scholars believe his descendants settled around the Black and Caspian Seas on Russia's southern border. In *The Jeremiah Study Bible*, I identify this region as home to the former "-stan" nations (Kazakhstan, Kyrgyzstan, and so on), all former satellites of the Soviet Union. What unites the sixty million residents of this region today is their religion: Islam.

Meshech and Tubal

Meshech and Tubal were also grandsons of Noah (Genesis 10:2). The descendants of these two men established cities or territories bearing their names. C. I. Scofield identifies Meshech as "Moscow" and Tubal as "Tobolsk."[2] Other scholars and experts identify them as territories in modern Turkey.

Persia

Persia is mentioned in Ezekiel 38:5 and about thirty-five more times in Scripture. Persia became Iran in 1935, and then the Islamic Republic of Iran in 1979. Today, Russia is Iran's strongest ally and Israel's strongest enemy.

Russia and Iran will become intimate bedfellows when it comes to moving against Israel in the latter days.

Ethiopia

Ethiopia (Ezekiel 38:5) is one of two North African nations that will join the alliance, approaching from Israel's south. Ethiopia was founded by Cush, another grandson of Noah (Genesis 10:6), and originally represented the land south of Egypt. Today that region is the modern country of Sudan, another declared enemy of Israel.

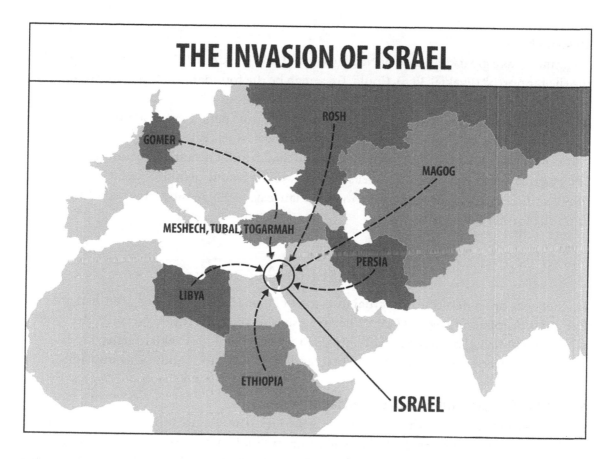

THE INVASION OF ISRAEL

Libya

Libya is the only nation on Ezekiel's list that retains its ancient name today. Founded by Put, another of Noah's grandsons (Genesis 10:6), Libya is the land west of Egypt. Today, Libya is another of Russia's Islamic-nation friends.

Libya's longtime dictator, Muammar Gaddafi, was overthrown in the Arab Spring uprisings in 2011. Since then, the country has been in political turmoil. But there is evidence that Libya is seeking to purchase military armaments from Russia.[3]

Gomer

Gomer, a grandson of Noah (Genesis 10:2–3), has a name that strikes a chord with the modern name "Germany," according to some scholars. Nobody needs to remind the world of Germany's history with the Jewish people in World War II. If Germany becomes part of an alliance with Russia against Israel, it would not be the first time anti-Semitism has played a part in her history.

Togarmah

Togarmah was a great-grandson of Noah (Genesis 10:3). Ezekiel helpfully locates this people in "the far north" (Ezekiel 38:6). Could Togarmah be the foundation of the modern nation of Turkey, as some believe?

Regardless of their exact modern identities, these nine peoples were identified as parts of an alliance led by Gog, the leader, to come against Israel. Russia and Turkey will lead from the north, joined by Iran from the east and Sudan and Libya from the south and possibly Germany from the west. Ezekiel says there will be "many peoples" with Gog (Ezekiel 38:9), so there may be other nations in the alliance as well—possibly the "-stan" nations from the former Soviet bloc.

The Russian Attack

Ezekiel goes on to describe the actual invasion of Israel (Ezekiel 38:7–17). But remember: Ezekiel is prophesying *against* Gog. When God says, "I am against *you*" (verse 3), the "you" is Gog, not Israel. God is the speaker in this prophecy, through Ezekiel against Gog.

We now need to answer the why, where, and when questions about this invasion.

Why Will Russia and Her Allies Attack Israel?

From Russia's perspective, there are three reasons. First, the alliance will come to *seize* Israel's land (Ezekiel 38:11–12). Second, they will come to *steal* Israel's wealth (Ezekiel 38:12–13). Third, they will come to *slaughter* Israel's people (Ezekiel 38:11–12, 16). This slaughter will be the culmination of the Arab hatred for Israel that has been simmering since the days of Ishmael and Isaac (Genesis 21:8–19).

Where Will the Russian Invasion Occur?

It will be in the land of those who have been regathered from the nations and are dwelling safely: the land of Israel (Ezekiel 38:8). Ezekiel confirms this many times in chapter 38. This will be a lopsided invasion! Russia is nearly 800 times larger than Israel in terms of land. Add in the size of the other alliance members, and the odds are overwhelmingly against Israel.

When Will the Russian Invasion Occur?

Two of three events that will precede the invasion have already happened, but the third will occur in due time. The events are:

1. Israel Must Be Present in Her Land

Ezekiel makes this point clearly in 36:24; 38:8, 12; 39:25, 27–28. Prior to 1948, the Jews as a nation had not been in the land since AD 70, when they were driven out by the Romans who destroyed everything, making the land uninhabitable. After World War II, persecuted European Jews began pouring into Israel, and the United Nations declared Israel a nation in May 1948. Hundreds of thousands of Jews from all over the world began streaming into their homeland.

An important note about the progress of Ezekiel's prophecy: Ezekiel 36–37 describes the regathering of Israel; Ezekiel 38–39 describes the invasion of Israel; Ezekiel 40–48 describes Israel in the Millennium. So the invasion of Israel takes place between the regathering and the Millennium. That is, between the *national* and the *spiritual* rebirth of the nation.

2. Israel Must Be Prosperous in Her Land

Ezekiel 36:11 describes the growth and prosperity of Israel when she is back in her land, and that has certainly been fulfilled. Indeed, Israel's wealth is one of the reasons for the invasion by the Russian alliance. By all standard measures—technology, innovation, start-up companies, education, wealthy citizens—Israel surpasses all countries of her size in the world and many that are much larger.

3. Israel Must Be Peaceful in Her Land

This is the condition that remains to be realized: peace in the land. Ezekiel 38:8, 11, and 14 suggest that Israel thinks she is secure—that there is no need for strong defenses. Something unusual must happen to make this embattled nation think she is secure, and the prophet Daniel tells us what it will be: The Antichrist will establish a peace treaty that protects Israel (Daniel 9:27). Because of peace between Arabs and Israelis, Israel will feel secure. But she will also be a ripe target for an unexpected invasion. The Antichrist's peace treaty will begin the seven-year Tribulation period. So, after the beginning of the Tribulation is when the invasion of the Russian alliance will happen.

The Russian Annihilation

The alliance will come upon Israel "like a cloud, to cover the land" (Ezekiel 38:15–16). There is no human way Israel could survive. And yet she will, because God will intervene (Ezekiel 38:18–19).

In addition to the three reasons for the invasion I mentioned previously, there is a fourth: to set the stage for judgment against Russia and other nations that have a history of rebelling against God (Ezekiel 39:7–8). "Then the nations shall know that I am the LORD, the Holy One in Israel" (verse 7). God will allow the greed and hatred of the alliance to be a reason for the judgment they deserve. It will be a destruction such as the world has never seen.

Monumental Convulsions

There will be unrivaled earthquakes and destruction. The entire earth will feel the reverberations of God's destruction of the armies (Ezekiel 38:19–20).

Military Confusion

In the midst of the destruction, the invading armies will turn on each other in confusion (Ezekiel 38:21). This will parallel what happened to the enemies of Judah in the days of King Jehoshaphat (2 Chronicles 20:22–25).

Major Contagion

Because of the myriad of dead bodies, disease will break out, resulting in further chaos and judgment (Ezekiel 38:22).

Multiple Calamities

There will be natural disasters: "Flooding rain, great hailstones, fire, and brimstone" (Ezekiel 38:22), similar to what happened at Sodom and Gomorrah.

All these judgments will extend to the homelands of the alliance nations (Ezekiel 39:6). It is not just the armies that will be judged but the populations of their nations as well.

The Russian Aftermath

The disposal of the bodies and equipment of the invaders will be monumental (Ezekiel 39).

The Birds and the Beasts

The scavengers of the animal kingdom will be called by God to help dispose of rotting corpses (Ezekiel 39:17–20). God calls it a "sacrificial meal" (verse 17).

The Burnings

Equipment—tons and tons of it—will have to be burned, scrapped, recycled, and otherwise disposed of (Ezekiel 39:9–10). Ezekiel describes weapons of his day because that's all he knew. But instead of swords, shields, bows, and arrows being destroyed, it will be modern military hardware.

The Burials

It will take Israel "seven months" to bury what remains of the dead in a place called "the Valley of Hamon Gog" (Ezekiel 39:11–12).

Two things will happen in this terrible conflict: a rebellious coalition of nations will be judged, and God will prove His faithfulness to His people Israel. As always, those who purpose to rise against God are themselves taken down. Those who choose to sow violence reap a harvest of greater violence and destruction (Galatians 6:7).

Five times in Ezekiel 38 and 39, God repeats His desire to make His name known among the nations (38:16, 23; 39:6–7, 23). This is not egotistical on God's part. Rather, it is for our benefit. God doesn't need to know how great His name is, but we do. His faithfulness—His greatness—is just another way for us to realize who He is.

We live in a world beset by trouble and tribulation among nations. And there is certainly trouble yet to come. But God is in control. He uses even the sins of the nations to accomplish His purposes, making His name known and drawing mankind to Himself.

APPLICATION

Personal Questions

1. How do we know that a spiritual rebirth is coming for the nation of Israel (Ezekiel 36:24–28; 37:14, 26–27)? What will be its characteristics?

2. To whom is the prophecy of Ezekiel 38–39 directed (Ezekiel 38:3; 39:1)?

   a. How many nations or peoples will join with Gog to come against Israel? List their names (Ezekiel 38:2–3, 5–6).

   b. Who is going to lead these nations against Israel (Ezekiel 38:3–4)?

   c. What does "hooks into your jaws" (verse 4) suggest about God's power and control over these nations?

d. How does God "whistling" to call Assyria to punish Israel compare with His sending the Russian alliance (Isaiah 5:26; 7:18)?

e. What does this say about God's control of the nations (Job 12:23; Daniel 2:21; Acts 17:26–27)?

f. What does "be a guard for them" mean for Gog? What is his role in the alliance (Ezekiel 38:7)?

g. Geographically, what is the connection between "far north" (Ezekiel 38:6, 15) and Russia from Jerusalem's point of view?

h. Ezekiel wrote his prophecy while in captivity in Babylon. Check a map—what modern country is directly "far north" of Babylon?

Group Questions

1. Why is Ezekiel 38:8 a good description of the nation of Israel in both Ezekiel's day and our day (see also 36:3)?

   a. How did Ezekiel portray the nation in the vision he saw in Ezekiel 37:1–14?

   b. What time indicator is given in Ezekiel 38:8? How do we know this invasion hasn't already happened? ("After _____ days . . . in the _____ years.")

2. Based on information from this lesson, give the "big idea" of these sections of Ezekiel:

   a. Ezekiel 36–37: the _____ of Israel

   b. Ezekiel 38–39: the _____ of Israel

   c. Ezekiel 40–48: the _____ of Israel

3. Based on size and numbers, why would the coming Russian invasion of Israel be a certain victory for the alliance, humanly speaking?

   a. Who saves Israel? Why (Ezekiel 39:7)?

   b. What comfort do you take from this prophecy concerning future world events? Who is in charge?

DID YOU KNOW?

According to Orthodox Church tradition, the disciple Andrew first brought the Gospel to the region of Belarus, Russia, and Ukraine. The baptism of Vladimir the Great and his family in Kiev in AD 988 marks the official beginning of Christianity in Russia and the beginning of the Russian Orthodox Church, which is in full communion with the Eastern Orthodox Church. Prior to the Bolshevik Revolution in Russia in 1917, Christianity was the dominant religion of Russia. After 1917, the Union of Soviet Socialist Republics became officially atheistic based on the teachings of Marx and Lenin. Since the fall of the Soviet Union in 1991, the Russian Orthodox Church has gradually gained restored freedom while maintaining its distance from the state.

Notes
1. H. W. F. Gesenius, *Gesenius' Hebrew-Chaldee Lexicon* (Grand Rapids, MI: Eerdmans, 1957), 752.
2. C. I. Scofield, *The Scofield Study Bible* (New York: Oxford University Press, 1909), 883.
3. Mustafa Fetouri, "Libya Looks to Russia for Arms," *Al-Monitor*, April 20, 2015, http://www.al-monitor.com/pulse/originals/2015/04/libya-us-uk-francerussia-uneast-west-armament-deal-morocco.html.

Babylon

REVELATION 18:1-24

*In this lesson we see the future revival and destruction of Babylon,
the center of the coming world economy.*

When we think of the world's great cities today, we think of New York, London, Tokyo, Rome, Sao Paulo, and others. But a city is coming in the future—an ancient city that has lain dormant for ages—that will dwarf today's world-class cities in opulence, commerce, finance, and sin.

OUTLINE

I. **The Reasons for the Destruction of Babylon**
   A. Babylon Is Judged Because of Her Sorceries
   B. Babylon Is Judged Because of Her Seductions
   C. Babylon Is Judged Because of Her Sins
   D. Babylon Is Judged Because of Her Self-Glorification
   E. Babylon Is Judged Because of Her Slavery
   F. Babylon Is Judged Because of Her Sacrifices

II. **The Reactions to the Destruction of Babylon**
   A. The Monarchs of the Earth Will Mourn
   B. The Merchants of the Earth Will Mourn
   C. The Mariners of the Earth Will Mourn

III. **The Rejoicing in Heaven over the Destruction of Babylon**

IV. **Our Response to the Destruction of Babylon**

OVERVIEW

Beginning in 1926, a man named George S. Clason wrote a series of pamphlets on principles of financial management, supposedly drawn from the wisdom of ancient Babylon, the world's original seat of commerce and finance. The pamphlets were eventually published in book form, *The Richest Man in Babylon.* What Clason couldn't have known then is that Babylon is still alive and will again be the capital of commerce in the world.

According to Revelation 18, Babylon will be rebuilt and will be the commercial capital of the world during the Tribulation. The late Dr. Henry Morris, a scientist and geologist, wrote in his commentary on Revelation that Babylon is located at the geographical center of the world's land masses—an ideal spot for a world center of commerce. He quotes the eminent historian Arnold Toynbee, who agreed: Babylon is the best place in the world to build a world cultural metropolis because of its location at the crossroads of Europe, Asia, and Africa.[1]

The United States believes in the importance of this region. In 2009, the U.S. opened the largest embassy in the world in Baghdad: twenty-seven buildings on 104 acres on the banks of the Tigris River. Long before modern experts identified the importance of Babylon, the prophets of old foresaw its importance in end-times prophecy.

Babylon's modern story begins with Iraq's former dictator, Saddam Hussein. He saw himself as a modern-day Nebuchadnezzar II, the king of Babylon in its original glory. Hussein invested more than $500 million in rebuilding ancient Babylon. He even had bricks inscribed with his name and the record of his acts, just as Nebuchadnezzar had done, and gold coins minted with his image and Nebuchadnezzar's. Obviously, Saddam Hussein's reign was cut short. But UNESCO (the United Nations Educational, Scientific, and Cultural Organization) is continuing the effort to turn ancient Babylon into a modern center for tourism and commerce.

Babylon is sixty miles south of modern Baghdad and was originally founded by Nimrod, the first world-level leader, if not dictator, responsible for the Tower of Babel (Genesis 10:8–10). According to Revelation, the Antichrist will be active in three cities: Rome (politics), Jerusalem (religion), and Babylon (commerce). Next to Jerusalem, Babylon is mentioned more than any other city in Scripture—and always in negative terms.

Both Jeremiah (51:26, 37, 43) and Isaiah (13:9, 19–20) prophesied that Babylon would one day become a desolate ruin. The fact is that those prophecies have never been totally fulfilled. Babylon is certainly not desolate today. Babylon changed hands from the Babylonians to the Medo-Persians to the Greeks and was never demolished throughout ancient history. So we know that the prophecy of Babylon's destruction is yet to be fulfilled, which means it must regain its glory.

Revelation 18 is an entire chapter devoted to the role and ruin of Babylon in the end times. We must remember that in Scripture Babylon represents more than a city—it is a metaphor for a greedy, corrupt world system dominated by man apart from God. From the days of the Tower of Babel to its role in the end of the world when the Antichrist controls world commerce from Babylon, it represents the rise and fall of man separated from God. Babylon represents humanism and rebellion from God, not just in one city but also in the world system at large. Babylon stands for the world as we know it today: humanistic, proud, and detached from God the closer we get to the end of the age.

The Reasons for the Destruction of Babylon

Revelation 18:1–2 pictures the destruction of Babylon: "Babylon the great is fallen!" The language John used when he wrote Revelation pictures an instantaneous action, not a gradual decline. Three times in this chapter we are told it will happen in one hour (verses 10, 17, 19). A world system on which people have built their whole lives will be gone in an hour.

There are six reasons why God pours out His judgment on Babylon.

Babylon Is Judged Because of Her Sorceries

John says Babylon "has become a dwelling place of demons, a prison for every foul spirit" (verse 2). The city will be a center of demonic activity, of depraved men and women seeking to advance their status in the world through commerce. Associated with demonic activity is the word "sorcery"—Greek *pharmaki,* from which our word "pharmacy" (drugs) is derived. There will no doubt be an unlimited use of drugs in Babylon as part of her depraved lifestyle.

Babylon Is Judged Because of Her Seductions

The nations and kings of the earth "have committed fornication with [Babylon], and the merchants of the earth have become rich through the abundance of her luxury" (verse 3). Babylon will one day be the richest, most liberated city on earth, home to every fleshly pleasure and pursuit. Immorality will replace morality in Babylon. The world will flock to Babylon to partake of her pleasures. Wealth will be multiplied for those who drink of Babylon's cup.

Wealth is on Babylon's horizon, with Iraq having one of the largest proven oil reserves in the world that remains largely untapped. That will happen in Babylon's revival. John Phillips, in his commentary on Revelation, suggests that the world's crime syndicates will relocate to Babylon to go after their share of the wealth that will soon be flowing in Babylon.[2] Everyone in the world with an evil thought will be seduced and intoxicated by the lure of Babylon.

Babylon Is Judged Because of Her Sins

Revelation 18:5 says that Babylon's "sins have reached to heaven, and God has remembered her iniquities." The word "reached" meant, in the original Greek, to be glued or stuck together, picturing Babylon's sins as having been joined together like bricks, piled on top of one another like bricks in a building. The image could not be more reminiscent of the Tower of Babel. God looks at modern Babylon's sins the same way He looked at ancient Babel's. Only this time, the "building" has reached all the way to heaven as an affront to a holy God. Just as God judged Babel for her sins, He will judge Babylon for hers—indeed, a double portion of judgment (verse 6).

Babylon Is Judged Because of Her Self-Glorification

Babylon will position herself as a "queen" who "will not see sorrow"—a prideful, self-appointed position. She prophesies about herself that she will not see sorrow—that she will not be destroyed; that she is impregnable and invulnerable to outside forces; that she is the ultimate manifestation of the power of man in the world. This is certainly the pride of Nebuchadnezzar manifested again (Daniel 4:28–30).

Babylon Is Judged Because of Her Slavery

Revelation 18:12–13 provides an inventory of the kinds of merchandise that will be found in Babylon—twenty-eight categories of goods in all, with gold and silver topping the list. This list is set in terms familiar to the ancient world: woods, metals, spices, condiments, livestock, and others. But at the end of the list is something unexpected: "bodies and souls of men," indicating trafficking in human beings for slavery of various sorts to include, no doubt, sexual slaves. Every kind of sexual debauchery known to man will be present in Babylon. It is estimated that more than twenty-seven million people are trapped in sexual slavery in the world today.[3] And God will judge Babylon for abusing precious human beings in such a perverted way.

Babylon Is Judged Because of Her Sacrifices

Found in Babylon will be "the blood of prophets and saints, and of all who were slain on the earth" (verse 24). In a city devoted to man, there will live some people who are devoted to God. But they won't live long. They will be martyred for their faith in a city that is anti-Christ. Remember, if true Christians do not submit to wearing the mark of the Beast, they will stand out conspicuously in Babylon and will be killed for their rebellion against the Antichrist and his system.

So, Babylon will be judged for many things: sorceries, seductions, sins, self-glorification, slavery, and the sacrifices of God's people. Her destruction is summarized in verses 8–10—a day of "death and mourning and famine. And she will be utterly burned with fire, for strong is the Lord God who judges her" (verse 8). That which man thinks is indestructible will all be destroyed in one hour of one day. Six times in verses 21–23 the word "anymore" is used, as in everything that once was Babylon will not be found "anymore"—no music, no money, no majesty, no merchants, no monarchs, no merriment, no morality of man. All of it will be gone.

The destruction of Babylon will cause reactions from kings and nations around the globe.

The Reactions to the Destruction of Babylon

Two words are used to describe the reaction of the kings of the earth to Babylon's destruction: "Alas, alas." In today's language, it would be like shaking one's head while moaning, "No, oh no! This can't be!" But it will be—a shock to those who viewed Babylon as untouchable.

The Monarchs of the Earth Will Mourn

"The kings of the earth who committed fornication and lived luxuriously with her will weep and lament for her, when they see the smoke of her burning" (verse 9). The kings of the earth will have treated Babylon like a harlot, using the great city as a source of pleasure and diversion. They were tied to her in body, mind, and spirit, partaking of her luxuries in an ongoing life of wanton pleasure. Suddenly, the source of their wealth and pleasure will be reduced to a smoking heap, as were Sodom and Gomorrah. The kings of the earth will weep and mourn for their loss.

The Merchants of the Earth Will Mourn

All the merchandise we saw earlier? All gone. Babylon is no longer the great mall for the world's merchandise that she was: "And the merchants of the earth will weep and mourn over her" (verse 11). Why? Because "in one hour such great riches came to nothing" (verse 17). The economic hub of the world—the gravy train for the merchants of the world—has been destroyed. The entire world will be thrown into economic and financial chaos because of the destruction of Babylon.

Psalm 52:7 says, "Here is the man who did not make God his strength, but trusted in the abundance of his riches, and strengthened himself in his wickedness." A perfect description of the mourning merchants of the end-time world when the source of their wealth is destroyed.

The Mariners of the Earth Will Mourn

Revelation 18:17–19 shows the trickle-down effect of the destruction of Babylon. The sea captains, piloting giant cargo ships around the globe, have suddenly lost their most profitable source of revenue: transporting goods to and from Babylon. During the Tribulation, the Persian Gulf will be flooded with merchant ships coming and going from Babylon, the great center of world commerce. There will no doubt be many in port on the day of Babylon's destruction, and many more coming and going in the waters of the Gulf. When they see the cloud of Babylon's destruction, they will weep and mourn over their loss.

But, if there is weeping on earth over Babylon's fall, there will be rejoicing in heaven.

The Rejoicing in Heaven over the Destruction of Babylon

Revelation 18:20 is an interesting parenthesis, an interlude, a snapshot of heaven's response to Babylon's fall: "Rejoice over her, O heaven, and you holy apostles and prophets, for God has avenged you on her!" This is a reference to what we have already seen in verse 24: the blood of prophets and saints who were killed in Babylon for their witness to Christ.

Monarchs, merchants, and mariners are mourning on earth while apostles, prophets, and saints are rejoicing in heaven! They rejoice over the destruction of a system that killed them, a system that set itself up in open rebellion against God. It was the spirit of Babylon that had been persecuting the martyrs of the Church for 2,000 years. Saints who died in obscurity are now remembered in heaven as the system that killed them is brought to account. They had been waiting in heaven for justice, crying out, "How long, O Lord?" (Revelation 6:9–11), and justice has now been served.

Those who dispensed wrath upon the people of God will one day feel His wrath themselves. The words of Deuteronomy 32:35, quoted by Paul in Romans 12:19, are fulfilled: "'Vengeance is Mine, I will repay,' says the Lord." No wonder there is rejoicing in heaven! The rejoicing is not over the death of lost souls but over the establishment of righteousness and justice. The righteous arm of the Lord requites those whose lives were taken by the sinful acts of men.

Our Response to the Destruction of Babylon

One last verse supplies the application for Christians today who study the future revival and downfall of Babylon: "Come out of her, my people, lest you share in her sins, and lest you receive of her plagues" (Revelation 18:4).

"My people" is a key phrase—God is speaking to us Christians who are His people today. We are surrounded today by the spirit of Babylon, the culture which will find its consummation in the Babylon of the future. And there is one message for us: Come out and be separate from the spirit and the city of Babylon.

There will be Christians living in Babylon at the time of her revival as a world city. Dr. Henry Morris speculated on how there might be Christians in Babylon in the end times:

Apparently, the same worldly allure will attract many believers to the final stage of Babylonian apostasy. The appeal of salary and prestige will entice many capable Christian business and professional men, architects, engineers, merchants, doctors, accountants, and others to participate in the planning and activation of this exciting and dynamic new metropolis. Christian workers in many construction and other trades will follow the enticement of high wages. No doubt, many of these Christians will rationalize their move to Babylon by the opportunity that will afford them to have a witness in the world's most important city, to the world's most important people.[4]

The danger in such a choice is obvious: getting caught up in the spirit and sin of Babylon. And thus, God's plea to "come out." Seven times in the Bible there is an exhortation to God's people to "come out" of Babylon. God is always warning His people against sharing in the sins, and thus the judgments, of the world. You may not be living in the city of Babylon today, but if you are partaking in her spirit, today is the day to come out.

APPLICATION

Personal Questions

1. Read Jeremiah 51:24–26. How is the ultimate destiny of Babylon described?

   a. How does "desolate forever" indicate that Babylon still has a life? (Is Babylon "desolate" today?)

   b. How does verse 43 indicate that we have not yet seen the final days of Babylon?

2. Psalm 52 is about the wicked and the righteous.

   a. How do verses 1–5 fit the character of Babylon as described throughout Scripture and Revelation 18?

   b. How is the character of the righteous man different (verses 6–9)?

    c. How does this dichotomy illustrate the need for God's people to "come out" of Babylon before getting trapped?

3. How is Proverbs 6:27 a warning to those who think they can live in Babylon without becoming defiled?

4. What have you learned about Babylon that you may not have known before?

Group Questions

Read Daniel 4:28–37 and discuss the following questions:

    a. How did Nebuchadnezzar, king of Babylon, describe the city over which he reigned as king of Babylon (verse 30)?

    b. For whose glory was Babylon built (verse 30)?

    c. What was God's overall response to Nebuchadnezzar's self-glorification (verses 31–32)? How does it parallel the response you have studied in Revelation 18?

    d. What was the first thing God told the king about His authority (verse 30)? How does this verify the words of Daniel spoken earlier in Daniel 2:21a?

    e. How would you describe the judgment issued to Nebuchadnezzar in verse 32a?

    f. How long would he remain in this condition (verse 32b)?

    g. What lesson was Nebuchadnezzar's punishment designed to teach him (verse 32b)?

    h. How was the judgment fulfilled (verse 33)?

i. What did Nebuchadnezzar do at the end of the "seven times" (verse 34)?

j. What lessons about God did Nebuchadnezzar learn and proclaim (verses 34–35)?

k. What happened to Nebuchadnezzar after his disciplinary experience (verse 36)?

l. What newfound perspective did he bring to his role as king (verse 37)?

m. How does the last line of verse 37 correlate with James 4:6?

n. What lesson is there in Nebuchadnezzar's experience about intruding into the domain of God's glory?

DID YOU KNOW?

The Hanging Gardens of Babylon were one of the Seven Wonders of the Ancient World. They were built by Nebuchadnezzar II, the king of Babylon mentioned in the book of Daniel, around 600 BC. They were a gift for the king's Persian wife who was homesick for the forests and lush vegetation of her homeland. The gardens were not so much "hanging" as "elevated" on platforms above the ground, high above the city floor. The Greek historian Strabo describes a screw-like device used to transport water into the gardens from below. The gardens are thought to have been destroyed in the second century BC by earthquakes.

Notes
1. Henry M. Morris, *The Revelation Record* (Wheaton, IL: Tyndale House, 1983), 348–349.
2. John Phillips, *Exploring Revelation—An Expository Commentary* (Grand Rapids, MI: Kregel Publications, 2001), 222.
3. Kevin Bales, *Disposable People: New Slavery in the Global Economy* (Berkeley, CA: University of California Press, 1999), passim and product description at Amazon.com, FreetheSlaves.net.
4. Morris, *The Revelation Record*, 357.

LESSON 5

America

SELECTED SCRIPTURES

In this lesson we examine the role of America in biblical prophecy.

America's activities are scrutinized by the worldwide media on a daily basis. How is it that the world's most powerful nation is not mentioned in the Bible? We can identify reasons for America's blessings but only speculate about her role in the world in the prophetic future.

OUTLINE

I. **The Sovereignty of God in the Founding of America**
   A. America Has Been the Force Behind World Missions
   B. America Has Been a Friend to the Jewish People
   C. America Has Been a Free Nation
   D. America Has Been Founded on God and His Word

II. **The Silence of the Bible on the Future of America**
   A. America Will Be Incorporated into the European Coalition
   B. America Will Be Invaded by Outside Forces
   C. America Will Be Infected with Moral Decay
   D. America Will Be Impotent Because of the Rapture

III. **The Spiritual Tensions Surrounding the End Times**
   A. The Tension Between the Material and the Spiritual
   B. The Tension Between Tomorrow and Today
   C. The Tension Between the International and the Individual

---

OVERVIEW

In the introduction to Peter Marshall and David Manuel's book *The Light and the Glory*, they ask a very profound question: "What if Columbus' discovering of America had not been accidental at all? What if it were merely the opening curtain of an extraordinary drama? Did God have a special plan for America? What if He dealt with whole nations as He deals with individuals? What if, in particular, He had a plan for those He would bring to America; a plan which saw this Continent as a stage for a new era in the drama of mankind's redemption?"[1]

That question raises the subject of this lesson: *What is the role of the United States of America in biblical prophecy?*

The Sovereignty of God in the Founding of America

In retrospect, though America is nowhere mentioned in the Bible, it certainly seems that God has had a plan for this nation in redemptive history. America has been blessed beyond any nation on earth. Why? Why has America outstripped all previous civilizations in terms of wealth, technology, and other achievements? That doesn't mean America has been perfect. But it does mean America's blessings are undeniable.

America Has Been the Force Behind World Missions

One reason for God's blessing has been our involvement in world missions—taking the Gospel of Christ to the ends of the earth. God blesses those who obey the Great Commission (Matthew 28:19–20) because He always blesses obedience. When the predominance of missionary activity in the world emanates from a country with a small percentage of the world's population, that is significant.

Following World War II, Americans started 1,800 missionary agencies and sent out over 350,000 missionaries.[2] Today, ninety-five percent of the world's population has access to some portion of the Bible in their language plus Christian radio, audio recordings, and other resources like the *Jesus* film.[3]

America Has Been a Friend to the Jewish People

America has also been blessed for being a friend to the Jewish people. God promised Abraham that He would bless those who blessed Abraham's descendants—and America has certainly done that. God said the Jews would be His chosen people forever, the "apple of His eye" (Zechariah 2:8).

As long as Jews have been in America, they have been afforded the full rights of all citizens and the right to maintain their religious heritage. And since the reconstitution of Israel as a nation in 1948, America has been Israel's staunchest ally and protector. "I will bless those who bless [the Jews]," God said (Genesis 12:3).

America Has Been a Free Nation

America's commitment to freedom, since the writing of the founding documents, has been based on biblical truth. Christianity and personal freedom go hand in hand. The first thing dictators and totalitarian rulers do is remove religious liberty from the people. Because America has maintained her identity as the "land of the free," Christianity has been allowed full-expression. Jesus said the truth is what sets men free (John 8:32). And because America was founded by seekers of spiritual freedom, the roots of personal freedom went deep into the soil of the new nation. Since its founding, immigrants have come from all over the world to live in America because they want the freedom and opportunity America offers.

In 2018, Freedom House reported that forty-five percent of the world's population lives in free societies—which means that fifty-five percent do not.[4] America represents freedom to the rest of the world, including religious freedom. And God blesses freedom.

America Has Been Founded on God and His Word

Finally, America was founded, and its government established, by people who honored God and His Word. That was certainly true of the Pilgrim founders and the early colonists, and mostly true of the founding fathers. While it may be debatable whether America is presently a Christian nation, there is no doubt that it was founded as one.

George Washington said, "It is impossible to rightly govern the world without God and the Bible." Benjamin Franklin requested that each session of the Constitutional Convention be opened in prayer: "The longer I live, the more convincing proofs I see of the truth that God governs in the affairs of men." All one need do is visit Washington, DC, and look at all the public buildings that have references to God inscribed on them—even on our coins, "In God We Trust." And sessions of Congress are still opened with a prayer.

Critics of Christianity can try to rewrite our nation's Christian heritage, but they will fail. History is history. America was established on God and His Word and has been blessed for it (Psalm 33:12; Proverbs 14:34).

The Silence of the Bible on the Future of America

Most modern nations are not mentioned in the Bible unless they also have roots in antiquity (like Syria, Israel, Persia, and regions of Asia Minor and southern Europe). The United States is less than 250 years old, so it is not surprising that the Bible is silent concerning it. We can say conclusively that the United States is not mentioned specifically in Scripture. This might seem puzzling since America is the world's superpower, and we are approaching the end of history when conflicts among nations are going to increase and a worldwide dictator, the Antichrist, will arise.

Here are several ideas that have been expressed concerning America's future in biblical prophecy.

America Will Be Incorporated into the European Coalition

Some believe that America will be incorporated into the revived Roman Empire. The reason for this is that America, along with Europe, is considered "the West" as opposed to Middle Eastern and Eastern (Asian) nations. Culturally and historically, America is tied more to Europe than any other part of the world, so the thinking is that America might join with European nations in an alliance.

America Will Be Invaded by Outside Forces

Others have suggested that America will be invaded or otherwise weakened by an outside force. Several nations in the world besides America (not to mention terrorists) have nuclear capability, and others might acquire it in the future. Only time will tell whether America is weakened by an outside force.

America Will Be Infected with Moral Decay

It has been well said that those who refuse to learn from history are doomed to repeat it. And what history tells us about the world's major civilizations is that most of them fell from internal weakness and decay, not from external conquerors. Or if they were conquered by invaders, they were so weak from moral decay that they could not mount a sustained defense. Babylon, Greece, Rome—empires that seemed invincible all gave way to greed and licentiousness. The average age of the world's great civilizations when they fell was 200 years. That means America is living on borrowed time.

The cycle of history in empires has gone something like this: they moved out of bondage to spiritual faith; from faith to courage; from courage to liberty; from liberty to abundance; from abundance to complacency; from complacency to apathy; from apathy to dependence; and from dependence back to bondage.[5] It is not hard to trace America's history on that path.

I would say we have passed the midpoint and are somewhere in the second half of that cycle—which is a scary thing to contemplate.

If that which resulted in God's blessing in the early years of this country is given up out of apathy, can we expect God to continue His blessing? Here are three national sins that Scripture says result in God turning His back on a nation.

1. Ingratitude

Thirteen times Israel went through a four-fold cycle: rebellion, retribution, repentance, and restoration, as told in the book of Judges. Later, when the prophet Jeremiah delivered God's warnings to the southern nation of Judah, he reminded them of how close they had been to the Lord in the infancy days of the nation (Jeremiah 2:1–2). Those were days of simple faith and obedience, of tender intimacy with the God of Israel—days long since abandoned by the nation. Jeremiah warns them that their idolatry was sure to incur God's judgment, and it did. America might listen to the same warning.

2. Idolatry

In verses 4–5, Jeremiah specifically accuses the nation of idolatry. In so many words, God asks the nation, "What have I done to make you worship other gods?"

Could God not ask the same question of America? Why would the most blessed nation on the face of the earth turn its back on God and worship the idols of greed, materialism, immorality, and self-interest? Gradually through the years we have pushed God out of the public square to the periphery of our nation's life. The farther away we push God from the center of our nation, the more His place is taken by chaos, factions, and economic struggles. We redouble our efforts, and things only get worse. Why would we turn our back on the God who has blessed and protected us?

Former President Herbert Hoover spoke these words: "We have overworked the word 'new.' The practical thing, if we want to make the world over, is to try out the word 'old' for a while. Some old things made this country. Some old things are slipping and if they slip too far, the light will go out of America—old virtues, old religious faith, whole truth, integrity, honor in public office, economy in government, individual liberty, willingness to sacrifice. Our greatest danger is not from invasion by foreign armies. Rather our great danger is suicide by compliance with evil."[6]

Even the church of Jesus Christ in America has fallen prey to the temptation to invent "new" ways of doing things—only to find that the tried and true biblical patterns are best after all. If the Church allows the culture to dictate how we "do" church, we will fade into irrelevance. Our mandate for doing church comes from the Word of God, not the world. The Bible may be old, but it is one of the old things to which we need to return in the Church and in our culture.

3. Indifference

Upon hearing Jeremiah's words, the people were indifferent (verses 6, 8). They didn't even bother to ask, "Where is the LORD . . . ?" They had become calloused, used to God's blessing. And they thought it would continue forever regardless of what they did. It's an attitude that is found in much of contemporary Christianity today: indifferent to the warnings of Scripture about becoming friends with the world rather than with God. Preachers are offering people words that make them feel good but which have no basis in Scripture. They are empty words of hope that vanish like the mist when the heat of tribulation bears down upon them. It may be a message of prosperity and success, but it leaves one spiritually bankrupt when life's difficulties come on the scene.

The final reason that America may have little impact on end-time events is actually a positive reason.

America Will Be Impotent Because of the Rapture

If the Rapture of the Church happened today and all true believers in Christ in America disappeared off the earth, millions of Christians and their small children—would vanish. Not only would America lose a large portion of her population, but she would also lose the best of her populace: the salt and light that has been preserving the nation's spiritual strength. If America lost her most faithful and patriotic citizens, she would be in no position to play a major role in end-time events. That may well be why America plays no significant role in the Last Days of planet earth: The best of her citizens have been taken to heaven.

The Spiritual Tensions Surrounding the End Times

There is always tension in spiritual truth, and end-times prophecy is no exception. We need to be aware of the following three realities as the history of the world draws to a close.

The Tension Between the Material and the Spiritual

We have looked at many material aspects of our world so far: nations, leaders, money, and others. And they are important. But as in all aspects of life, the material has to be balanced with the spiritual.

The Bible is clear that life in this era is a spiritual battle, a holy war. In the final analysis, the movements of men and material on the earth represent spiritual dynamics going on behind the scenes. The words of Zechariah 4:6 tell the final tale: "'Not by might nor by power, but by My Spirit,' says the LORD of hosts."

The Tension Between Tomorrow and Today

When we study prophecy, there is the possibility of becoming so heavenly minded (focused on tomorrow) that we are no earthly good (responsible for today). If we know all about the ten toes on Nebuchadnezzar's statue (Daniel 2) but are oblivious to the needs of our neighbor, then we have become like the Pharisees—making religion more important than people. To paraphrase Jesus' words about the Sabbath in Mark 2:27, "Man was not made for prophecy, but prophecy was made for man."

God's plans for the future will be fulfilled, but He has plans for us individually that are our responsibility to fulfill today.

The Tension Between the International and the Individual

It is so easy for us to sit back and be critical of nations and leaders—especially our own. This calls to mind Jesus' words about removing the plank from our own eye before we point out the speck in a brother's eye (Luke 6:41–42). The Bible wasn't written for nations; "nations" can't read God's Word and respond to it. Only individuals can do that. If nations change and do the right thing, it is only because individuals choose to obey God and make their voices heard and their actions seen.

We don't know the prophetic future of America, but we do know the future of Americans. As individuals, we must choose to obey God today.

APPLICATION

Personal Questions

Read Psalm 33:8–22.

a. Whose counsel ultimately directs the paths of world history (verse 11)?

b. From what you have learned so far, how has God used America and England, two nations with a Christian heritage, to shape the future of Israel?

c. When God is the Lord of a nation, what is the state of that nation (verse 12)?

d. Specifically, what nation is referred to here (verse 12)?

e. Could the promise of blessedness apply to any nation that makes God their Lord? Why or why not?

f. What picture of God's dealing with men and nations is portrayed in verses 13–15?

g. Of what ultimate strength are kings and armies in shaping the future (verses 16–17)?

h. To whom does God pay special attention (verses 18–19)?

i. As far as America's future is concerned, what should be our attitude (verses 20–21)?

j. If mercy is God withholding punishment that is deserved, what reasons does America have to pray for God's mercy (verse 22)?

Group Questions

1. As a Christian, what traits in America do you believe God continues to bless?

2. How could America best apply Jesus' teachings in Luke 6:39–42 in international relations?

3. What is the best way for a nation to become a light to other nations (Matthew 5:14–16)?

DID YOU KNOW?

While many of America's founding fathers were committed to the integrity of the Bible, Thomas Jefferson was not. He created a book called *The Life and Morals of Jesus of Nazareth*, or *The Jefferson Bible*, as it has come to be known. He took copies of Matthew, Mark, Luke, and John and cut out all the words spoken by Jesus Himself and pasted them onto pages in chronological order to obtain a code of morals and ethics based purely on the words of Jesus. He did not trust the records of the four evangelists—how they interpreted or presented Jesus' words and ministry. Jefferson didn't publish the book in his lifetime, but it was published by the National Museum in Washington in 1895.

Notes
1. Peter Marshall and David Manuel, *The Light and the Glory* (Old Tappan, NJ: Revell, 1977), 17–18.
2. Gordon Robertson, "Into All the World," CBN, http://www1.cbn.com/churchandministry/into-all-the-world, accessed November 1, 2007.
3. Luis Bush, "Where Are We Now?" www.missionfrontiers.org, 2003, accessed November 1, 2007.
4. Michael J. Abramowitz, "Democracy in Crisis," Freedom House, https://freedomhouse.org/report/freedom-world/freedom-world-2018.
5. Alexander Fraser Tytler, quoted in John Walvoord and Mark Hitchcock, *Armageddon, Oil and Terror* (Carol Stream, IL: Tyndale House, 2007), 65.
6. Herbert C. Hoover, *Current History* (Philadelphia, PA: Events Publishing Company, October 1951), 256.

PART 2

CULTURAL

SIGNS

Materialism

SELECTED SCRIPTURES

In this lesson we note financial trends that are building toward the Tribulation and the end of the age.

When it comes to money, life today is radically different from just a few decades ago. Today, the financial world operates electronically; wealth is concentrated in the hands of a minority of people; the middle class is vanishing; and oil has become an international bargaining chip.

OUTLINE

I. **The Proliferation of Global Technology**

II. **The Polarization of Prosperity and Poverty**

III. **The Priority of Oil and the Middle East**

IV. **The Preoccupation with Money and Material Things**

V. **The Passive Indifference to the Warnings of God**

OVERVIEW

In Part 3, we will discuss the order of end-time events: the Rapture, then the Tribulation, then the Second Coming of Christ, then the Millennium, and then the eternal state. Note that nothing needs to happen in order for the Rapture to take place—it could happen today. So, if the Rapture occurs just before the Tribulation, and if we see signs of the Tribulation growing more certain, that means the Rapture is growing closer as well.

Those signs include a one-world economic system that can eventually be controlled by a one-world ruler, the Antichrist. In this lesson we will examine financial signs of the end times to add to the growing body of evidence that the Tribulation (and thus the Rapture) is growing near.

The Proliferation of Global Technology

In Revelation 13, we learn that the mark of the Beast will be the only way to purchase or sell something during the Tribulation. A century ago, such a thing would have sounded like science fiction. But now the technology exists to make it a reality. When you pass through a grocery store checkout line, your ability to pay could easily be linked to permission to purchase.

A "cashless" society has been slowly developing, a society where all transactions are handled electronically instead of by currency. This is a necessary part of worldwide commerce, of course—removing the necessity for sending cash (or checks—a hard copy of cash) around the world. And if a person's bank account can be stored electronically, it would be just another step to store complete information on that person as well—such as whether they have permission to buy and sell (that is, whether they have the mark of the Beast). These changes happen so slowly, so incrementally, that hardly anyone notices over time. But compare today with thirty years ago and you'll see that a significant line has been crossed. In fact, the day is probably fast approaching when a surcharge may be levied on customers who choose to use cash instead of an electronic medium for purchases. Imagine—penalized for using money!

No money will change hands in the future. Paychecks and other checks will all be deposited electronically as many of them already are. Some are suggesting that physical money may be a way for germs to be transmitted—like flu viruses—providing another reason for the elimination of currency. Since credit and debit cards rarely leave your hand—you swipe your own card now—there's no danger of germ exchange with plastic.

The next major step toward the cashless society is transactions via cell phones. Consumers already use their cell phones (electronic wallets) to make transactions. America is actually behind some other parts of the world. Cell phones have replaced many laptops as the preferred means for accessing the Internet, to include electronic financial transactions. Cell phones now have all the capabilities of laptop or desktop computers.

As an addendum, let me mention that with the increase in these technologies come additional opportunities for ministry. At Turning Point, we offer strategies for disseminating solid Bible teaching via cell phones through various applications. Whatever technology is available to share the Gospel, we want to take advantage of every opportunity.

The Polarization of Prosperity and Poverty

Revelation 6–19 covers the time of the Tribulation on earth, so 6:5–6 reflects events early in the Tribulation. These verses describe the opening of the third seal (judgment) and the release of the black horse and rider upon the earth. The rider is holding a pair of scales in his hand, saying, "A quart of wheat for a denarius, and three quarts of barley for a denarius; and do not harm the oil and the wine" (verse 6). This is a picture of worldwide famine, a time when the poor will get poorer and the rich will be living in luxury.

A denarius was a day's wage, so a quart of wheat cost one day's wage. Barley, a cheaper grain, would be three quarts for a denarius. So it would take a day's wages just to buy food for a day, with nothing left over. It is a picture of extreme deprivation on earth for most people. But the hardships will not touch everyone equally. Verse 6 concludes by saying, "And do not harm the oil and the wine," meaning that while the basic staples will be in short supply, the finer things (oil and wine) will go untouched. Therefore, the average person will suffer while the wealthy do just fine.

A 2006 United Nations report showed that, increasingly, the wealth of the world is being consolidated in the hands of a smaller and smaller minority of people. Half the world's adult population owns barely one percent of global wealth. There is a massive polarization of wealth taking place in the world. The gap between rich and poor is growing wider day by day.

The Priority of Oil and the Middle East

Ezekiel 38:10–12 deals with a war that I believe will take place in the early days of the seven-year Tribulation. Others see it happening just prior to the Rapture. Either way, it could well be within our lifetime. The war involves a coalition of nations that plans to destroy Israel—and would, except for the intervention of the Lord.

The motivation of the coalition is oil. The Middle East was the site of the Garden of Eden, the site of lush forests that have decayed into the greatest reservoirs of oil on the planet. A geophysicist explained to a good friend of mine how the largest deposits of petroleum in the world lie under the sands in countries just to the east of Israel where the world was once covered by far-reaching forests and plant life like the world has never seen. The oil buried under the surface of the Middle East will become the motivation for wars in the years ahead. Satan could finance the Battle of Armageddon with oil derived from the decaying Garden he helped to ruin at the dawn of human history!

It is a fact that massive amounts of the world's oil reserves are controlled by Islamic nations—nations that hate Israel and America. God is going to use the world's hunger for oil to draw the nations of the world into the Middle East for a conflagration: "I will turn you around, put hooks into your jaws, and lead you out, with all your army, horses, and horsemen, all splendidly clothed, a great company with bucklers and shields, all of them handling swords" (Ezekiel 38:4). I believe it is possible, with the place that oil holds in our world's economy, that the stage is being set for just such a gathering of nations.

You've heard the expression, "Follow the money." In the end of days, it is going to be, "Follow the oil." Oil will represent wealth and mobility, and nations will go to war over it.

The Preoccupation with Money and Material Things

Everyone in the world is being, and will be more and more, affected by money and material things. In past generations in America, people lived in farming communities where natural resources—food, land, livestock—played an important role in sustenance. But today, everything revolves around the exchange of money.

In 2 Timothy 3:1–2, Paul wrote to Timothy to say that "in the last days perilous times will come: For men will be lovers of themselves, lovers of money." Paul lists many characteristics of people in the last days, and one of the first on his list is that people will be lovers of money. It's interesting that the first two—lovers of self and lovers of money—are mentioned together. So often, self-centered and selfish people are also greedy people. There have been many wealthy corporate executives convicted in recent years of defrauding stockholders, employees, and customers. They seemingly had no concerns except for their own accumulation of wealth. Individuals' loss of savings? Investors' loss of capital? Employees' loss of jobs? It didn't matter as long as they grew wealthier. That is the spirit of our age, and it will become more pronounced the closer we get to the end of the age.

Sadly, Paul says that some of these people will have "a form of godliness" without its true power. In other words, they will be religious people, professing Christians, even. The spirit of the age is not only among pagans; it has, and will, infect the Church of Jesus Christ. The love of money is at the core of modern society. Money drives commerce; money is power; money is a measure of worth and self-esteem.

No wonder Paul wrote to Timothy that "the love of money is a root of all kinds of evil, for which some have strayed from the faith" (1 Timothy 6:10). And no wonder Jesus said it is impossible to serve two masters, God and money (Matthew 6:24). Neither Paul nor Jesus said you cannot have money and love God. They just said you cannot love money and God at the same time.

Nothing has dominated the news cycles in our country in recent years more than money—that is, the economy. It is what our society depends on for happiness and well-being.

The Passive Indifference to the Warnings of God

People today are amazingly indifferent to what God says about the end of the age—even Christians! It's as if what the Bible says is not really meant to inform us, that it is just "Bible language" talking about "something" that really has little to do with me. That is certainly the view of the world, but it is also the view of many Christians.

Luke 17:26–30 is a prophecy from Jesus Christ Himself about "the day when the Son of Man is revealed" (verse 30). Jesus compares that coming generation with the generation that experienced the Flood in Noah's day and the destruction of Sodom and Gomorrah in Lot's day. The reference is not to the people's wickedness or debauchery; it is simply to their ordinariness. They were going about business as usual and never saw the judgment that was coming. The verbs Jesus uses say it all: they ate, drank, married, bought, sold, planted, built—they were just living their lives without any awareness of what was happening around them.

One of the biggest challenges preachers have is getting people's attention. They are so caught up in the mundane (but demanding) affairs of their lives that a worship service is more of an opportunity just to sit and rest for an hour than it is to pay attention to the truths of the Word of God. When they leave, things continue on just as they did before they came in. And Jesus said it will be the same way in the end times—which certainly can include our day.

In the letters Christ dictated to the apostle John when he was exiled on the island of Patmos, there are some similar descriptions (Revelation 2–3). The seven churches Christ addressed were literal churches, but I also believe the seven churches are pictures of the stages of the Church in the 2,000 years since Christ. The Laodicean church represents the Church on earth prior to the return of Christ to earth (Revelation 3:14–18).

About this church (the Church in our day) John Stott wrote:

> The Laodicean church was a halfhearted church. . . . It describes vividly the re-spectable, sentimental, nominal, skin-deep religiosity which is so widespread among us today. Our Christianity is flabby and anemic. We appear to have taken a lukewarm bath [in] religion.[1]

If you attend a strong, Bible-believing, Christ-honoring church, you may think that's an overstatement. But not all churches are like yours. There is a large part of professing Christianity that is very nominal—very much like John Stott describes it. They are, to use Christ's words in Revelation, "lukewarm, and neither cold nor hot" (Revelation 3:16).

Jesus said some people's hearts will grow cold in the end times (Matthew 24:12), but in Revelation He described hearts that are neither "cold nor hot." A lukewarm heart is a heart that is passively indifferent. It doesn't matter whether they attend church or not: "It doesn't hurt, so why go?"

The cure for the lukewarm church is found in Revelation 3:20, where Jesus is standing at the door of the Laodicean church: "Behold, I stand at the door and knock. If anyone hears My voice and opens the door, I will come in to him and dine with him, and he with Me." While that verse is often used in terms of personal evangelism, its context is the Church. Jesus wants His entire Church to hear His knock and open the door and allow Him to come in. He wants to reclaim His rightful place as the Lord of the Church. What a sad indictment of the condition of the Church today—that the Lord of the Church needs to ask to enter!

This is a warning and a rebuke not only to Christians but also to pastors who are the leaders of local churches. It is just as easy for churches to get caught up in "playing church" as it is for Christians to get caught up in "living life." In any case, Christ and His plan for the ages can be completely ignored and overlooked. No wonder Jesus asked, "Nevertheless, when the Son of Man comes, will He really find faith on the earth?" (Luke 18:8).

The picture of Christ knocking on the door of His Church was captured famously years ago in a painting by artist Holman Hunt. Christ is standing outside a door; weeds have grown up around the dwelling. And, most notably, there is no handle on the outside of the door! The intent of the artist was clear: Christ will not open the door to the Church or a person's heart by force. The door can only be opened from the inside by the occupant.

Have you opened the door of your heart to Christ? Don't be one of those too busy with the cares of this world to note the changing seasons of the ages. He is coming soon!

APPLICATION

Personal Questions

1. Read 2 Peter 1:12–21.

   a. What role was Peter playing with those to whom he wrote (verses 12–13)?

   b. What was the source of all that he had taught those he mentored in the faith (verses 16–18; see Matthew 17:5)?

   c. To what "prophetic word" is Peter referring in verse 19?

   d. What metaphor does Peter use about the role of prophetic words in the believer's heart (verse 19)?

   e. To what does the last part of verse 19 refer? What is "the day" (see 2 Timothy 1:12)?

   f. What comfort do verses 19–20 give the student of the end times as he seeks out God's plans for the near future?

   g. How much emphasis do you give in your Bible reading to understanding Scriptures related to the end times?

   h. What principles does Proverbs 2:1–5 offer about seeking God's truth?

2. Compare Matthew 6:19–20 with James 5:1–6. What principles were the rich violating?

   a. What evidence of a middle class do you find in the James passage?

   b. What signs do you see in America of a "vanishing" middle class—of the rich getting richer and the poor getting poorer?

Group Questions

1. In what sense could Luke 18:8 have been written about Christ's first coming to earth (see John 1:11)?

2. Read 2 Timothy 3:1–9.

   a. Discuss the characteristics of those who will populate the "last days."

   b. What does "form of godliness" mean in verse 5?

   c. How do people "deny" the power of godliness? What is the power of godliness (verse 5)?

   d. What command does Paul give Timothy concerning such people (verse 5)?

   e. What does verse 7 suggest about the danger of head knowledge alone when it comes to Scripture?

3. Discuss the rebuke Jesus gave to the Pharisees and Sadducees in Matthew 16:1–3.

   a. What positive trait did the sons of Issachar possess (1 Chronicles 12:32)?

   b. What signs of the times are you learning about in this study?

DID YOU KNOW?

Federal Reserve Bank officials use several designations for discussions about money in the U.S. economy. M0 (M zero) is the total of physical currency in the system plus account balances at the central bank that can be exchanged for physical currency. M1 is physical currency plus the balances in demand (checking or savings) accounts. M2 is M1 plus other accounts like money market funds and certificates of deposit under $100,000. According to the Federal Reserve, M1 increased 142 percent, to just under $2 trillion, in the two years ending in November 2009 as a result of all the new currency the Treasury Department printed and put into the system. M2, at the end of 2009, was $8.36 trillion dollars—four times the amount of actual currency. In other words, if everyone in America wanted their cash at one time in hard dollars, there wouldn't be enough to go around. The "fractional banking system" on which our economy is based is only required to keep a small percent of customers' balances on hand.[2]

Notes

1. John Stott, *What Christ Thinks of the Church* (Grand Rapids, MI: Zondervan, 1964), 116.
2. Figures from wikipedia.com, s.v. "money supply."

Immorality

ROMANS 1:18–32

This lesson defines the issues playing a role in our culture today and offers insights into how the Christian can make a difference in an age where anything goes.

We live in a time that is historically unprecedented in its open idolatry, debauchery, and pursuit of immorality, but as we look to God's Word we gain understanding on how to live for Christ during a time of moral decline.

OUTLINE

I. **The Expression of Our Moral Decline**
   A. Depravity in Our Minds
   B. Depravity in Our Marriages
   C. Depravity in Our Military
   D. Depravity in Medicine

II. **The Explanation of Our Moral Decline**
   A. The Historical Explanation
   B. The Biblical Explanation

OVERVIEW

We live in an age of decadence, where the shameful acts of yesterday are the celebrated triumphs of today. Perversions are seen as normal, purity is labeled as puritanical, and the pursuit of personal pleasure is king. As Christians, we should not be surprised at the depths to which humanity continues to sink because Scripture clearly speaks of man's propensity to sin and God's holy intolerance of it. It is no wonder that we have found ourselves in a place where "anything goes."

"Anything Goes" is the memorable toe-tapping song written by Cole Porter in 1934. If you listen closely to the lyrics, you will find they celebrate the moral freefall of the American twentieth century. "We've rewound the clock," say the lyrics. Profanity and nudity are in vogue, and "now God knows—anything goes."

"Anything Goes" represents the moral relativism that has infected our culture, leaving the West on the brink of spiritual collapse. Ironically, it's a philosophy that ruined Cole Porter's own life. His secretary lamented that her boss never found the strength that came from faith in God. We're living in a world where anything goes, but nothing satisfies. That is why it is vital for Christ-followers to resist the siren calls of our decadent age.

The Expression of Our Moral Decline

The Bible anticipated these times. In speaking about His Second Coming, the Lord Jesus said, "But of that day and hour no one knows, not even the angels of heaven, but My Father only. For as the days of Noah were, so also will the coming of the Son of Man be" (Matthew 24:36–37).

Those words take us back to Genesis 6:5, which is a description of the society swept away by the Flood: "Then the LORD saw that the wickedness of man was great in the earth, and that every intent of the thoughts of his heart was only evil continually."

In 2 Timothy 3:1–5 we are reminded "that in the last days perilous times will come: For men will be lovers of themselves . . . without self-control, brutal, despisers of good . . . lovers of pleasure rather than lovers of God, having a form of godliness, but denying its power."

This rejection of God and His standards is a symptom of our isolation from God. It began at the Fall of man and continues to this day. Depravity is the root cause of America's moral decline.

Depravity in Our Minds

The Internet offers many benefits for us today, but it created an avenue for destructive behavior that is staggering in its reach: pornography. Online pornography is an addictive and destructive trap that brings lurid material into the hearts and souls of consumers. Even worse, over one quarter of Internet pornography is child related.[1] It is a sickening trend, which brings with it a depravity of the mind and soul, with innocent children being abused—causing emotional scars that last a lifetime. Sexually explicit content is not limited to the Internet; television today contains material that in earlier decades would have never been allowed. There are not adequate words to describe the sex, violence, and addictive nature of some of today's options for so-called entertainment.

In Noah's day, every thought was only of evil continually, but today we have the technology to take the most lurid fantasies of the human mind and project them onto a screen a child or adult can hold in his or her hand.

All this has led to the coarsening of Western culture. We've become a profane people with fewer restraints on behavior and language and with a lessening respect for human life, even innocent life in the womb.

Depravity in Our Marriages

Another aspect of our sexually demanding society is vehemence of the LGBTQ movement (lesbian, gay, bisexual, transgender, questioning), which won a great legal victory in 2015. In the case of Obergefell v. Hodges, the Supreme Court of the United States, in a 5-4 vote, took it upon itself to "redefine" marriage.

But God Himself defined the marriage covenant in Genesis 2 in the Garden of Eden before human governments were established. It wasn't human government, Mosaic Law, or church councils that established the definition of marriage. God did it before any of those institutions came into existence.

The Lord established the formula for marriage just like He established the law of gravity or the axioms of physics. God ordained marriage as a lifelong covenant union between one man and one woman, and this is the only proper God-given arena for the exercise of sexual relations.

Depravity in Our Military

Today, Bible-believing members of our Armed Forces face new restrictions on expressing their religion, and our military chaplains are on the front lines of intense politically correct pressure. While at this point there is no official policy banning voluntary prayer, religious services, or pastoral counseling, there have been several instances where Christian chaplains have experienced difficulties for praying in Jesus' name, counseling from a Christian perspective, and expressing biblical standards for sexuality.

We have yet to see the full moral effect of the U.S. military's recent policies of allowing homosexuals to serve in the military and the inclusion of women in combat roles. But it should be clear to any objective thinker that these decisions cannot but foster increased moral deterioration, not to mention diluting the effectiveness of our forces in combat.

Depravity in Medicine

Dr. Paul Church is one of Boston's most-loved physicians, a urologist who invested twenty-eight years practicing medicine at Beth Israel Deaconess Medical Center and teaching at Harvard University. One day, hospital officials noticed that on the hospital's online portal, Dr. Church had posted concern about the health dangers of same-sex activity.

In September 2014, the hospital launched a formal investigation into Dr. Church's views, and that began a long and losing battle for Dr. Church, who has now been expelled from the hospital.[2] Sadly, we have reached the point where political correctness trumps public health concerns. As the Bible puts it: "For the time will come when people will not put up with sound doctrine. Instead, to suit their own desires, they will gather around them a great number of teachers to say what their itching ears want to hear. They will turn their ears away from the truth and turn aside to myths" (2 Timothy 4:3–4, NIV).

The Explanation of Our Moral Decline

It's time to ask the question: *How did Western morality arrive on such a slippery slope?* What happened to us? It can be explained in two ways: historically and biblically.

The Historical Explanation

The historical explanation dates back to the eighteenth-century Enlightenment. Throughout the Middle Ages, the Western world, for all its darkness and depravity, at least had an understanding of objective truth. The existence of God was granted, which provided a basis for belief in absolute values of right and wrong. But hard on the heels of the Reformation, the secular thinking of the Enlightenment (or the Age of Reason) radiated from France like a forcefield across Europe and to the New World.

As philosophy detached itself from religion, morality was liberated from divine authority. This newfound "freedom" and doctrine of the perfectibility of humanity set the stage for all kinds of mischief—the Communist movement of Karl Marx, the theological liberalism of Julius Wellhausen, and the evolutionary hypotheses of Charles Darwin.

Darwin's evolutionary ideas spread to all other areas of thought, including non-scientific philosophical arenas. We are constantly changing and forever evolving, said the enlightened thinkers, and that includes our values. Darwinian morality replaced biblical codes of conduct and character.

The rising tide of humanistic secularism was shoehorned into America's education system by John Dewey, a shy, bookish educator who hailed from Vermont. Dewey's core principle was the rejection of absolute unchangeable truth. Final truth, he believed, was illusionary.[3]

About that time, the American judicial system entered the picture and began mandating secularism, almost as though it were the nation's new official religion. In 1963, the Supreme Court of the United States prohibited school officials from organizing or leading Bible reading or prayer exercises in schools. We've now had two generations to see how that has worked out.

Against this backdrop, moral relativism entered the pop culture with a vengeance between the 1920s and 1960s—remember, Cole Porter wrote "Anything Goes" in 1934—and set the stage for the sexual revolution of the 1960s through the 1980s. Hollywood jumped on the bandwagon, and America's moral values turned downward like economic charts of the Great Depression.

The culture today is reaping the seeds of moral relativism and a secular world view.

The Biblical Explanation

While we can trace the philosophical decline of our moral foundations, the true explanation is found in humanity's rebellion against the holy character of God.

A culture begins to collapse, said Paul, when it rejects the reality of creationism and of a Creator. Romans 1:18–20 says, "For the wrath of God is revealed from heaven against all ungodliness and unrighteousness of men, who suppress the truth in unrighteousness, because what may be known of God is manifest in them, for God has shown it to them. For since the creation of the world His invisible attributes are clearly seen, being understood in the things that are made, even His eternal power and Godhead, so that they are without excuse."

The existence and complexity of Creation demands a Designer. This presents an insolvable problem for modern humanity, for the existence of a Creator implies His authority over all His creation. If we're subject to a Maker, we're not autonomous, for morality is intrinsically rooted in His holy character.

To escape these implications, our society has chosen to believe the unbelievable—that everything came from nothing in an unexplainable explosion, that primordial sludge was jolted from death to life, that molecules developed from randomness into complexity, and that human beings are the resulting accidents. That's the foundation of secularism, and it leads downward in belief and behavior. It leads to ingratitude.

We Have Rejected God Through Ingratitude

Paul wrote, "Because, although they knew God, they did not glorify Him as God, nor were *thankful,* but became futile in their thoughts, and their foolish hearts were darkened" (Romans 1:21, emphasis added).

We Have Rejected God Through Idolatry

The rejection of the Creator-God means only one thing—humanity must construct its own gods. Romans 1:22–23 goes on to say, "Professing to be wise, they became fools, and changed the glory of the incorruptible God into an image made like corruptible man."

Anything that comes before Jesus Christ in your affections or priorities—that's your idol. In Colossians 3:5, the apostle Paul told his readers, "Therefore put to death your members which are on the earth: fornication, uncleanness, passion, evil desire, and covetousness, which is idolatry."

Our goals, ambitions, dreams, obsessions, addictions, pleasures, or opinions can become our gods. But make no mistake—when we reject the Creator-God of Scripture, we must find a substitute. We must have an idol, which leads to the next downward step—a lust-driven life.

We Have Rejected God Through Immorality

Paul continues in Romans 1:24–25 to say, "Therefore God also gave them up to uncleanness, in the lusts of their hearts, to dishonor their bodies among themselves, who exchanged the truth of God for the lie, and worshiped and served the creature rather than the Creator, who is blessed forever. Amen."

Only the true God of heaven is holy enough to empower His people to live according to the dictates of His holiness. All other gods lead to an erosion of morality, to sensuality, to sexual sins, and to lust-driven lives. How sad to follow this downward course when God longs to give us an upward path. But the steps keep descending. The next stop on the way to the days of Noah is a sex-saturated society.

We Have Rejected God Through Iniquity

When a culture denies its Creator, erects its own gods, and succumbs to a lust-driven existence, it inevitably becomes sexsaturated. Romans 1:26–27 says plainly: "For this reason God gave them up to vile passions. For even their women exchanged the natural use for what is against nature. Likewise also the men, leaving the natural use of the woman, burned in their lust for one another, men with men committing what is shameful, and receiving in themselves the penalty of their error which was due."

This downward spiral of decency finally leads to the basement of debauchery—total moral collapse.

The history of the world is littered with the stories of cultures who descended this staircase, never to return. Our pathway from the Enlightenment to Postmodernism isn't new. The same thing happened in the days of Noah. It happened to Sodom and Gomorrah. It happened to the ancient empires of Assyria, Babylon, Greece, and Rome. It even happened to ancient Judah in the days of the prophet Ezekiel.

The Lord's glory dwelt in His temple for 400 years. But by the time of King Zedekiah, the temple of the Lord was a different place, for the nation of Judah had followed step-by-step the sequence of sin described in Romans 1: the rejection of the Creator, the proliferation of idols, lust-driven hearts, and a sexually saturated age that led to total moral collapse.

As the Babylonians began their assault on Judah, one of the early victims was Ezekiel. In chapters 8–11 of his book, Ezekiel described how he was given the awful privilege of watching the glory depart from Judah. The biblical word for this is "Ichabod"—the glory has departed (1 Samuel 4:21). All hope for Israel was gone—decimated by the Babylonians.

The Church of Jesus Christ and its message are the only things standing between this world and the judgment of God. Our Lord has placed us here for times like these, and we mustn't be drawn into the corruption of our culture. Instead, we're to shine like stars in the night as we firmly hold out the Word of life to a crumbling culture (Philippians 2:15–16).

The Bible tells us to remain fully committed to Christ, to keep ourselves unspotted from the world, to hold our convictions without fear, and to preach the Gospel without compromise. It's easy to condemn our age—and we certainly have the biblical authority to speak the truth and expose sin—but we also need to demonstrate Christ to our world.

Without succumbing to the ways of the world, we should reach out in love to the people of the world, reflecting the heart of Christ to everyone we meet. Let's remember the truth of John 3:16—despite everything, God loves this world.

Our times are not lost on our Lord. He understands our culture, and He loves its people. We're engaged in our times because Jesus died for times like these, and we are living in a world for which He offered Himself on the cross.

I hope you feel as I do, that it's an honor to represent Jesus Christ to my generation, even in times like these. It's an honor to be a light in a darkened age.

Keep yourself unspotted from the world, but don't disengage from the world. Let's love our neighbors and rescue the perishing. We are here in these days as His ambassadors on assignment, serving the One who told us to go into all the world with the Gospel—even into a world where "anything goes."

APPLICATION

Personal Questions

1. Read Genesis 6:1–8.

   a. What were the conditions on earth like as defined in verse 5?

   b. Describe the implications of the words "every" and "only" in verse 5.

   c. Verse 6 mentions two reactions that God had to this situation. What were they?

   d. What was God's plan of action in the face of this (verse 7)? Why?

   e. What do you think the purpose of verse 8 is in light of the preceding passage?

2. Read Romans 2:1–11.

   a. According to verse 1, what can be said of those who judge? Why is that?

   b. How does God judge (verse 2)?

   c. What are the implications of verse 3, especially for Christians living today?

   d. What does God's goodness lead to (verse 4)? Why do you think that is?

e. What two attributes build up the wrath of God against you (verse 5)? When will this come to fruition?

f. To whom is eternal life bestowed (verse 7)?

g. List the four results of living a disobedient, self-seeking life (verses 8–9).

h. To whom will this occur? Be specific (verses 8–9).

i. What three things come to those who work for good (verse 10)?

j. Rephrase verse 11 in your own words and then explain how it relates to this study.

Group Questions

Read Romans 2:12–16 and discuss the following questions:

a. How is it possible to sin "without law" and "perish without law"?

b. Why is it that the doers and not the hearers of the law are justified as stated in verse 13?

c. What, according to verse 15, bears witness to the law in the unbeliever's heart? What is the implication of this reality?

d. What will God judge one day? How (verse 16)?

e. What kind of material and ideas has Romans 2:1–16 given you that can aid you in approaching nonbelievers with the truth of God's Word? Discuss as a group what you have learned about the inner working of unbelievers from this passage.

DID YOU KNOW?

The Scopes Trial of 1925 was a landmark event and the biggest trial of the Roaring Twenties. The American Civil Liberties Union (ACLU) wanted to try a case against the Butler Act, a Tennessee Law that banned the teaching of evolution in state-funded schools. They found a willing participant in a small-town teacher by the name of John Scopes and financed a trial that featured two of the most prominent lawyers in America: William Jennings Bryan and Clarence Darrow. This trial set the stage for future conflicts where state-funded schools would teach evolution in defiance of previously established biblical standards.

Notes
1. Cited by Harry Leibowitz, World of Children Award Co-Founder and Board Chairman, "The Numbers: Child Sexual Imposition in the United States," *Huffington Post*, February 12, 2016, www.huffingtonpost.com/harry-leibowitz/ the-numbers-child-sexua\-_b_9101508.html.
2. Jack Minor, "Doc Faces Boot for Citing 'Gay,' Health Dangers," *WND*, June 27, 2015, http://www.wnd.com/2015/06/doc-faces-boot-for-citing-gay-health-dangers/.
3. David Breese, *Seven Men Who Rule the World from the Grave* (Chicago, IL: Moody, 1990).

Radical Islam

EZEKIEL 38:1-6

In this lesson we are introduced to the fastest-growing religion in the world.

The Muslim religion has existed for 1,500 years, yet it has only been in the last few decades that Westerners have become aware of the power and presence of Islam in the world. A minority of the world's Muslims are militant extremists for whom chaos is part of their life's mission.

OUTLINE

I. **The History of Islam**

II. **The Habits of Islam**
   A. To Recite the *Shahadah*
   B. To Pray (*Salat*)
   C. To Fast (*Sawm*)
   D. To Give Alms (*Zakat*)
   E. To Make the Pilgrimage to Mecca (*Hajj*)

III. **The Hatred of Islam**

IV. **The Hopes of Islam**
   A. Islam Hopes to Rule the World
   B. Islam Hopes to Return Their Messiah

V. **The "How To's" Regarding Islam**
   A. Do Not Compare Islam with Christianity
   B. Do Not Consider Allah as God
   C. Do Not Confuse Jihad with Salvation
   D. Do Not Connect the Qur'an with the Bible
   E. Do Not Conclude That All Muslims Will Be Lost

OVERVIEW

The Arab countries of the Middle East have grown in their power and influence in the world today, and most of their citizens subscribe to the religion of Islam. But it is not just oil reserves and the accompanying wealth that make the Arab-Islam countries a force to be considered. It is also because Islam is the fastest-growing religion in the world. However, many Americans know very little about this religion that is permeating countries around the world.

In this lesson, we will focus on the tenets of the Muslim religion to increase our awareness of this rapidly growing segment of the world's religious community.

The History of Islam

The word "Islam" means "submission" in Arabic. Therefore, a Muslim is "one who submits to god." Of the 1.8 billion Muslims in the world today, approximately four million live in the United States. The largest concentration of Muslims is not in the Middle East but in the Asia-Pacific region.[1]

The founder of Islam, Muhammad, was born in Mecca (in present-day Saudi Arabia) in AD 570. His parents died when he was young, and he was raised by his paternal grandfather. He worked as a merchant until the age of twenty-six, when he married a woman who was a wealthy, forty-year-old caravan owner. Together they had six children.

Muhammad was exposed to numerous religious influences in Mecca, and according to his own testimony, he received what he considered to be a divine revelation while meditating in a cave at age forty. The revelations continued throughout his life and were eventually compiled into what is now known as the Qur'an, regarded by Muslims as the word of god. There were more than 360 deities in the Arabic pantheon, and Muhammad chose the name of one of them, Allah, to be the true god.

As Muhammad's followers grew, they slaughtered everyone in their path who would not testify that "there is no god but Allah, and Muhammad is his messenger." Muhammad and his followers eventually fled to Medina, where he became head of the first Muslim community in AD 620. Muhammad died in AD 632.

After his death, the Islamic world splintered as the followers of Muhammad tried to choose his successor. Today, Sunni Arabs comprise about ninety percent of the Islamic world, believing that Muhammad's gifts died with him. For Sunnis, the Qur'an is their sole authority. (Saddam Hussein was a Sunni Arab, the minority branch of Islam in Iraq.)

The other major branch of Islam is the Shiites, who identified with Muhammad's son-in-law after Muhammad's death. The Shiites believe that their leaders (imams) have spiritual authority equal to the Qur'an. They also believe that the Twelfth Imam was concealed hundreds of years ago but is still alive, to be one day revealed as the Muslim "Mahdi," or messiah.[2] The Sunni and Shiite Muslims today have a contentious relationship.

The Habits of Islam

The primary practices of the Muslim faithful are referred to as the five pillars of Islam.

To Recite the Shahadah

The Shahadah is the Muslim creed: "There is no god but Allah, and Muhammad is his messenger." In prayer, Muslims repeat this prayer over and over almost as a mantra.

To Pray (Salat)

Muslims pray five times each day—the call to prayer wafting out across Arab cities from the local mosque. Muslims stop wherever they are at the moment and kneel down toward Mecca, first performing a ceremonial cleansing with water (or sand if water is unavailable). The prayers are memorized and recited in Arabic.

To Fast (Sawm)

The most important fasting time for Muslims is during the lunar month of Ramadan, in which they refrain from eating food during daylight hours. Ramadan is set aside for meditation and reflection and ends with a joyous celebration.

To Give Alms (Zakat)

Muslims are required to give 2.5 percent of their income to the poor and needy.

To Make the Pilgrimage to Mecca (Hajj)

The fifth pillar is the once-in-a-lifetime pilgrimage to Mecca, required of all who are physically and financially able. The journey usually takes at least one week and includes stops at many other Islamic holy sites along the way.

The Hatred of Islam

In the Middle East, we have seen Muslim extremists engage in all manner of violence. Indeed, America was the target of extremist violence and hatred on September 11, 2001. Associated with these attacks is the Arabic word "jihad"—a word unknown to most of us in the West a few decades ago. Jihad is often called the sixth pillar of Islam—it means "struggle." Spiritually, jihad refers to the struggle of the individual to submit to Allah, while outwardly it refers to defending the Muslim religion and culture. A big part of jihad is martyrdom, the culture of death. Martyrdom for the sake of Islam is considered a privilege and a great honor.

The Muslim hatred for Israel began in modern times in 1948 when Palestine was returned to Israel as a homeland. And because America is an ally of Israel, Americans have become targets of jihad as well. Experts believe that there are millions and millions of Muslims who are willing to die as martyrs to defeat their perceived enemies. Those who are violent extremists don't represent all of Islam, but they have given the religion and culture a bad name by their actions.

The Hopes of Islam

The hopes of Islam are some of the least known aspects of the religion to Westerners.

Islam Hopes to Rule the World

Radical Islamists have one ultimate goal: to cover the globe with the teachings of Muhammad and bring all into submission to Allah. Ayatollah Khomeini, the former leader of Iran, once said, "The governments of the world should know that Islam cannot be defeated. Islam will be victorious in all the countries of the world and Islam and the teaching of the Qur'an will prevail all over the world."[3] This doesn't always mean a violent jihad.

Islam Hopes to Return Their Messiah

In 2005, Iranian president Ahmadinejad spoke before the United Nations to explain his country's continued pursuit of nuclear technology. He opened his remarks with this prayer: "Oh Allah, the almighty and merciful, hasten the emergence of your last repository, the promised one, that perfect and pure human being. The one that will fill this world with justice and peace."

He was praying for the return of the Twelfth Imam, a figure in Shiite Muslim teaching who parallels the Jewish Messiah in terms of significance. Because the Shiites believe the Twelfth Imam will only return during a time of worldwide chaos, creating that chaos on earth is a way to hasten his return. This makes reasonable negotiations for international stability with a country like Iran out of the question, since instability is what must precede the Imam's return.

Remember, modern Iran is ancient Persia. The rise of radical Islam within Iran correlates perfectly with Ezekiel 38:1-6. There the prophet foretells an alliance between "Gog, of the land of Magog, the prince of Rosh, Meshech, and Tubal" and "Persia, Ethiopia, and Libya," plus "Gomer" and "Togarmah." Gog and Magog represent modern Russia. Never in history has there been an alliance between Russia and Persia—until now. Russia is providing extensive military and technological support to Iran. Ezekiel 38 foretells that this alliance will one day come against Israel and would completely overwhelm Israel without the intervention of God (which will happen).

From the Shiite Muslim perspective, creating chaos works to their advantage because it hastens the return of their Imam (messiah). What they don't realize is that the true Messiah will arrive at just the right moment to save Israel and destroy her enemies (Revelation 19:11).

The "How To's" Regarding Islam

This is not lightweight material—thoughts of international alliances leading to wars in the future can give any of us pause. And we must be careful as we think about the fastest-growing religion in the world. Here are five cautions when it comes to how to regard Islam.

Do Not Compare Islam with Christianity

Being a Muslim is not the same as being a Christian. Jesus Christ said that there was only one way to reach God the Father and that way was Him—Jesus (John 14:6). And there are many other differences:

- Christians do not call for the genocide of a particular race; radical Islam does (the Jews).
- Christians do not send suicide bombers to kill innocent people; radical Muslims do.
- Christians don't work for worldwide chaos to set the stage for the return of their Messiah; radical Shiite Muslims do.
- Christians work for the salvation of Muslims; Muslims call for jihad against those with whom they disagree.

So Christianity and Islam are not two different, parallel paths heading for the same place. They are different paths going in opposite directions.

Do Not Consider Allah as God

Allah is not God. Psalm 86:10 says, "You alone are God." They are not the same God under different names. Their character and teachings are so different that they could not be the same.

- Allah was chosen by Muhammad out of a pantheon of 360 Arabic deities; Jehovah God is eternal and self-revealing.
- Allah is not a trinitarian god; Jehovah God is Trinitarian: Father, Son, and Spirit.
- Allah did not die for man's sins; Jehovah God sent the Son of God to die for man's sins.
- Allah says, "Kill those who don't believe, and you can come to heaven"; Jehovah God died for those who don't believe so they can go to heaven.

Do Not Confuse Jihad with Salvation

Salvation is totally different in Islam and Christianity. Titus 3:5 says it is "not by works of righteousness which we have done, but according to His mercy He saved us." Whether good works during Ramadan or through jihad, Islam is a works-based religion. Christianity is totally based on "grace . . . through faith" (Ephesians 2:8–9).

Ergun Caner, a friend of mine and former Islamic follower who became a Christian, says, "Islam teaches that Allah's love and forgiveness is conditioned upon one's righteousness. The Bible teaches that God's love and forgiveness is unconditional, based not on how good one has been but on the death of Jesus. Salvation is not founded upon the enduring work of each person but on the finished work of Jesus Christ."

A converted Palestine Liberation Organization (PLO) bomber who came to Christ explained it this way: In Islam the only way to get to heaven is to die as an offering to God. In Christianity, Jesus Christ died in our place so we might go to heaven.

Do Not Connect the Qur'an with the Bible

The Qur'an is not "another Bible." Muslims believe that the Qur'an is the mother of all holy books and that the Bible is subservient to the Qur'an. But such a ranking is patently impossible! The Bible was written through divine inspiration by over forty authors over a period of 1,400 years with a consistent message from cover to cover. The Qur'an, on the other hand, is a self-contradicting book supposedly given by the angel Gabriel to Muhammad. But since the latter could neither read nor write, the teachings of the Qur'an were translated and collected by those who heard Muhammad teach. Anyone who reads the Qur'an and then reads the Bible will find no similarity between them in terms of content and quality.

The last point may be the most important because it has to do with the work being done by the Spirit of God to get the Gospel into Muslim contexts—and the fruit that is being born.

It would be possible to think that we are at a stand-off with the militant Muslim world, and to a degree that is true, for this reason: We have nothing they want. It is difficult to negotiate with people for whom negotiation produces no benefit. We have nothing to offer Islam except our souls since they want to cover the earth with the teachings of the Qur'an. And most Christians in the West—indeed, most people in the West—are not going to give up their beliefs or way of life.

So what do we do? We must remain strong: "Be strong in the Lord and in the power of His might" (Ephesians 6:10). We must maintain love toward those that hate us while, at the same time, we defend ourselves against theological error and compromise. And we continue to offer the Gospel of salvation to those who have not yet met the true Messiah, Jesus Christ.

The result is that the Gospel is making incredible inroads into the Muslim world. Our own Turning Point radio broadcasts, along with others, are heard in many Arabic-speaking countries. We get letters from listeners in those countries who tell us what finding Christ has meant to them. And when they ask us to send materials to them, they warn against there being any indication that the materials are religious in nature as it could cost them their lives.

Do Not Conclude That All Muslims Will Be Lost

The promise in 2 Peter 3:9 certainly applies to Muslims just as it does to any other person: "The Lord is . . . not willing that any should perish but that all should come to repentance." We should never assume that any person or group of persons will be lost. Concerning Muslims, the evidence is certainly to the contrary: Many Muslims are embracing Jesus Christ as they encounter His Gospel.

Jesus Christ died for every militant Muslim terrorist just as He died for you and for me. In fact, it is for just such sinners as those who create havoc in the world that Christ died. Remember: "Those who are well have no need of a physician, but those who are sick" (Matthew 9:12). If you have a hard time hoping and praying that Muslims will become your brothers in Christ, then you need to remember that you were once the enemy of God as well until He reached out and brought you to Himself (Colossians 1:21). Yes, we need to protect ourselves from our enemies. But we also need to pray that they will be reconciled to God through Christ. (And pray for the safety of Christian missionaries who are risking their lives to take the Gospel to Islamic populations.)

Two points in closing this lesson: First, do not fear what is happening in the world around us. And second, look up—the signs of the end of the age are indicating that our redemption is drawing nigh.

APPLICATION

Personal Questions

1. List and describe the five habits (or pillars) of Islam.

    a. What habits sound similar to Christian spiritual disciplines?

    b. What makes the habits of Islam different than Christian spiritual disciplines?

2. Explain the meaning of jihad.

    a. What does jihad refer to spiritually for Muslims?

    b. And what does it refer to outwardly?

    c. Why is martyrdom a large part of jihad?

3. What are the two main hopes of Islam?

    a. What is the goal of radical Islam?

    b. How does the Shiite teaching about the Twelfth Imam make it difficult to have peaceful international relations with a Shiite Muslim country?

4. Describe what you have learned about Islam from this lesson.

    a. How will this information help you share the Good News with Muslims?

    b. How do Matthew 9:12 and Colossians 1:21 help you pray for Muslims to come to know Christ as Savior?

Group Questions

1. Discuss the history of Islam.

   a. Share with the group what you learned about Muhammad from this section.

   b. What is the difference between Shiite and Sunni Muslims? Why is knowing this difference important in understanding Islam?

2. As a group, discuss the five "How To's" regarding Islam.

   a. What does John 14:6 tell us about the path of Christianity and the path of Islam?

   b. What does Psalm 86:10 tell us about God?

   c. Describe the differences between Allah and God in character and teaching.

   d. How do Titus 3:5 and Ephesians 2:8–9 describe salvation?

   e. What does Islam teach about salvation?

   f. Explain the difference between how the Qur'an was written and how the Bible was written.

3. What should we not conclude about Muslims?

   a. How does this impact our interactions with those who believe in Islam?

   b. How should we be praying for Muslims?

DID YOU KNOW?

Although Islam is the world's fastest-growing religion, Muslims are converting to Christianity in record numbers. Open Doors tells the story of a refugee family from Syria who gave their hearts to Christ after having a vision of the Lord Jesus: "[After that] we decided to follow Him. . . . We left our old Islamic customs." Although they face persecution back home, they said, "The most important thing is that we know Jesus Christ as our Savior. . . . God is with us." The Lord is working in mighty ways in the Middle East. The pastor of a church in Lebanon talked about the great numbers of Muslims turning to Jesus: "God is waking up a sleeping church [in the Middle East]; a new nation of believers is being born."[4]

Notes

1. "Archived: Statistics by Tradition" (2004), The Pluralism Project, Harvard University, http://www.pluralism.org/resources/statistics/nimer_stats.php.
2. Information on the history of Islam is from Winifred Corduan, *Pocket Guide to World Religions* (Downers Grove, IL: InterVarsity Press, 2006).
3. Christopher Hugh Partridge, *Introduction to World Religions* (Minneapolis, MN: Fortress Press, 2005), 365.
4. Information from "Muslims Converting to Christianity in Unprecedented Numbers," Parts 1 and 2, Open Doors USA, https://www.opendoorsusa.org/christian-persecution/stories/muslims-turn-to-christ-in-unprecedented-numbers-pt-1/, and https://www.opendoorsusa.org/christian-persecution/stories/muslims-turn-to-christ-in-unprecedented-numbers-pt-2/.

Persecution

SELECTED SCRIPTURES

In this lesson we consider the growing trend toward persecution of Christians in America and how to prepare for it.

When we speak of persecution, most Christians think of physical torture or punishment. But that is too narrow. Persecution encompasses all manner of oppression against a person's faith commitments. In that sense, the persecution of Christians in America has already begun.

OUTLINE

I. **The Substance of Christian Persecution**

II. **The Stages of Christian Persecution**
   A. Stage One: Stereotyping
   B. Stage Two: Marginalizing
   C. Stage Three: Threatening
   D. Stage Four: Intimidating
   E. Stage Five: Litigating

III. **The Story of Christian Persecution**
   A. Persecution of Christians in the Bible
   B. Persecution of Christians in History
   C. Persecution of Christians in Today's World

    IV. The Side Effects of Christian Persecution

        A. Suffering Promotes Character

        B. Suffering Provokes Courage

        C. Suffering Proves Godliness

        D. Suffering Produces Joy

        E. Suffering Provides Rewards

    V. The Strength to Face Christian Persecution

        A. Determine to Stand for Truth

        B. Draw Support from One Another

        C. Derive Your Security from the Lord

OVERVIEW

In the last few years, an increasing number of churches, businesses, and individuals have come under legal attack for standing on their biblical principles. These attacks have mostly been generated when Christians have resisted the decay of biblical sexual-moral standards in the U.S.

Jesus scolded the Pharisees for their inability to discern the signs of the times in their day (Matthew 16:3). The signs of *our* time could not be more clear: America is growing increasingly hostile toward biblical Christianity. The Bible is no longer America's moral compass. Those who hold to biblical principles are cited as intolerant at best and law-breakers at worst.

The Substance of Christian Persecution

America's biblical foundation began to erode in the post-World War II prosperity, which resulted in the protest culture of the 1960s. Freedom has been replaced by license. "If it feels good, do it" is now the guiding principle of American culture, pushing Christianity to the margins of the marketplace.

The Pew Research Center reports that Christianity is declining sharply in America. In 2014, about seventy percent of American adults identified as Christians.[1] But this figure is misleading. According to a study by sociologists C. Kirk Hadaway and Penny Long Marler published in *The Journal for the Scientific Study of Religion*, less than twenty percent of Americans regularly attend church on a weekly basis.[2] This statistic gives us a better indication of actual Christian commitment.

Dr. Paul Nyquist, the president of Moody Bible Institute in Chicago, writes, "Get ready. An exciting, yet terrifying era is beginning for American believers. As cultural changes sweep our country, we'll soon be challenged to live out what the Bible says about confronting and responding to persecution."[3]

The Stages of Christian Persecution

Five stages of religious suppression and persecution are taking place in America.

Stage One: Stereotyping

Today, Christians are often stereotyped as ignorant, uneducated, backward, inhibited, homophobic, hateful, and intolerant. Movies and television portray Christians as the cultural "bad guy," the unreasonable character who is judgmental and out of step with the mainstream.

While it's true that some professing Christians do a poor job of representing the faith, these stereotypes do not reflect the reality of authentic Christianity. They grow out of the rising cultural prejudice against the Christian faith. Our duty is to live our convictions in a way that shows these slanderous pictures to be gross distortions of the truth.

Stage Two: Marginalizing

Many would prefer for Christianity not only to be criticized but also to be marginalized—to be pushed so far to the periphery of society that it is, for all practical purposes, eliminated. If Christianity can't legally be eliminated, they want to force it behind closed doors. They want Christianity's influence on American culture to be removed—for example, the secularization of holidays like Christmas and Easter. And it's happening. Christian student organizations are now barred from many university campuses. Courts have eliminated Christmas carols in some public schools, and doctors and small business owners are being forced to serve homosexual clients.

Stage Three: Threatening

Many individuals have been fired from companies for expressing their religious beliefs and practices *on their own time*. The very thought that a practicing Christian might bring some harm or disrespect to a government agency or a company is driving these terminations. Or, more likely, it is the fear of a lawsuit by intolerant groups against agencies and companies.

Companies figure it is easier to fire the Christian than to go through a lengthy adjudication of the employees' rights.

Stage Four: Intimidating

In 2001, California parents sued to prevent psychological testing on first-, third-, and fifth-graders because the tests contained explicit sexual questions. They lost. The court's ruling: "Parents have no due process or privacy right to override the determinations of public schools as to the information to which their children will be exposed."[4] This is only one example. Similar cases of loss-of-rights now occur regularly, and people are being forced into compliance by the government.

Stage Five: Litigating

Christian small business owners who have declined the business of homosexual patrons have been taken to court and fined. Some have lost their businesses, and some have received death threats. Public schools have long been the target of activists like the ACLU. When they took steps to prevent any kind of religious expressions at the graduation ceremonies of a Florida high school, the students themselves struck back. They rose together and recited the Lord's Prayer on their own, motivating many in attendance to join them.[5]

Unless there is a great turnaround, we can expect lawsuits and court judgments to escalate against Christians who practice their faith. According to one writer, "Persecution could well accelerate to include Henry VIII style seizure of church property and monies because of Christian leaders' refusal to bow to the doctrines of the State . . . even jail time for Christians is quite possible."[6]

Christians in America are not likely to experience the kinds of persecution and torture seen in other countries today. And yet, I never imagined a few decades ago that what is now happening in America to Christians would be possible. So who knows what the future holds?

The Story of Christian Persecution

God's people have always been persecuted, even in the Old Testament (Hebrews 11:35–38). Christ was persecuted, as were His apostles—as He warned them they would be (Matthew 10:16–20). To be persecuted for righteousness' sake means that we are hated or opposed solely for being a follower of Christ. When we are doing what is right and living for God, yet suffer because of it, that is persecution.

In America, we have traditionally held a too-narrow view of persecution—that it refers only to physical attacks. But persecution can include mental, spiritual, and emotional oppression brought about through any number of means, all for simply being a Christian. And *Christianity Today* magazine reminds us that "most persecution is not violence. Instead, it's a 'squeeze' of Christians in five spheres of life: private, family, community, national, and church."[7]

Why does the Christian message, and those who follow it, motivate such antagonism? Because it requires submission to God. Those antagonistic to the Gospel feel judged, and rightly so. Not judged by other Christians, but by God Himself. And without a proper understanding of God's *right* to judge sinners, that produces a backlash against God and His people. Ultimately, all are without excuse, as Paul wrote in Romans 1:20–21. Because they don't like—and cannot silence—the message, opponents attack the messenger.

Persecution of Christians in the Bible

Persecution in the New Testament begins with Christ's birth in Bethlehem, when Herod tried to kill Him when He was just a baby. Jesus was persecuted as an adult, as was John the Baptist, the apostles, the deacon Stephen, the Christians living in Jerusalem, and the apostle Paul in extreme measure (2 Corinthians 11:22–29). All the apostles died grisly deaths at the hands of Christ's opponents.

It is amazing that the early Christians in Jerusalem, in the midst of persecution, bound themselves to one another and to the Lord and continued on. They pooled their resources and took care of each other (Acts 4:32–35). In fact, they even rejoiced that their persecution provided a great opportunity for God to display Himself (Acts 4:29–30).

Persecution of Christians in History

The Roman emperor Nero impaled Christians on stakes and set them afire as torches. He sent them into the arenas to be eaten by wild animals and killed by gladiators. He executed both Peter and Paul. Emperor Domitian declared himself to be "Lord and God" and demanded Christians worship him. When they refused, they were killed. The apostle John was exiled to Patmos by Domitian. Until Constantine became emperor and declared Christianity legal in AD 313, Christians were persecuted in the Roman Empire.

Millions more Christians have been killed in various parts of the world since the first century for various reasons. Stories abound of Christians willingly suffering persecution for the sake of their Savior. Catholic Queen Mary of England—called "Bloody Mary" for her execution of more than 300 Protestants—sentenced Henry VIII's former chaplain, Nicholas Ridley, to be burned. "As he was being tied to the stake, Ridley prayed, 'Oh, heavenly Father, I give unto thee most hearty thanks that thou hast called me to be a professor of thee, even unto death.'"[8]

Persecution of Christians in Today's World

Worldwide, each month hundreds of Christians are killed for their faith, churches are attacked, and numerous acts of violence are committed against individual Christians and Christian groups. Those figures add up to more than 12,000 incidents of serious persecution of Christians per year. This does not include the more than 200 million Christians who, according to the World Evangelical Alliance, are presently denied fundamental human rights just because of their faith. The top ten persecuting countries are: North Korea, Iraq, Eritrea, Afghanistan, Syria, Pakistan, Somalia, Sudan, Iran, and Libya.[9] America could soon join this list.

The Side Effects of Christian Persecution

Let me suggest five ways persecution can be a positive thing for a Christian.

Suffering Promotes Character

The New Testament clearly teaches that tribulation—and that would include persecution—builds character (Romans 5:2–5; James 1:2–4). If you want proven character, persecution is one way to get it.

Suffering Provokes Courage

Courage is a reflection of the life of Christ in the Christian. Jesus was not a coward. He entrusted Himself to the Father and drank from the bitter cup of persecution. Peter and John told the Jewish officials that they would not stop preaching the Gospel, that it was their duty to obey God rather than man (Acts 4:19–20; 5:29). The apostle Paul's post-conversion life was a living display of courage (Philippians 1:20–21).

Suffering Proves Godliness

Paul wrote that all who want to live a godly life for Christ will suffer persecution (2 Timothy 3:12). Professing Christians who are not suffering may need to examine the depth of their godliness. Suffering is a form of cleansing and maturing (Hebrews 12:6; 1 Peter 5:10). Jesus learned obedience through the things He suffered (Hebrews 5:8), and so can we. *Suffering* for Christ is a sure sign we are *living* for Christ (Romans 8:16–17).

Suffering Produces Joy

When Paul and Silas were confined to jail in Philippi, they contented themselves with "praying and singing hymns to God" (Acts 16:22–25). Peter and John went away from their persecution "rejoicing" at the privilege of suffering for Christ (Acts 5:41).

Suffering Provides Rewards

What are some of the rewards promised to those who endure persecution?

- Those who endure will be avenged (Revelation 6:9–11; 16:5–7; 18:20; 19:2).
- They will be rewarded with white robes, signifying holiness and purity (Revelation 6:11).
- They will be given perfect and abundant lives free of sorrow (Revelation 7:14–17).
- Heaven will rejoice over them because they did not shrink from death (Revelation 12:11–12).
- They will find eternal rest (Revelation 14:13).
- They will reign with Christ for 1,000 years (Revelation 20:4, 6).
- They will receive the crown of eternal life (James 1:12).
- They will have no more death to fear (1 Corinthians 15:54; Revelation 20:14).

The Strength to Face Christian Persecution

The time to prepare to face persecution is before it happens. If we wait until persecution arises, our emotions will rule the day. We must decide in the calm of commitment what we will do if persecution comes. Following are three things we can do to prepare.

Determine to Stand for Truth

In his famous Harvard commencement address, Aleksandr Solzhenitsyn said, "A decline in courage may be the most striking feature that an outside observer notices in the West in our days."[10] We as Christians must turn that criticism on its head. It is imperative that fear of rejection, criticism, or loss does not cower us into hiding our light. To live worthy of the Gospel is to stand for God's truth without bending. As Paul urged the Corinthians, "Watch, stand fast in the faith, be brave, be strong. Let all that you do be done with love" (1 Corinthians 16:13–14).

We must be prepared to take whatever criticism or persecution comes our way. We must be willing to be "fools for Christ's sake" (1 Corinthians 4:10). Paul gave us our rules of engagement: "Being reviled, we bless; being persecuted, we endure; being defamed, we entreat" (1 Corinthians 4:12–13). And we must be prepared to defend our faith (1 Peter 3:15–16).

Draw Support from One Another

Hebrews 10:24–25 says it best: "And let us consider one another in order to stir up love and good works, not forsaking the assembling of ourselves together, as is the manner of some, but exhorting one another, and so much the more as you see the Day approaching." When persecution comes, we need the support of the Body of Christ. We need the Church, and the

Church needs us. The worst place to be in the midst of persecution is alone. Elijah survived the persecution of Queen Jezebel by discovering there were 7,000 more in Israel who were standing firm against the wicked queen and king (1 Kings 19:14–18).

We, too, need the company of others like ourselves with whom we can share encouragement, struggles, and victories. In today's culture, this need is greater than ever. Now in the minority and under attack, it's easy for us to feel alone and discouraged, as Elijah did. But in the company of fellow believers, we draw strength, discipline, knowledge, encouragement, support, and love from each other. A courageous example can spur any one of us to say, "If she can do it, by God's grace so can I."

Derive Your Security from the Lord

We must keep our eye on the prize when the pressure of persecution hits. We belong to Christ; we are on our way to heaven; nothing can separate us from the love of God in Christ; all things work together for the good of those who belong to Him. The greatest temptation in the face of persecution is to do *anything* to save our life. But remember Jesus' words: "For whoever desires to save his life will lose it, but whoever loses his life for My sake will find it" (Matthew 16:25).

According to C. S. Lewis, we are in "enemy-occupied territory." There will be attacks, even some casualties. But our citizenship is in heaven. We are simply waiting here on earth for Him to appear from heaven to transform us into His own image (Philippians 3:20–21).

What will you do if repression and coercion in America ultimately lead to persecution? Don't wait until it happens to decide who you serve. Draw a line in the sand and stand on the side of Christ. Trust your past, present, and future to the One who has promised to save you forever.

APPLICATION

Personal Questions

1. Read Hebrews 11:35–40.

   a. What is the overall context of this passage? (Remember: Hebrews 11 is the "Hall of Faith" chapter.)

b. Why were some of these martyrs willing to die, refusing to be released from torture (verse 35)?

c. How does verse 36 suggest that personal ridicule qualifies as persecution? Have you suffered this kind of persecution for your faith?

d. How is being "tempted" a form of persecution (verse 37)? Would someone lay a trap hoping for your moral failure?

e. What is true even when a Christian dies from persecution (verses 39–40)?

f. Why is citizenship in heaven the ultimate hope for those who are persecuted (Philippians 3:20)? Who can take that away from you?

2. What was the first act of persecution recorded in the New Testament (Matthew 2:1–16)?

3. What happened to John the Baptist (Mark 6:25–29)?

4. How was Jesus treated during His short time on earth?

a. Luke 4:28–30:

b. Luke 13:31:

c. John 5:16–18:

d. John 8:37–40:

5. What did Jesus learn through His persecutions (Hebrews 5:8)?

6. Why is discomfort or suffering the only place where obedience can be learned?

Group Questions

1. Read the following verses and discuss what happened to Peter and the apostles in Jerusalem after Christ's ascension:

   a. Acts 4:1–3, 18:

   b. Acts 5:17–18:

   c. Acts 12:1–4:

2. How did the apostles react to this persecution (Acts 4:19–20; 5:29)?

3. What did they ask God to do for them (Acts 4:29–30)? Given how the Jewish leaders would respond, what were they asking God for? (More _____.)

4. What was the Early Church in Jerusalem forced to do (Acts 8:1)?

5. Explain what the Early Church father Tertullian meant when he said, "The blood of the martyrs is the seed of the church."

6. Summarize and discuss the kinds of things the apostle Paul suffered for the Gospel (2 Corinthians 6:4–5; 11:22–29).

7. Discuss your "persecution quotient." How would you respond if persecution of Christians in America begins to affect your livelihood or your life?

DID YOU KNOW?

The most comprehensive account of Christian persecution was compiled by John Foxe in England and published in 1563. It is still in print today as *Foxe's Book of Martyrs*, its original title being too long: *Actes and Monuments of these Latter and Perillous Days, Touching Matters of the Church.* Written during the reign of Protestant Queen Elizabeth I, it was originally published in five books. It covered the earliest Christian persecutions, the Catholic Inquisitions in the medieval period, the early English Protestant movement, the separation of the Church of England from Rome, and finally the persecutions of Protestants by Catholic Queen Mary who herself was responsible for executing more than 300 Protestant leaders in England.

Notes
1. "America's Changing Religious Landscape," Pew Research Center, May 12, 2015, http://www.pew forum.org/2015/05/12/americas-changing-religious-landscape/, accessed April 11, 2016.
2. Kelly Shattuck, "7 Startling Facts: An Up Close Look at Church Attendance in America," *Church Leaders,* http://www.churchleaders.com/pastors/pastor-articles/139575-7-startling-facts-an-up-close-look-at-church-attendance-in-america.html, accessed April 11, 2016.
3. J. Paul Nyquist, *Prepare* (Chicago: Moody Publishers, 2015), 10.

4. "Ninth Circuit Decision Denies Parents' Rights," *Education Reporter,* December 2005, http://www.eagleforum.org/educate/ 2005/dec05/9th-circuit.html, accessed April 6, 2016.

5. Bob Unruh, "Graduating Students Defy ACLU," *WND,* June 5, 2009, http://www.wnd.com/2009/06/100274/, accessed April 7, 2016.

6. Fay Voshell, "Persecution of Christians in America: It's Not Just 'Over There,'" *American Thinker,* May 10, 2015, http:// www.americanthinker.com/articles/2015/05Ipersecution_of_christians_in_america_its_not_just_over_there.html.

7. "Inside the Persecution Numbers," *Christianity Today,* March 2014, 14.

8. "Bishops Ridley and Latimer Burned," Christianity.com, http://www.christianity.com/church/church-history/timeline/ 1501-1600/bishops-ridley-and-latimer-burned11629990.html, accessed April 9, 2016.

9. "Christian Persecution," Open Doors USA, https://www.opendoorsus..org/christianpersecution/, accessed April 7, 2016.

10. Aleksandr Solzhenitsyn, "Harvard Commencement Address," June 8, 1978.

Spiritual Warfare

SELECTED SCRIPTURES

*In this lesson we will learn about Satan's character
and his strategies in attacking Christians.*

Approaching the end of the age before Christ's return, we can expect an intensification of spiritual warfare. But too many Christians have failed to prepare themselves. In order to protect ourselves against the attacks of Satan, it is important to know who Satan is and what he does.

OUTLINE

I. Who Satan Is

    A. Satan Is the Great Deceiver

    B. Satan Is the Great Divider

    C. Satan Is the Great Destroyer

II. What Satan Does

    A. The Strategy of Indifference

    B. The Strategy of Ignorance

    C. The Strategy of Infiltration

    D. The Strategy of Intervention

    E. The Strategy of Intimidation

OVERVIEW

From the beginning of time, war has been easy to define and identify—opposing armies had names, home territories, consistency in dress and weapons. Army A and Army B met on a battlefield, were engaged in skirmishes or battles, and moved from place to place geographically.

In the modern era, the Vietnam War introduced "guerilla warfare," and American forces weren't quite prepared for the change. Hit-and-run tactics, booby traps, soldiers dressed like civilians—it was a new kind of war. And today, in the modern war on terrorism, things have changed even more. Today, more than fighting against armies and soldiers, we are fighting against a religiously inspired ideology where the chief weapons are fear and intimidation. This is a war in which there are no rules. Terrorists, we have learned, can appear to be normal citizens at one moment and soldiers the next.

Christians should understand the war on terrorism better than anyone since spiritual warfare shares many similarities. Satan and his demons are invisible, they play by their own rules, they set traps and ambushes, they use deceit and trickery, and their weapons are spiritual instead of physical. Sadly, even though every Christian is a target of Satan and his demons, not every Christian knows it. Too many Christians are ill-equipped to be victorious in the battle to which they have been called.

And the battle is on! First Timothy 4:1 says that in "latter times" many will give "heed to deceiving spirits and doctrines of demons." And Revelation 9:8–11 paints a frightening picture of how earth will suffer during the Tribulation when demons are given free rein to attack. The Roman Catholic Church, both in Italy and in the United States, has increased its training for priests and bishops in the area of spiritual warfare and exorcism. Spiritual attacks are increasing throughout Christendom, in Catholic and Protestant settings alike.

More than 2,000 years ago a small book was written that is still being read by military strategists today: *The Art of War* by Sun Tzu. Consider his words from chapter 3:

- If you know the enemy and you know yourself, you need not fear the result of a hundred battles.
- If you know yourself but not the enemy, for every victory gained, you will also suffer a defeat.
- If you know neither the enemy nor yourself, you will succumb in every battle.[1]

The key principle is the first: In battle, you must know yourself and your enemy! In spiritual warfare, the Christian's enemy is Satan and his demonic hordes: "For we do not wrestle against flesh and blood, but against principalities, against powers, against the rulers of the darkness of this age, against spiritual hosts of wickedness in the heavenly places" (Ephesians 6:12). Without knowing our enemy well enough to know his strategies, we are doomed to defeat.

One of the most important things to realize in spiritual warfare is that people are not our enemy. Satan is the enemy! Yes, Satan may use people in destructive or hurtful ways in our life. But if that happens and we attack the person, we are not attacking the enemy. Only defending ourselves against the true enemy will bring victory in spiritual warfare.

I once made a list from the Bible of all the verbs—the action words—associated with Satan. And it is a frightening list: He beguiles, seduces, opposes, resists, deceives, sows, hinders, buffets, tempts, persecutes, blasphemes, and does many more similar things. All his actions are deceitful, divisive, and destructive, and they try to diminish and deface the glory of God. For the remainder of this lesson, we will define who Satan is and what he does in an attempt to know the enemy.

Who Satan Is

Satan is three things: a deceiver, a divider, and a destroyer. Almost everything he does can be placed under one of these three headings.

Satan Is the Great Deceiver

John 8:44 is the classic text on this point: "There is no truth in [Satan]. When he speaks a lie, he speaks from his own resources, for he is a liar and the father of it." We often say a person today speaks in his "native tongue" or "native language"—meaning the language they know best, the language in which they can conduct personal and commercial business. For Satan, that is the language of lies! There is no truth in him. Everything that comes from his mouth is intended to deceive since lies are his native tongue. The apostle John confirms this in Revelation 12:9: "Satan, who deceives the whole world."

Satan Is the Great Divider

Satan's strategy is to divide and conquer. When he was cast out of heaven, he took a third of the angels with him. He divided the first human family, pitting Cain against Abel. He tempted Ananias and Sapphira to divide their loyalty between God and money. Wherever you see Satan at work, you'll find division. Conversely, whenever you find disputes and division, you'll find Satan. And, yes, Satan goes to church. In the first century, there was one church; today there are hundreds of denominations resulting from divisions through the centuries. And the Church is weaker as a result. Satan delights in weakening and destroying by division.

So much division in the Church and elsewhere begins with words. James says the tongue "is set on fire by hell. . . . It is an unruly evil, full of deadly poison" (James 3:6, 8). When we find words hurting and dividing, guess who is delighted in those situations?

Satan Is the Great Destroyer

Satan will do anything to destroy, delay, demolish, or dismantle God's work. Job, from the Old Testament, is a prime example. When Satan was given access to Job, he destroyed everything (including Job's health) except Job and his wife—he even destroyed Job's wife's attitude toward her husband. He will destroy everything he possibly can for the purpose of destroying the faith of the people of God. Satan knows he can't destroy God, so his next tactic is to destroy the faith of the people of God. Fortunately, Job resisted and kept the faith and saw God bless him richly at the end of his test. In Revelation 9:11, Satan's "name in Hebrew is Abaddon, but in Greek he has the name Apollyon"—and both names in their respective languages mean "destroyer."

Warning: Satan will take any opportunity, however small and seemingly insignificant, to destroy a lifetime of faithfulness to God. Be on your guard.

What Satan Does

In order to be on our guard, we must know *how* Satan does his deceiving, dividing, and destroying work. This is war; we must believe our enemy has strategies he works against us.

The Strategy of Indifference

Satan wants nothing more than for you to be indifferent toward him, to think he doesn't exist. He will therefore do whatever he can to create that appearance. If he can make you think he's a cartoon figure created by Hollywood, with a red suit, pitchfork, horns, and pointed tail, he will.

A 2009 survey by the Barna Group asked 1,871 professing Christians whether or not they agreed that "Satan is not a living being, but a symbol of evil." Forty percent agreed, along with nineteen percent more who agreed "somewhat," and eight percent who weren't sure what they believed. That means sixty-seven percent of the professing Christians did not believe Satan is an actual spiritual being. Only twenty-six percent disagreed, with nine percent disagreeing "somewhat."[2]

There are two reasons why it is easy for Satan to hide himself: first, he's invisible; second, he does his work through worldly means such as media, arts, politics, economics, and education. He even transforms himself into an "angel of light" (2 Corinthians 11:14), meaning he can do things that appear good. But the truth is that "the whole world lies under the sway of the wicked one" (1 John 5:19).

Why would the apostle Paul give us complete instructions on how to put on the armor of God if we were not at war with an actual, powerful spiritual being (Ephesians 6:10–18)? The word "against" appears six times in that passage. Who are we to "stand against" if not an actual being? Spiritual warfare is like standing in a rushing stream that is constantly, every second of every day of every year of your life, rushing against you. It never lets up.

In his book *This World: Playground or Battleground?*, A. W. Tozer described how serious Christians used to see this world as a battleground. Today, however, the spiritual world has become not a battleground, but a playground. Instead of being here to fight, we're here to frolic. Instead of being here to view earth as a foreign land, we've made ourselves very much at home here. Rather than living in expectation of eternity with God, we're pursuing life as we want it now with little thought for the future.[3]

Satan is delighted that we are taking him far less seriously than we used to.

The Strategy of Ignorance

In 1982, an American missionary and professor, Paul Hiebert, published a groundbreaking article titled "The Flaw of the Excluded Middle."[4] As a missionary to India, he had discovered that he was ill-equipped to handle the spiritual realities that Indians took for granted—that realm between heaven and earth where spirits and humans encounter one another. He had been trained in the scientific method in America, which didn't take into account that which could not be seen nor measured. The non-scientific Indian natives were the opposite: They knew full well that unseen powers exist. Hiebert's article was a call for Western missionary training to incorporate this unseen "excluded middle" into their worldview.

The problem in the West was ignorance. In the early 1980s, many theologically astute, evangelical missionary leaders (and other Christian leaders) knew little of what the Bible is clear about: There is a spiritual war taking place. It was as if leaders thought a giant glass canopy had been installed around the earth at the end of the first century, preventing Satan and his demons from having access to Christians. But in other cultures, where science had not explained away supernatural phenomena, the war was all too real.

There is still too much ignorance in the Church today. There are still too many Christians who are suffering from spiritual attacks and have no idea why. God said, "My people are destroyed for lack of knowledge" (Hosea 4:6) for a reason.

The Strategy of Infiltration

If we are indifferent and ignorant about Satan, it is easy for him to infiltrate our lives. Resisting infiltration is pictured perfectly in Ephesians 4:26–27: "'Be angry, and do not sin': do not let the sun go down on your wrath, nor give place to the devil." Paul's point is obvious: Being angry unto sin is a good way to allow the devil to get a "foothold" (NIV) in your life. Sin of any kind is the devil's turf. If we willingly embrace sin and do not repent and keep a clean heart before God, it's like issuing an invitation to the devil—like giving him a "place" in our life. The principle is the same as in Proverbs 6:27: "Can a man take fire to his bosom, and his clothes not be burned?" If we play with fire, we're going to get burned; if we play with sin, we're going to get attacked by the devil.

The idea of a "place" or "foothold" comes from the rocky, mountainous terrain of the Bible lands. In order to gain entrance into an enemy stronghold built into the side of a mountain, warriors would have to climb—and a tiny toehold or foothold, big enough to insert a sandal, might make all the difference in capturing the stronghold. Satan will take any tiny advantage we give him—just enough to get his foot in the door of our life.

The Strategy of Intervention

The idea of staging an intervention in a person's life to arrest the progress of some kind of injurious or unwise behavior is well known. The goal is to intervene—to break the normal cycle of behavior and substitute clinical help or other better behaviors.

Satan loves to intervene in our lives to do just the opposite: distract us from our healthy spiritual behaviors and tempt us with bad behaviors. If he can distract us from the spiritually productive priorities in our life and occupy us with the things of this world, his intervention will be successful. If we are too busy to pray, study the Bible, serve others, attend church or Bible studies, then we will not grow spiritually. We will remain babes in Christ.

A devotional reading sent to me by a friend concludes with this question: "Have you figured out the difference between being busy and being successful in what God has called you to do? Sometimes being busy—B-U-S-Y—just means Being Under Satan's Yoke."[5] There's nothing wrong with being busy, of course, as long as we are busy with the right things. And as long as we don't get so busy that we begin to think of our busyness as a way of impressing God. Even that is a trap of Satan to distract us from true spirituality.

The Strategy of Intimidation

Some Christians are confused about the power of Satan and are intimidated by him; they believe Satan is the opposite counterpart of God.[6] That is false! Satan is in no way equal to God. As a created angel, Satan's opposite in heavenly places is Michael the archangel, not God.

Yes, Satan has powers we do not have—powers that must be respected. But they need not be feared. Why? Because "He who is in you is greater than he who is in the world" (1 John 4:4). The Holy Spirit who lives in us to manifest the life of the Lord Jesus Christ (Galatians 2:20) is far more powerful than Satan. Again, referring to Ephesians 6 and the believer's spiritual armor, Paul would not have given us this armor and told us to use it if it were not sufficient to prevent our being destroyed by Satan. So there is no need to be intimidated by Satan—as long as we have our armor on and are filled with the Spirit.

Napoleon Bonaparte is said to have felt he could conquer the world if it were not for Britain, the nation that defeated him at Waterloo. Satan is the same way. If he could rid history of the cross and resurrection of Jesus Christ, he too might conquer the world. First John 3:8 says, "For this purpose the Son of God was manifested, that He might destroy the works of the devil." Satan can't get rid of Jesus, but Jesus can destroy the works of the devil.

APPLICATION

Personal Questions

Read 1 John 5:18–19.

    a. What does verse 19 say about Satan's domain, his area of influence?

    b. What evidence of his influence do you see in the world that would support verse 19?

    c. Explain how verse 19 and Deuteronomy 10:14 can both be true.

    d. How far does Satan's influence in the world extend? (Use Job 1:12 and 2:6 as examples.)

    e. What security does verse 18 provide against the attacks of the devil?

f. Based on the promise of protection to "whoever is born of God," what does this suggest about the vulnerability of those not born again of God?

g. How do you know that the promise of verse 18 applies to you?

Group Questions

1. What do you think it means to be a "son of the devil" as described in John 8:44 and Acts 13:10?

   a. In what ways would the normal resemblance between fathers and sons apply in this spiritual realm?

   b. What insight does this spiritual father-son metaphor offer to the New Testament idea of "adoption" (Romans 8:15; Ephesians 1:5)?

   c. By whom have Christians been adopted? What does that mean for you personally?

2. What two words precede the phrase "of the devil" in Ephesians 6:11 and 2 Timothy 2:26?

   a. What do these two words suggest about the character and strategies of Satan?

   b. What do they suggest about the need to practice the admonition of 1 Peter 5:8?

3. Read Ephesians 6:10–18. Discuss the purpose of spiritual armor.

   a. How is that purpose expressed in more detail in verse 11?

   b. How does verse 12 dispel the notion that we are at war with the "idea" of evil?

c. List the six elements of armor in verses 14–17 and what each represents as a spiritual weapon.

1)

2)

3)

4)

5)

6)

d. What do the first two words of verse 11 and the first word of verse 14 suggest about the believer's role in his own defense?

DID YOU KNOW?

Christians often wonder if they can be demon-possessed. The answer is no. Unlike non-believers (Matthew 4:24; 8:16, 28), there are no examples in the New Testament of Christians being described as possessed by a demon. In fact, the Greek word used in these instances is not literally translated as "demon-possessed." *Daimonizomai* is best translated as "demonized," or demon-influenced or afflicted. If a person has no spiritual or moral defense mechanisms to use in resisting the devil, then yes—that person could be completely dominated by Satan's influence, or "possessed." Christians can be influenced (tempted, harassed) by Satan and his demons but not dominated due to the presence of the Holy Spirit.

Notes

1. Sun Tzu, *The Art of War* (Hollywood, FL: Simon & Brown, 2010), 11.
2. The Barna Group, "Most American Christians Do Not Believe that Satan or the Holy Spirit Exist," Barna.org, April 10, 2009, accessed January 24, 2010.
3. A. W. Tozer, *This World: Playground or Battleground?* (Camp Hill, PA: Christian Publications, Inc., 1989), chapter 1.
4. Paul G. Hiebert, "The Flaw of the Excluded Middle." *Missiology*, 10:35–47, January 1982. Reprinted in Ralph D. Winter and Steven C. Hawthorne (eds.), *Perspectives on the World Christian Movement: A Reader* (3rd edition) (Pasadena, CA: William Carey Library, 1999), 414–421.
5. Bob Gass, *The Word for Today,* September/October/November 2010 (Alpharetta, GA: Bob Gass Ministries), 21.
6. Randy Alcorn, *If God Is Good: Faith in the Midst of Suffering and Evil* (Colorado Springs, CO: Multnomah, 2009), 51.

Apathy

MATTHEW 24:36-51

In this lesson we are warned against looking at the present and future from the world's perspective.

The saying, "He can't see the forest for the trees," applies to many in our world. The obligations and options we must deal with can blind us to history's grand purpose. We can grow cavalier, careless, even callous about God's plan to consummate history with the return of Christ.

OUTLINE

I. **Jesus Warns Against a Cavalier Attitude**

II. **Jesus Warns Against a Careless Attitude**

III. **Jesus Warns Against a Calloused Attitude**

OVERVIEW

The Old and New Testaments are filled with the promises of the Second Coming of Christ. In the Old Testament, there are 1,845 references and a total of seventeen Old Testament books that give it prominence. Of the 216 chapters in the entire New Testament, there are

318 references to the Second Coming, or one out of every thirty verses. Twenty-three of the twenty-seven New Testament books refer to this great event. For every prophecy of Christ's First Advent to this earth, there are eight concerning His Second Coming. Now, in light of that massive evidence, can we really say, "Well, it's just not relevant"?

My friend, if Christ's return were not relevant, God would not have mentioned it. If He had not wanted us to know about it, He could easily have omitted it. But the truth is that anyone who claims to be a teacher/preacher of the Word of God must regularly visit this truth.

In Matthew 24:36–44, we read these words:

> But of that day and hour no one knows, not even the angels of heaven, but My Father only. But as the days of Noah were, so also will the coming of the Son of Man be. For as in the days before the flood, they were eating and drinking, marrying and giving in marriage, until the day that Noah entered the ark, and did not know until the flood came and took them all away, so also will the coming of the Son of Man be. Then two men will be in the field: one will be taken and the other left. Two women will be grinding at the mill: one will be taken and the other left. Watch therefore, for you do not know what hour your Lord is coming. But know this, that if the master of the house had known what hour the thief would come, he would have watched and not allowed his house to be broken into. Therefore you also be ready, for the Son of Man is coming at an hour you do not expect.

These are the words of the Lord in response to the three questions the disciples had asked Him. Jesus had told them about the cataclysmic events that would come at the end of the age, and the disciples were curious, just as we are. So they asked, "Lord, when? When is this going to happen?" The Lord answered them, but He didn't answer them. He didn't give them what they wanted to know; He gave them what they needed to know.

Here's what He told them. First of all, this is going to happen at an unknown day and hour. No one knows when it is. Second, this is going to take place in such a way that no one will be able to discern the date. We read in Matthew 24:42, "Watch therefore, for you do not know what hour your Lord is coming." Verse 44 says the same thing: "Therefore you also be ready, for the Son of Man is coming at an hour you do not expect." Verse 50 says the same thing: "The master of that servant will come on a day when he is not looking for him and at an hour that he is not aware of." And in Matthew 25:13 we find it again: "Watch therefore, for you know neither the day nor the hour in which the Son of Man is coming."

First of all, He didn't give the disciples a date. Then, second, He told them no one would know the day. Believers today need to heed the voice of the Lord as well, for the coming of the Rapture of the Church—when the Lord takes us out of here—is going to occur when we do not expect it.

So what? Some might say, "If you can't know, no big deal." Yet the Scriptures remind us over and over again that we are to be prepared. If we don't know about something and we don't care about it, how in the world can we be prepared for it?

Notice how frequently the New Testament addresses this issue. In Romans 13:11–14, Paul wrote:

> And do this, knowing the time, that now it is high time to awake out of sleep; for now our salvation is nearer than when we first believed. The night is far spent, the day is at hand. Therefore let us cast off the works of darkness, and let us put on the armor of light. Let us walk properly, as in the day, not in revelry and drunkenness, not in lewdness and lust, not in strife and envy. But put on the Lord Jesus Christ, and make no provision for the flesh, to fulfill its lusts.

In 1 Corinthians 1:7, Paul commended the first generation church in Corinth, saying, "You come short in no gift, eagerly waiting for the revelation of our Lord Jesus Christ." Paul also reminded Philippian believers in Philippians 3:20, "Our citizenship is in heaven, from which we also eagerly wait for the Savior, the Lord Jesus Christ."

The writer of Hebrews told all the believers who received his epistle, "Let us consider one another in order to stir up love and good works, not forsaking the assembling of ourselves together, as is the manner of some, but exhorting one another, and so much the more as you see the Day [of our Lord's return] approaching" (Hebrews 10:24–25).

James said, "Establish your hearts, for the coming of the Lord is at hand" (James 5:8).

Peter wrote, "But the end of all things is at hand; therefore be serious and watchful in your prayers" (1 Peter 4:7).

John said, "Little children, it is the last hour; and as you have heard that the Antichrist is coming, even now many antichrists have come, by which we know that it is the last hour" (1 John 2:18).

And Jesus' last words recorded in the Bible are these: "Surely I am coming quickly" (Revelation 22:20).

If we go back through all these passages, we find that in almost every single case, future truth impacts present responsibility. It is the knowledge that His coming is soon that puts a little bit of urgency into our step and a little bit of determination into our service.

A lot of Christians think they have forever to win their friends and their families. But as our Lord speaks of His Second Coming, He reminds us that it is possible for us to have wrong attitudes. So let's look at three of the attitudes our Lord warned against.

Jesus Warns Against a Cavalier Attitude

In Matthew 24:37–39, Jesus uses an illustration that would have brought immediate recognition to every one of His listeners. He said, "But as the days of Noah were, so also will the coming of the Son of Man be. For as in the days before the flood, they were eating and drinking, marrying and giving in marriage, until the day that Noah entered the ark, and did not know until the flood came and took them all away, so also will the coming of the Son of Man be."

Jesus said that when He comes back, it is going to be like it was before the flood of Noah. Genesis 6:5 tells us what the Lord saw when He looked down: "Then the LORD saw that the wickedness of man was great in the earth, and that every intent of the thoughts of his heart was only evil continually."

We may not be quite there yet, but we are headed in that direction. This world is not getting better; it is getting worse. And that's the way it was just before the Flood.

In this passage, Jesus was not talking about people doing bad things, just normal things. They were just eating and drinking. Just marrying and giving in marriage. Just taking life as it was.

No matter how intense the signs and the message of Noah were, they didn't pay any attention. How long did Noah preach to those people about the Flood? One hundred and twenty years! That's a long time to preach one message: "It's going to rain." But that's what he did. And rather than turning to God in repentance, they didn't do anything. The Bible says that's the way it will be before Jesus comes back again. What are people going to be doing? Just what they are doing.

Nobody has time for prophecy. "I don't want to talk about the Lord's coming. I've got to go to a wedding." "We're having a dinner at our house." "We've got kids being born into our family." "I've got grandchildren." "I've got a career to pursue." So people just take the Bible in a cavalier way. They look forward to the future, and they don't listen to the Word of God.

Jesus said the days before the Second Coming will be just like that. People will continue to live the way they have always lived in spite of the cataclysmic warnings and predictions. They will think only of the present. They will make plans for the future to ensure their physical comfort. They will not give one thought to the possibility that the prophets were right about the times.

The apostle Peter said:

> Beloved, I now write to you this second epistle (in both of which I stir up your pure minds by way of reminder), that you may be mindful of the words which were spoken before by the holy prophets, and of the commandment of us, the apostles of the Lord and Savior, knowing this first: that scoffers will come in the last days, walking according to their own lusts, and saying, "Where is the promise of His coming? For since the fathers fell asleep, all things continue as they were from the beginning of creation" (2 Peter 3:1–4).

Doesn't that sound familiar? But he goes on to say in verses 5–6, "For this they willfully forget: that by the word of God the heavens were of old, and the earth standing out of water and in the water, by which the world that then existed perished, being flooded with water."

What is Peter saying? He is saying that the last days will be just like it was in Noah's time. Just because God's judgment doesn't arrive on people's time schedule, they assume it won't come at all. But then all of a sudden it does happen and, because they did not believe, it's too late.

Jesus Warns Against a Careless Attitude

Jesus tells a little story in Matthew 24:43–44: "But know this, that if the master of the house had known what hour the thief would come, he would have watched and not allowed his house to be broken into. Therefore you also be ready, for the Son of Man is coming at an hour you do not expect."

Jesus isn't comparing Himself to a thief, but He does use that illustration. In fact, the Bible refers to it quite a few times. Notice Luke 12:39: "Know this, that if the master of the house had known what hour the thief would come, he would have watched and not allowed his house to be broken into." And 1 Thessalonians 5:2: "For you yourselves know perfectly that the day of the Lord so comes as a thief in the night." And 2 Peter 3:10: "But the day of the Lord will come as a thief in the night, in which the heavens will pass away with a great noise, and the elements will melt with fervent heat; both the earth and the works that are in it will be burned up."

Revelation 3:3 reads, "Remember therefore how you have received and heard; hold fast and repent. Therefore if you will not watch, I will come upon you as a thief, and you will not know what hour I will come upon you." In Revelation 16:15 we read, "Behold, I am coming as a thief. Blessed is he who watches."

Jesus is saying, "Don't get careless about this just because you don't see it happening yet."

Jesus Warns Against a Calloused Attitude

Let's look at Matthew 24:45–51:

Who then is a faithful and wise servant, whom his master made ruler over his household, to give them food in due season? Blessed is that servant whom his master, when he comes, will find so doing. Assuredly, I say to you that he will make him ruler over all his goods. But if that evil servant says in his heart, "My master is delaying his coming," and begins to beat his fellow servants, and to eat and drink with the drunkards, the master of that servant will come on a day when he is not looking for him and at an hour that he is not aware of, and will cut him in two and appoint him his portion with the hypocrites. There shall be weeping and gnashing of teeth.

Jesus warns against a calloused attitude. He tells a story of two slaves who work for an absentee master. One slave is good and faithful, and the other is evil and faithless. The good slave represents believers who will be on the earth before the Lord's return, while the evil servant represents unbelievers. Every person in the world holds his life, his possessions, and his abilities in trust from God, and all will be held accountable to the Lord for what they have done with that trust. In the case of this evil servant, the dominant attitude is one of calloused procrastination. He doesn't believe the master is going to come back any time soon, so he has no motivation to cease doing evil. Christ's words warn him to be careful because he doesn't know the schedule.

I've heard people say something like, "I believe in the coming of the Lord, but I've got some things I want to do, and I've got this all figured out. When I first begin to see anything that looks like the Second Coming, I'm going to get my life together, and then I'll be ready to go."

I question the sincere faith of anybody who reasons like that. That's just not the way a real Christian reasons. But even if you could reason like that, how stupid it would be to live that way. The Bible tells us that in such an hour as you think not, He comes!

A man told me not long ago that he wanted to become a Christian, but it wasn't convenient for him then. Can you imagine standing before the Lord someday and saying, "I was going to accept You, but it just wasn't convenient." Well, because it wasn't convenient for that man to accept Christ, it won't be convenient for him to get into heaven.

There is going to be a day when that decision has to be made or it will no longer be available. We can't keep hearing the warnings, hearing the Scripture, listening to our friends, watching what we know to be the evidence of God's work in this world, and not do what we need to do.

If you haven't trusted Him yet, why don't you do it today? Receive Him as your Savior and your Lord.

APPLICATION

Personal Questions

Read the parable told by Jesus in Matthew 24:45–51.

   a. What responsibility did the master give the servant (verse 45)?

b. In what general sense is this responsibility similar to that given in Genesis 1:28?

c. What is the master's attitude when he arrives and finds the servant carrying out his assigned responsibility (verses 46–47)?

d. How does this situation contrast with what God found His "managers" doing in Genesis 6:5–6?

e. Contrast the manager's response in Matthew 24:47 with God's response in Genesis 6:7.

f. What is the master's response when he returns and finds his servant disobeying his commands (verse 51)?

g. What is the danger of choosing not to be a faithful steward (verse 50)?

h. What is the message of the parable (Matthew 24:44)?

i. Is this parable for unbelievers alone who face the prospect of judgment if they aren't prepared for Christ's return (verse 51)?

j. How should believers in Christ, whose eternal life is secure, apply Christ's teaching about the unknown day and hour of His return?

k. What does a Christian, who is not living faithfully for Christ when He returns, stand to lose (1 Corinthians 3:11–15)?

Group Questions

Read Romans 13:8–14 and discuss the following questions:

a. How do verses 8 (cleaning up all debts) and 12 (the day of the Lord is near) connect? When one's physical life is almost over, how does one "get his finances in order"?

b. Just as one doesn't make large purchases and incur large obligations at the end of physical life, what should our primary focus be as the end of life on earth approaches? If one violates the commandments, what debt(s) does he incur (verses 8–10)?

c. What reason does Paul give in verse 11 for owing no one anything except love?

d. In what sense is your own salvation "nearer than when [you] first believed" (verse 11)?

e. It has been 2,000 years since the promise of Christ's return was given. Why is it easy to get lulled into complacency about it happening in your lifetime?

f. When Paul said, "the day is at hand" (verse 12), did he mean chronologically or theologically?

g. How do verses 12–14 parallel verses 48–50 in Jesus' parable (Matthew 24)?

h. Taken in light of the any-moment return of Christ, why is "put on the Lord Jesus Christ" a good image for the Christian lifestyle? How would you feel if Christ arrived and you were clothed in the garments of this world?

i. What aspects of your life would you be proud, or ashamed, for Christ to see if He returned today?

DID YOU KNOW?

The latest effort to explain away the Genesis account of Noah's Flood came in the late 1990s. Two geologists theorized that melting glaciers, which covered much of Europe and Asia, caused oceans worldwide to rise. When the Mediterranean Sea rose, it cut through modern Turkey and breached the strait known today as the Bosporus, flooding the freshwater Black Sea and destroying all human and animal life in the area. Undersea explorer Robert Ballard has since found evidence of human settlements beneath the Black Sea. This local flood was supposed to have given rise to flood legends that exist in many ancient cultures. However, this latest theory in no way conforms with the Genesis account of a worldwide flood.

PART 3

HEAVENLY

SIGNS

LESSON 12

Rapture

1 THESSALONIANS 4:13-18

In this lesson we define and discover the details of the coming event known as the Rapture.

As He prepared to leave this world, Jesus told His disciples He would return and take them to the place He had prepared for them. Later, the apostle Paul provided the details of this event. Since it could happen at any time, the Rapture is a strong motivation for a consecrated, expectant life.

OUTLINE

I. **The Rapture Is a Signless Event**

II. **The Rapture Is a Surprise Event**

III. **The Rapture Is a Sudden Event**

IV. **The Rapture Is a Selective Event**

V. **The Rapture Is a Spectacular Event**

VI. **The Rapture Is a Sequential Event**
   A. The Return
   B. The Resurrection
   C. The Redemption
   D. The Rapture and the Reunion

VII. The Rapture Is a Strengthening Event
A. Expectation
B. Consecration
C. Examination

OVERVIEW

Two publishing events have helped insert the Rapture of the Church into cultural conversations around the world. The first was *The Late Great Planet Earth,* written by Hal Lindsey, and released in 1970.

The second was the twelve-volume series of books known as "The Left Behind Series," *Left Behind* being the title of the first volume that was released in 1995. The books were co-authored by Tim LaHaye and Jerry Jenkins. The ninth volume, *Desecration,* was released shortly after the terror attacks of September 11, 2001, and sold enough copies before the end of 2001 to be the world's bestselling book of that year.

These authors have done the Church a great service by reminding her of the incredible importance of the prophetic Scriptures. The Rapture is perhaps the most important piece of prophecy for today's Christians to understand since it could very well impact them personally. In this lesson, we will discover what the Rapture is, defend it biblically, and explain its personal and practical importance for the Christian.

In summary, the Rapture is an event where all who have put their trust in Christ, living and deceased, will suddenly be caught up from earth, be joined with Christ in the air, and taken to heaven. Paul describes the Rapture in 1 Thessalonians 4:13–18.

"Rapture" is not a biblical word. It is derived from the Latin translation of 1 Thessalonians 4:17, which translates Greek *harpazo* (to catch up or carry away) as *rapiemur* from the Latin *rapio.* The Greek *harpazo* occurs fourteen times in the New Testament with four variations of meaning, each of which contributes to understanding what Paul is describing in verse 17: "Then we who are alive and remain shall be caught up together with [the dead] in the clouds to meet the Lord in the air."

First, *harpazo* can mean "to carry off by force." Christ will use His power to remove living and deceased believers from the last enemy, death. Second, *harpazo* can mean "to claim for oneself eagerly." Christ purchased us with His blood and so will return to claim those who are His. Third, *harpazo* can mean "to snatch away speedily." The Rapture will occur "in the twinkling of an eye" (1 Corinthians 15:52). Fourth, *harpazo* can mean "to rescue from the danger of destruction." This meaning supports the idea that the Rapture will save the Church from the danger of the seven-year Tribulation.

This coming event is part one of Christ's two-part return to earth. First, to remove the Church from the world. Second, seven years later, to establish His kingdom on earth. For every prophecy in Scripture about Christ's first advent there are eight about His second.[1] The 260 chapters of the New Testament contain 318 references to the Second Coming of Christ.[2]

Will the Rapture occur at Christ's Second Coming? The short answer is, "Yes, but . . ." The Rapture sets in motion the end-time events leading to Christ's Second Coming. The two stages—Rapture and Return—will be separated by a seven-year Tribulation on earth. The purpose of the Rapture is to spare Christ's own from the horrors of the Tribulation, according to Revelation 3:10.

The physical return of Christ will happen at the end of the Tribulation as described in vivid detail in Revelation 19. The apostle John's vision of Christ's return echoes what Zechariah saw in the Old Testament: a giant battle and Christ returning to the Mount of Olives, bringing His saints with Him (Zechariah 14:1, 3–5). Jude states what will happen when Christ returns: judgment of the ungodly (Jude 14–15).

The prophets saw what appears to be the Tribulation—"the time of Jacob's trouble" (Jeremiah 30:7)—not the Rapture. But that is not surprising; they didn't differentiate clearly between the First and Second Advents of Christ. The prophets "inquired and searched carefully" (1 Peter 1:10–11) but saw more of the big picture than the details. And they didn't see the Church at all, which is who the Rapture affects. The prophets saw the future like seeing successive mountain peaks through a telephoto lens. They saw the peaks (events), but not the distance that separates them.

Three New Testament passages tell us about the Rapture: John 14:1–3; 1 Corinthians 15:50–57; 1 Thessalonians 4:13–18. Paul's words in 1 Thessalonians are the most complete and form the basis for this lesson. First, we must note that Paul gained his understanding of the Rapture via special revelation from God—he called it a "mystery" in 1 Corinthians 15:51, meaning a truth not previously revealed. The revelation was "by the word of the Lord" (1 Thessalonians 4:15). Second, Paul passed on the content of this revelation to meet a practical concern of the Christians in Thessalonica. They were concerned about the fate of Christians who died before Christ's Second Coming (1 Thessalonians 4:13–18) and about the timing of the Rapture—whether it had already happened (2 Thessalonians 2:1–2).

Now, seven characteristics of the Rapture.

The Rapture Is a Signless Event

Unlike the Second Coming, no signs will precede the Rapture. It could occur at any moment. This is called the doctrine of *imminency*—that is, the Rapture is imminent; it could happen at any moment. Specifically, nothing in God's prophetic program must take place as a prerequisite to the Rapture. Things *may* happen but nothing *must* happen. That means we don't know when it could happen. It could be today or years from today.

Bible expositor A. T. Pierson wrote, "Imminence is the combination of two conditions, viz., certainty and uncertainty. By an imminent event we mean one which is certain to occur at some time, uncertain at what time."[3] Without any warning, Jesus Christ will return to rapture His saints and take them to heaven. Christians must live prepared lives, ready to meet their Savior at any moment.

The Rapture Is a Surprise Event

While many through the years have predicted the date of the Rapture and Jesus' Second Coming, Jesus' words in Matthew 24:36–39 should be taken literally: No one, including Jesus and the angels, knows the time of His return. Only God the Father knows. Not knowing when Jesus will come for His Church causes us to be ready at all times.

The Rapture Is a Sudden Event

Paul wrote that the Rapture will take place "in a moment, in the twinkling of an eye" (1 Corinthians 15:52). "Twinkling" likely refers to the amount of time it takes for light, traveling at 186,000 miles per second, to be reflected on the retina of one's eye. In less than a nanosecond, the Lord will call believers to Himself!

The Rapture Is a Selective Event

All three of the major passages that teach about the Rapture make it clear that it involves believers only (including innocent children too young to believe). In John 14:1–3, Jesus is speaking to His disciples who are obviously believers. His words, "I will come again and receive you to Myself," are what we call the Rapture—the uniting of Jesus Christ with His faithful followers.

In 1 Corinthians 15, Paul talks about "those who are Christ's at His coming" (verse 23). He concludes the passage by talking about their abounding in the work of the Lord (verse 58), an obvious reference to Christian believers. Three times in 1 Thessalonians 4:13–18 he refers to believers as "brethren" (verse 13), as those who "believe that Jesus died and rose again" (verse 14), and as the "dead in Christ" (verse 16). The question is this: *Were Jesus and Paul talking about you?* Will you be a participant in the Rapture?

The Rapture Is a Spectacular Event

The actual Second Coming of Christ is described as a glorious event in Revelation 19:11–14, and rightly so. For that reason, the Rapture has traditionally played second fiddle to the Second Coming. But the Rapture itself will be a spectacular event.

One verse is all we need: "For the Lord Himself will descend from heaven with a shout, with the voice of an archangel, and with the trumpet of God" (1 Thessalonians 4:16). These are not three distinct sounds but one sound described three different ways.

This sound will be like a shout, ringing with commanding authority like the voice of an archangel. It will also be like the blare of a trumpet in its volume and clarity. And the sound will be heard only by those who have trusted Christ as Savior. Jesus shouted, "Lazarus, come forth!" in John 11:43. His shout of "Come forth!" at the Rapture will not name a single individual, but will be heard by every believer in every grave around the world.

Based purely on how the Rapture will sound—it will be a spectacular event.

The Rapture Is a Sequential Event

In 1 Thessalonians 4, Paul identifies five aspects of the Rapture in their sequential order.

The Return

The initiating event is Christ's return from heaven (verse 16). This fulfills the prophecy given by the angels the day Christ ascended into heaven—that the disciples would see Him return in like manner (Acts 1:11). Jesus ascended; Jesus will return. The same person who left earth will return.

The Resurrection

"The dead in Christ will rise first" (verse 16). "Sleep" is a biblical metaphor for death (John 11:11; Acts 7:60; 13:36). Those who have been "asleep" in Christ will be "awakened" and raised from the dead. How bodies dead for centuries, not to mention bodies that have been cremated or destroyed in explosions, will be recomposed and raised, we do not know. But they will be.

The Redemption

Following the resurrection of the dead, believers who are alive will rise to meet Christ in the air. They will experience the same physical transformation as the deceased, then resurrected, believers. Paul says in 1 Corinthians 15:51–52, "We shall not all sleep, but we shall all be changed—in a moment, in the twinkling of an eye, at the last trumpet." We will become like Christ's resurrected, glorified body, fit for heaven.

The Rapture and the Reunion

There are three reunions that will take place (verse 17).

Translating living saints to heaven has happened before the Rapture. In fact, four raptures have already occurred. In the Old Testament; Enoch was taken to heaven without dying (Genesis 5:24), as was Elijah (2 Kings 2:1, 11). We have already mentioned Christ being taken up to heaven (Acts 1:11), and the apostle Paul also was taken up to "the third heaven" and returned to earth (2 Corinthians 12:2–4).

There are two raptures that are yet to occur. During the Tribulation, God's two witnesses will be taken to heaven while they are still living (Revelation 11:12). The primary Rapture yet to occur, of course, is the Rapture of the Church just before the beginning of the Tribulation.

First, dead bodies will reunite with their spirits which Christ will have brought with Him from heaven (verse 14). Deceased bodies will be reunited with their spirits. Second, resurrected believers will meet living believers. It will be a reunion of saints from every era of history, uniting finally as the one, universal Church. Third, together these groups will experience the joy of reunion with their Lord. They met Him first at their conversion, now they meet Him face to face.

The Rapture Is a Strengthening Event

The Rapture can change our life; it is a source of personal comfort and hope. The reason Paul wrote to the Thessalonians about it was to ease their concerns about their departed loved ones. Death is not final. The resurrection of believers who have died will reverse the effects of death. All who have lost loved ones to the sting of death can be comforted in the knowledge that they will see them again. But it is also a source of strength. Jesus promised His disciples, on the night He was arrested, that He would return for them (John 14:1–3).

It is no wonder that Paul told the Thessalonians to comfort themselves with the truth concerning the Rapture (1 Thessalonians 4:18).

The Rapture can impact our life now, in three ways, while we wait for it to happen.

Expectation

The letter from Paul to Titus puts in words how the expectation of the Rapture should impact our life:

> For the grace of God that brings salvation has appeared to all men, teaching us that, denying ungodliness and worldly lusts, we should live soberly, righteously, and godly in the present age, looking for the blessed hope and glorious appearing of our great

God and Savior Jesus Christ, who gave Himself for us, that He might redeem us from every lawless deed and purify for Himself His own special people, zealous for good works (Titus 2:11–14).

Consecration

I am told that Robert Murray M'Cheyne, a brilliant young Scottish preacher who died at age twenty-nine in 1843, wore a wristwatch with the words "The Night Cometh" engraved on its face. Every time he checked his watch, he was reminded that time is marching on. We won't always have time to win souls to Christ and to consecrate our own lives for His service. The apostle John exhorted his readers to "not be ashamed before Him at His coming" (1 John 2:28). The any-moment imminent return of Jesus for His Church is life's greatest stimulus for living a consecrated life.

Examination

Jesus warned that He is "coming quickly" (Revelation 22:12). That means we should live every day as if He was coming that day. But will we be ready? Will we be found with heart and hands dedicated to serving Him at the moment we see Him face to face? Even more important, have we committed ourselves by faith to Christ so we are assured of being part of His Church that is called into His presence at the Rapture?

When the Rapture occurs, there will be no opportunity to make a decision. Be sure today that you have said yes to Christ so you will be prepared to rejoice at His appearing.

THE RAPTURE	THE RETURN (SECOND COMING)
Christ comes in the air (1 Thessalonians 4:16–17)	Christ comes to the earth (Zechariah 14:4)
Christ comes for His saints (1 Thessalonians 4:16–17)	Christ comes with His saints (1 Thessalonians 3:13; Jude 1:14)
Believers depart the earth (1 Thessalonians 4:16–17)	Unbelievers are taken away (Matthew 24:37–41)
Christ claims His bride	Christ comes with His bride
Christ gathers His own (1 Thessalonians 4:16–17)	Angels gather the elect (Matthew 24:31)
Christ comes to reward (1 Thessalonians 4:16–17)	Christ comes to judge (Matthew 25:31–46)

THE RAPTURE	THE RETURN (SECOND COMING)
Not in the Old Testament (1 Corinthians 15:51)	Predicted often in the Old Testament
There are no signs. It is imminent.	Portended by many signs (Matthew 24:4–29)
It is a time of blessing and comfort (1 Thessalonians 4:17–18)	It is a time of destruction and judgment (2 Thessalonians 2:8–12)
Involves believers only (John 14:1–3; 1 Corinthians 15:51–55; 1 Thessalonians 4:13–18)	Involves Israel and the Gentile nations (Matthew 24:1–25:46)
Will occur in a moment, in the time it takes to blink. Only His own will see Him (1 Corinthians 15:51–52)	Will be visible to the entire world (Matthew 24:27; Revelation 1:7)
Tribulation begins	Millennium begins
Christ comes as the bright morning star (Revelation 22:16)	Christ comes as the Sun of Righteousness (Malachi 4:2)

Some content taken from *The End,* by Mark Hitchcock. Copyright © 2012. Used by permission. All rights reserved. www.tyndaledirect.com.

APPLICATION

Personal Questions

1. Which Scripture passages in the New Testament mention the Rapture?

   a. What do these passages teach about who will be raptured?

   b. What do these passages tell us about how Paul gained understanding about the Rapture?

   c. Why did Paul write to the Thessalonians about the Rapture?

   d. How do Paul's words to the Thessalonians bring comfort and understanding to you?

2. Describe the differences between the Rapture and the Second Coming of Christ.

    a. When does each event occur?

    b. What is the purpose of each event?

3. Does the imminency of the Rapture impact how you live and how you interact with others?

    a. If so, how does it impact your life?

    b. If not, what changes do you need to make in your life in light of Christ's imminent return?

4. As you serve a Savior you've never seen, what does it mean to know you will one day be united with Him?

Group Questions

1. How would you summarize the Rapture?

2. Explain the four different meanings of the Greek word *harpazo* and how each definition relates to the Rapture.

3. Discuss the seven characteristics of the Rapture.

    a. Explain what is meant by the imminency of the Rapture.

    b. Who knows when the Rapture will occur?

    c. How long will the Rapture take?

    d. What will the sound that occurs at the Rapture be like (1 Thessalonians 4:16)?

4. What are the five aspects of the Rapture?

    a. Discuss the four raptures that have already occurred.

    b. What are the three reunions that will occur as part of the Rapture?

5. Share how the Rapture strengthens your faith.

    a. What hope does the Rapture give us?

    b. How does the imminency of the Rapture impact how we live here on earth?

DID YOU KNOW?

Have you ever thought about what people on earth will be experiencing in the moments after the Rapture? Dr. Tim LaHaye did. While he was traveling, he observed a flirtatious interaction between a married pilot and an unmarried flight attendant. He imagined the pilot's wife was a believing Christian and wondered what the pilot would do if some of his passengers were suddenly raptured. These thoughts sparked the *Left Behind* series, which Dr. LaHaye wrote with Jerry B. Jenkins. Their popular, fictional series about the Rapture and subsequent end-time events opened the eyes of many to the imminency of Christ's return and the reality of the end times.[4]

Notes

1. "The Second Coming of Christ" preceptaustin.org, February 21, 2015, www.preceptaustin.org/the_second_coming_of_Christ.htm.
2. Chuck Swindoll, "Does the Bible Teach that Jesus Will Return?" Jesus.org, n.d., www.jesus.org/early-church-history/promise-of-the-second-coming/does-thebible-teach-that-jesus-will-return.html.
3. Arthur T. Pierson, *Our Lord's Second Coming as a Motive to World-Wide Evangelism* (published by John Wanamaker, n.d.). Quoted by Renald Showers in *Maranatha—Our Lord, Come!* (Bellmawr, NJ: The Friends of Israel Gospel Ministry, Inc., 1995), 127.
4. Jerry B. Jenkins, "Jerry B. Jenkins, The Tim LaHaye I Knew," *Christianity Today*, July 25, 2016, https://www.christianitytoday.com/ct/2016/july-web-only/jerry-b-jenkins-tim-lahaye-i-knew-tribute-left-behind.html.

LESSON 13

Resurrection

1 CORINTHIANS 15:35-49

In this lesson we discover the nature of the believer's resurrection body.

Much speculation has been offered about what those who populate heaven will look like. Will they appear as angels? As "ghosts"? The Bible makes it clear that believers will have corporeal bodies that are recognizable but which are free from all the limitations of bodies on planet earth.

OUTLINE

I. **The Requirement of Resurrection Is the Death of the Body**

II. **The Result of Resurrection Is a Different Kind of Body**
   A. Our New Bodies Will Be Indestructible
   B. Our New Bodies Will Be Identifiable
   C. Our New Bodies Will Be Incredible
   D. Our New Bodies Will Be Infinite

OVERVIEW

As we begin this lesson on the Resurrection, here is an epitaph from Benjamin Franklin, that ties in perfectly with the message of this lesson:

[Benjamin Franklin] . . . lies in the grave like the cover of an old book, with its contents torn out, stripped of its lettering, but which will appear once again in a new and more eloquent edition, revised and corrected by the author.[1]

Those words eloquently describe the ultimate "extreme makeover" every Christian will one day receive from God. In 1 Corinthians 15, Paul deals with the doctrine of the resurrection—both the resurrection of Christ and of the believer. As part of that doctrine, he talks about the change that will occur in our physical bodies when we are resurrected at the end of this age.

The Requirement of Resurrection Is the Death of the Body

There is a prerequisite for having a resurrection body: First you have to have a dead body! I think Paul is having a little fun with the Corinthians when he says, "Foolish one, what you sow is not made alive unless it dies" (1 Corinthians 15:36).

Here Paul is obviously picking up on the teaching of Jesus, who said in John 12:24, "Most assuredly, I say to you, unless a grain of wheat falls into the ground and dies, it remains alone; but if it dies, it produces much grain."

The biblical perspective on death is different from the world's. Death is to be embraced, not feared. Death is the precursor to the wonderful resurrection body God has planned for the believer. If we did not die, we would be stuck with our current body for all eternity. Paul strikes a positive note right up front, saying that death is not to be feared. It's what has to occur before we can be changed. Without death there is no resurrection.

The Result of Resurrection Is a Different Kind of Body

In the next two verses, Paul makes an important point: The seed is one thing, the body of the plant it produces is another. In other words, sow one shape or form and reap another—a kernel of corn is radically different from the tall, green stalk that emerges from the earth. Applied to the human body, the body that dies and is buried in the earth is raised as a totally different kind of body. On the day of our resurrection, the body that comes out of the ground will be very different from the body that went into the ground.

Paul gives us four ways in which the bodies that come out of the ground will be different from the bodies that were buried in the ground.

Our New Bodies Will Be Indestructible

There has only been one body that was perfect—incorruptible—and that was the body of Jesus Christ. This was prophesied by the psalmist who wrote, "Nor will You allow Your Holy One to see corruption" (Psalm 16:10). Our bodies, however, are "sown [buried] in corruption."

Our present bodies get old, wear out, and eventually die. Things stop working like they once did, all part of the aging process of "corruptible" bodies. Despite the claims of science, there is nothing that will ever grant us immortality on this earth. On the other hand, our resurrected bodies will be incorruptible—they will last forever! They will not age, wear out, or be susceptible to disease.

I ride a bike now for exercise, and I have learned that it is much easier to go with the wind than against it. But that won't be true in heaven because my resurrection body will not get tired, strained, or become short of breath. Our bodies will be perfect in every way—indestructible!

Our New Bodies Will Be Identifiable

Second, we are not going to be ghost-like apparitions that all look the same. Our new bodies will be identifiable. Paul says our new bodies will be "raised in glory," which literally means "brilliance."

I don't know if we're going to have a brilliant "glow" or not. We have to look at Philippians 3:20–21 to get an idea of what Paul is probably talking about here. There Paul says that our "lowly body" will be conformed to Christ's "glorious body." Our new bodies will be like the body of the Lord Jesus Christ. The apostle John wrote that "it has not yet been revealed what we shall be, but we know that when He is revealed, we shall be like Him, for we shall see Him as He is" (1 John 3:2). Paul concludes this thought in verse 49 of 1 Corinthians 15 by saying, "And as we have borne the image of the man of dust [Adam], we shall also bear the image of the heavenly Man [Christ]."

The best glimpse we have of what Jesus' glorified body was like (and thus what our resurrected bodies will be like) is in the forty-day period between His resurrection and ascension. We can identify four characteristics of His body during that period:

- *Jesus said that His body was real (Luke 24:39).* Jesus, when He met with the disciples after His resurrection, invited them to touch Him to see that His body was real: "Handle Me and see, for a spirit does not have flesh and bones as you see I have." Jesus had a physical, corporeal body after His resurrection from the dead.

- *Jesus ate on at least two occasions (Luke 24:42–43; John 21:12–13).* People ask me this question about heaven more than any other: "Are we going to eat in heaven?" Apparently so, since Jesus ate in His post-resurrection body. He ate a piece of fish and some honeycomb on one occasion (Luke 24), and (apparently) shared fish and bread with His disciples on the shores of the Sea of Galilee (John 21).

It seems that the role of food changes from being a necessity to a pleasure. We won't need to eat to stay alive because our bodies will be incorruptible. But we will enjoy the pleasure of eating just as Adam and Eve would have done in the Garden of Eden before they sinned.

- *Jesus told Thomas to touch His body (John 20:27).* When Thomas doubted that Jesus had really been raised from the dead, Jesus encouraged him to reach out and touch His wounds, to see that it was really Jesus in the body in which He had been crucified.

- *Jesus told Mary not to hold on to Him (John 20:17).* When Mary encountered Jesus in the garden after His resurrection, He cautioned her not to cling to Him—to throw her arms around Him. He would not have said that had it not been possible for her to cling to Him; that is, if His body had not been a true physical body.

So, if our bodies are going to be like Jesus' body, we will be physical, we will be recognizable, we will be able to eat, and we'll be able to communicate. Jesus was as recognizable and communicable after His resurrection as He was before His death. Paul says in 1 Corinthians 13:12, "Now I know in part, but then I shall know just as I also am known." In heaven, we will know and be known.

On the Mount of Transfiguration, Moses and Elijah were recognized by the disciples (Matthew 17:1–4), and Jesus said that in the kingdom "many will come from east and west, and sit down with Abraham, Isaac, and Jacob in the kingdom of heaven" (Matthew 8:11). It would be hard to sit down with Abraham if you couldn't tell who he was!

Our New Bodies Will Be Incredible

Paul says our bodies are sown in weakness (death is the ultimate weakness), but "raised in power." When we come out of the grave, we will come out as power personified. The weakness we experience now will be a thing of our past life.

When a group from our church went to Africa on a missions trip, we experienced just what physical weakness is all about. Our task was to work in the vegetable gardens that were being planted as a source of food for African villagers. We went out strong in the morning; but when we returned in the evening, we looked bad—like we'd been run over by a truck! The work was hard, and as the week wore on, our stamina decreased markedly. In this life we simply do not have the power we need to do all we would like to do.

On one occasion after His resurrection, Jesus just appeared in a room where the disciples were. He didn't use the door—He was just there (John 20:19). Will we have that same kind of power in our resurrected bodies—the ability to transport ourselves from one place to another? To the degree that we are like Jesus in His resurrected body, I would think so, though we can't know for sure.

The point is that we can't even imagine what it will be like to live in bodies that are not limited as our current physical bodies are. Jesus was not constrained by the limitations of His earthly body, and neither will we be in the resurrection.

Our New Bodies Will Be Infinite

Finally, Paul draws a distinction between a natural body and a spiritual one. In this passage, he points to Adam as the image bearer for our natural body and to Christ, the last Adam, as the image bearer for the spiritual body we will receive.

What is a "spiritual" body? First, Paul doesn't mean it is an immaterial body. We've already seen that Jesus had a physical body, and so will we—a body that can be touched and felt. Instead, a spiritual body is one that is not controlled by the physical appetites of the fallen, carnal human nature. Instead, our bodies will be spiritual, controlled by the Holy Spirit. The basic difference between natural bodies and spiritual bodies is that one is at home on the earth, and the other is at home in heaven. That's why Paul says our natural bodies cannot inherit the kingdom of God (1 Corinthians 15:50).

Our current bodies are completely unsuited for heaven, which is why God will give us new ones when we are resurrected from the dead. Our spiritual bodies will welcome the control of the Spirit, and we will no longer have to contend with the flesh. If you have ever had a brief period of time, even just a few moments, where you felt completely in step with the Spirit of God, you have tasted heaven. It will be a time when our desires and the desires of God are one. There will be no conflict, no competition between Spirit and flesh. Our whole desire will be to do the will of God. Watch for those moments in this life and, when they happen, remind yourself that you are headed for an eternity of such bliss if you know Jesus as your Savior.

So, Paul summarizes the order of events in verses 51 and 52: Some will be alive when Christ comes, and some will be "asleep," having already died. But all will be changed in a moment of time when the last trumpet sounds and the dead are raised and changed from corruption into incorruption.

From 1 Thessalonians 4, we can add the specific order of the changes that will take place. The dead in Christ will rise first; then those who are alive when Christ returns will join them in the air, and all will be changed. Instantaneously—"in the twinkling of an eye" (1 Corinthians 15:52)—our corruptible, natural, weak, and limited bodies will become incorruptible, spiritual, powerful, and limitless bodies.

I sincerely hope I am alive when that happens—when Christ returns for His Church at the Rapture. I believe we ought to all have that longing and hope, to hear the trumpet and the archangel's shout, to see our Savior in the clouds, and to experience the transformation of our bodies. What a glorious moment to live for! What a blessed hope we have, to know that whether we are alive or not when He comes, we shall all be changed!

Joni Eareckson Tada is one of many saints who have experienced physical disabilities and limitations in this life, and she has written beautifully about her hope and God's promise for a new body:

> I still can hardly believe it. I, with shriveled, bent fingers, atrophied muscles, gnarled knees, and no feeling from the shoulders down, will one day have a new body, light, bright, and clothed in righteousness—powerful and dazzling. Can you imagine the hope this gives someone spinal-cord injured like me? Or someone who is cerebral palsied, brain-injured, or who has multiple sclerosis? Imagine the hope this gives someone who is manic-depressive. No other religion, no other philosophy promises new bodies, hearts, and minds. Only in the Gospel of Christ do hurting people find such incredible hope.[2]

No wonder Paul said that if in this life only we have hope, we are most miserable (1 Corinthians 15:19, KJV). But we have hope beyond this life. And that hope is in Jesus. One day all of the pains and the aches and the deformities and the deficiencies that we carry in our earthly bodies are going to be taken away when we get our heavenly bodies. We will know the joy of living in the perfection and glory that God intended for us from the beginning.

This truth about our new physical bodies is not the least of the reasons I am passionate about taking people to heaven with me. I don't want anyone to miss what God has planned for those who are His.

The reality of a new body is part of the expectation of glory that heaven represents. Since we have never lived in perfect, limitless, spiritual bodies, it's very difficult to imagine what it will be like. The surest way to find out is to experience the change yourself by being one of those Christ calls to Himself when He comes for His own. Make sure you have entrusted yourself to Him by faith and that you enter eternity with your ultimate "extreme makeover"!

APPLICATION

Personal Questions

1. Turn to 1 Corinthians 15:36–43.

   a. What must happen to believers before being resurrected (verse 36; see also John 12:24)?

   b. According to Paul, the body is sown in _____ and raised in _____ (verse 42).

   c. Is there anything on earth that will grant you immortality? Only where will you have eternal life?

   d. We will be buried in dishonor and weakness, but raised in what (see verse 43)?

2. What reason do you have, as a follower of Christ, not to be afraid of death?

   a. Paul says death will be swallowed up in what (1 Corinthians 15:54)?

   b. How quickly will believers be changed when Christ returns for His Church (verse 52)?

3. Read John 20:16–17, 24–28.

   a. What is the implication of Jesus' words to Mary concerning the nature of His resurrected body (verse 17)? (Is it possible to "cling to" a spirit?)

   b. What physical evidence did Jesus offer Thomas of His resurrection (verse 27)?

4. In what should you have hope, if not in your life on earth (see 1 Corinthians 15:19–20)?

5. What assurance do you have that you will be granted a heavenly body (verse 20, NIV)?

Group Questions

Read 2 Corinthians 5:1–10 and discuss the following questions:

a. What metaphor does Paul use to describe our earthly body (verse 1a)?

b. What is waiting for us when our earthly sojourn is finished (verse 1b)?

c. What is implied in verse 2 concerning the difference between earthly life and heavenly life?

d. What is the meaning of verse 3 concerning our heavenly existence? Will we be "spirits" or corporeal bodies in heaven?

e. How did Paul reverse that image in verse 4?

f. Who did the Old Testament saints see doing the "swallowing" in this life (verse 4; see Psalm 69:15; Proverbs 1:12)?

g. What guarantee have we been given that death is going to be "swallowed up by life" (verse 5; see Ephesians 1:13)?

h. What tension do Christians live with while on earth (verse 6)?

i. Since we have never seen heaven or our new heavenly bodies, what should be the basis of our hope (verse 7)?

j. Given a choice, where would Paul rather be (verse 8)?

k. In either place, what should be our highest priority as Christians (verse 9)?

l. What motivates our desire to be well-pleasing to the Lord (verse 10; see also 1 Corinthians 3:11–15)?

DID YOU KNOW?

Several resurrections from the dead were recorded in the New Testament. Jesus raised the deceased son of a widow from the dead (Luke 7:11–15), as well as His friend Lazarus (John 11:38–44). He also brought the daughter of Jairus, a synagogue ruler, back to life (Mark 5:22–24). The apostle Peter raised a young man named Eutychus from the dead in Troas (Acts 20:7–12). The bodies of those raised from the dead were not, however, "resurrection bodies"—mortality putting on immortality (1 Corinthians 15:53–54). Each of those raised from the dead died a second time later in their lives to await their immortal resurrection.

Notes

1. Benjamin Franklin, quoted in John Newton Brown, ed., *Fessenden & Co's Encyclopedia of Religious Knowledge* (Brattleboro: Fessenden & Co., 1836), 1257.
2. Joni Eareckson Tada, *Heaven: Your Real Home* (Grand Rapids, MI: Zondervan, 1995), 53.

Heaven

SELECTED SCRIPTURES

In this lesson we learn why heaven is such an important place for the Christian.

Everyone has heard the expression, "Oh, this is just heaven!" Granted, it's a figure of speech, but it betrays the casual approach most people take to something that is biblically serious. Since heaven is the eternal home of Christians, we should know all there is to know about it.

OUTLINE

I. **The Prominence of Heaven**

II. **The Plurality of Heaven**
   A. The First Heaven (Isaiah 55:9–10)
   B. The Second Heaven (Genesis 1:14–17)
   C. The Third Heaven (2 Corinthians 12:2–4)

III. **The Place Called Heaven**

IV. **The Preciousness of Heaven**
   A. Our Redeemer Is in Heaven
   B. Our Relationships Are in Heaven
   C. Our Resources Are in Heaven

D. Our Residence Is in Heaven
E. Our Reward Is in Heaven
F. Our Riches Are in Heaven
G. Our Reservation Is in Heaven

OVERVIEW

When a Sunday school teacher quizzed her class of fifth-graders about how one gets to heaven, she got all correct answers: One doesn't get there by being good, giving away money, or being a nice person. "Well, then," she asked, "how *does* one get to heaven?" Before any of the regular students could answer, a boy who was visiting the class that week shouted out, "You have to be dead!"

That's the correct answer, isn't it? Unless Jesus Christ returns and takes us off the earth to be with Him in heaven, we have to die to get there. Worldwide, nearly two people die every second. That means more than 6,000 people every hour are passing from life to death and going either to heaven or to hell—more than 151,000 people every day.[1]

A 2003 Harris Poll found that eighty-two percent of Americans believe in heaven and sixty-three percent said they expected to go there when they die. In spite of all that interest in heaven, there is little talk about heaven in American churches whether evangelical, mainline Protestant, or Catholic.[2]

Other polls from the Barna and Gallup organizations tell us there is little difference between the morals and lifestyles of Christians and non-Christians. And I believe the absence of a focus on heaven is in large part to blame. When we lose sight of the fact that God has a wonderful destination prepared for those who are His, we start trying to create heaven on earth. We start investing our time and talent and treasure in creating a place that we know in our heart is what we were created for (Ecclesiastes 3:11). We know there is supposed to be a heaven; and when we stop seeking the biblical heaven, we try to create an earthly one.

The problem with that strategy is that we could never approximate on earth what God has created for us in heaven—so we try harder. And we begin pursuing the pleasures of this world. We begin doing what Solomon writes about in Ecclesiastes, looking for pleasure and satisfaction in wine, women, and wealth. He finally recognized the futility (vanity) of his ways, but many Christians have not. If we do not feed the hunger for heaven with biblical truth, we will feed it the superficial baubles and bangles of this world.

The Prominence of Heaven

While heaven isn't being talked about much in churches, it seems to be popping up in the popular culture. A book called *The Five People You Meet in Heaven,* by Mitch Albom, was on *The New York Times* bestseller list for more than a year—but it has nothing to do with heaven. It has to do with evaluating how you treated people on earth when you meet them in heaven. The famous *Left Behind* series has sold millions of books and deals a lot with heaven. And a book called *Heaven* by an evangelical author, Randy Alcorn, was published in 2004 and sold 100,000 copies in just a few months. So people are reading about heaven—we're just not talking about it in church very much.

Heaven is mentioned more than 500 times in Scripture. Both the Old Testament word (*sha-mayim*) and the New Testament word (*ouranos*) for heaven refer to high and lofty places. Heaven is a consistent theme in the Bible. It is discussed in our culture, but the average Christian knows little about it.

The Plurality of Heaven

The Bible speaks of three heavens. Paul, when writing to the Corinthian believers, talks about being "caught up to the third heaven" (2 Corinthians 12:2), a place he then refers to as "Paradise" (verse 4). We have to conclude that if Paul visited the third heaven, there must be a first and second heaven as well.

The First Heaven (Isaiah 55:9–10)

We could call this heaven the "atmospheric" heaven—a place mentioned numerous times in Scripture: "For as the heavens are higher than the earth. . . . For as the rain comes down . . . from heaven" (Isaiah 55:9–10). This heaven is the atmosphere surrounding the earth—the domain of clouds and birds (Genesis 1:20).

The Second Heaven (Genesis 1:14–17)

This heaven is mentioned early in the book of Genesis and is the domain of the heavenly bodies: the sun, moon, stars, planets, and galaxies besides our own. We refer to this today as "outer space," where satellites and planetary space probes travel.

The Third Heaven (2 Corinthians 12:2–4)

When Paul described being caught up to the third heaven, he didn't say where it was. In fact, he seemed not to know: "Whether in the body I do not know, or whether out of the body I do not know" (2 Corinthians 12:2). We can only assume it was a place beyond the atmospheric and stellar heavens—the dwelling place of God.

Jesus taught His disciples to pray, "Our Father in heaven . . ." (Matthew 6:9), and He referred in Matthew 5:16 to "Your Father in heaven." Psalm 11:4 says, "The LORD's throne is in heaven." That must be the heaven to which Paul was taken by God—either physically or spiritually—the heaven where God dwells. This is the heaven that is our destination as believers in Christ.

The Place Called Heaven

John 14 is a classic text on the subject of heaven where we learn from Jesus Christ Himself as He raised the subject with His disciples.

The disciples of Christ were greatly troubled at the timeline that had been laid out for them concerning Jesus' future: He would die, be buried, be resurrected, and then return to heaven. Not understanding the complete picture of Christ's mission, they were understandably sorrowful at this news that He was going to leave them. But in John 14:1–4, He gives them a truth to comfort them in their sorrows: "I'm going to prepare a place for you in My Father's house so that you can one day join Me there forever" (paraphrase).

Then Jesus replied to Thomas's doubts (verse 5) by saying, "No one comes to the Father except through Me" (verse 6). That is, not just His disciples would be joining Him in heaven, but also all who believed in Him. Heaven is a real place being prepared by Christ to receive all those who belong to Him. Jesus didn't leave His disciples or us to find heaven on earth. He went to prepare heaven for us.

While heaven is referred to in Jesus' parables by many metaphors (country, city, kingdom), the picture I like best is the one here in John 14: the Father's house. Those who grew up in a warm and loving house know it as a place you long to return to. When we were younger, my wife and I would drive 2,000 miles round trip over a weekend just to spend a few hours in "the father's house." When my dad eventually became a widower and sold his home, I hated to see us lose it because of what it represented: the place to which we could always return.

Fortunately, we don't have to worry about losing our heavenly Father's house since Christ has gone to heaven to prepare it for us. It is a permanent, heavenly abode where we will dwell forever in God's presence. Heaven is not a feeling or an emotion or a point of view or an attitude. It is not a place we create by our actions here on earth. It is a "place" (Greek *topos*, in John 14:2; a physical, locatable place).

Where, exactly, is the place called heaven? We can't say with certainty because the Bible doesn't say. But Ephesians 4:10 says it is above all the heavens, where Christ ascended; and in Acts 1:10–11, the disciples were gazing "up into heaven" where Jesus had gone. If language means anything, we have to assume that Jesus' destination was "up."

But depending upon where you are standing on earth, "up" is a different direction—it just means perpendicular to the surface of the planet. But in Isaiah 14, we get a different perspective. Addressing God, Satan says, "I will exalt my throne above the stars of God; I will also sit on the mount of the congregation on the farthest sides of the north" (verse 13). Satan refers to heaven as the "farthest sides of the north." Regardless of where you are on the globe, north is always pointing in the same direction. So it may be reasonable to conclude that heaven is somewhere in the northern heavens beyond the range of the astronomers' most powerful telescopes. Astronomers even tell us that this part of outer space contains fewer stars and galaxies than other parts.

So, even if we don't know exactly where the third heaven is, we know it's a specific place where Jesus is preparing a place for us.

The Preciousness of Heaven

Everything that should be precious to a follower of Christ applies to heaven because that's where Christ is, where He will be forever, and where we will be with Him. Here are seven reasons why heaven is a precious place.

Our Redeemer Is in Heaven

Hebrews 9:24 says Christ has entered "into heaven itself, now to appear in the presence of God for us." The descriptions of heaven in Revelation suggest it is going to be a stunningly beautiful place, but I believe all that beauty will pale into insignificance when we behold the beauty of our Redeemer, Jesus Christ. When we see the One who suffered and died to pay the penalty for our sins . . . when we see the scars of His suffering, I think nothing will look as beautiful as He will look to our eyes when we see Him as He really is.

Our Relationships Are in Heaven

My father told me as he grew old and began to see his friends pass away, "One of the hard things about getting old is you have more friends in heaven than you do on earth." That's true, but what a wonderful truth! My wife and I have lost all four of our parents, but we know where they are—they are in heaven. And we rejoice that one day we will be reunited with them.

The writer to the Hebrews made an interesting choice of words when he wrote, "To the general assembly and church of the firstborn who are registered in heaven" (12:23). It sounds like checking in at a hotel, doesn't it? You leave earth and arrive in heaven and are registered there. So when we get there, we will look up our friends and loved ones and be reunited for all eternity.

Our Resources Are in Heaven

First Peter 1:3–4 says that our inheritance is "reserved in heaven." When you became a Christian, God became your Father. And when God is your Father, you are one of His heirs, which means you have an inheritance waiting for you in heaven. Peter says that our inheritance has preceded us to heaven—it is already there waiting for us to arrive and claim it. Unlike earthly inheritances, our heavenly inheritance is not dependent on the economy as to its value. It has been perfectly established in heaven and will never change.

Our Residence Is in Heaven

Philippians 3:20 says that "our citizenship is in heaven." That doesn't mean we reside there now, but it does mean that's our official, permanent residence. When we fill out paperwork in this life, we have to declare our place of birth and our residence—but that's all just temporary. Our real place of birth is heaven (the phrase in Greek, "born again," can also be translated in John 3:3, 7 as "born from above," CEV), and therefore our citizenship is in heaven. When we die, we simply go to our permanent home to live for eternity.

Our Reward Is in Heaven

Jesus told His disciples to "rejoice and be exceedingly glad, for great is your reward in heaven" (Matthew 5:12). We will spend an entire lesson in this section on the rewards of heaven. As a preview, we can note here that there are five crowns that can be earned by Christians on earth, crowns which will be awarded in heaven.

Some think it is not very spiritual to be looking forward to heaven in order to receive a reward. But God is big on rewards! All throughout Scripture, God makes promises that have positive benefits as their rewards. God motivates us to faithfulness by offering rewards. That is perfectly reasonable since our fallen human nature is not inclined to be faithful or obedient. So God motivates us to be faithful and then rewards us when we are. It's a great program!

Amazingly, we will end up casting all those crowns and rewards at the feet of Jesus in honor and praise of Him (Revelation 4:10; more on this in an upcoming lesson).

Our Riches Are in Heaven

Another reason why heaven is so precious is that our riches are in heaven. In Matthew 6:19–21, Jesus tells His followers not to lay up treasures on earth, but to lay them up in heaven where they would be eternally safe: "For where your treasure is, there your heart will be also" (verse 21).

How do we store up treasure in heaven? By investing on earth in the only things that are going to be transferred to heaven, and that is the souls of men and women and boys and girls.

The Word of God and the human soul are the only eternal things on earth. So to build equity in heaven, we have to build the Word of God into the lives of people on earth.

Our Reservation Is in Heaven

Revelation 21:27 says that "only those who are written in the Lamb's Book of Life" will be allowed into heaven. If you belong to Christ, then your name is recorded in that book in heaven. Jesus once told His disciples to rejoice that their names were "written in heaven" (Luke 10:20)—and we should likewise rejoice.

As we study the end-time events that are all around us, it's the right time for you to confirm that your name is written in the Lamb's Book of Life. If you have never asked God to forgive your sins through Christ's death in your place on the cross, do so now. Heaven is not a place you want to miss!

APPLICATION

Personal Questions

1. Read 2 Corinthians 12:2–4.

    a. Where was the apostle Paul "caught up" (verse 2)?

    b. Where did he say that place was located (verse 3), and what did he refer to that place as (verse 4)?

2. Turn to John 14:1–4 in your Bible.

    a. What did Christ tell His disciples in verse 1? For what reason did He say this? Does this verse give you comfort today?

    b. Where did Christ go to prepare a place for believers (verse 2)?

    c. What did Christ promise to believers in verse 3?

3. According to Matthew 5:12, what did Jesus tell His disciples would be waiting for them in heaven?

   a. Jesus told His followers to do what in Matthew 6:19–21?

   b. Are there any "treasures" you are storing up on earth? What can you do to avoid this habit?

4. Read Revelation 21:27.

   a. Where will the names of those who are saved be written?

   b. Have you asked God to forgive your sins through Christ's death on the cross? If not, think about praying that prayer today, so that you do not miss out on the place He is preparing for you.

Group Questions

1. What does the plural "heavens" in Genesis 1:1 suggest about how many heavens there are?

   a. Which heaven did the apostle Paul visit (2 Corinthians 12:2)?

   b. If there is a "third heaven," at least how many divisions of heaven must there be?

   c. What characterizes the layer of heaven that is nearest to earth (Genesis 7:11; Psalm 78:23; Daniel 7:13)?

   d. What characterizes the next highest level of heaven (Genesis 1:14–19; Psalm 19:4–6)?

   e. What other word did Paul use to describe the "third heaven" (2 Corinthians 12:4)?

   f. What do you learn about this part of heaven from Revelation 2:7?

   g. Though 2 Corinthians 5:8 doesn't use the word "heaven," how is it consistent with Luke 23:43?

2. Discuss the details about heaven that you can discover from John 14:1–4:

   a. What Jesus called it (verse 2):

   b. Why Jesus was going there (verse 2):

   c. Who the future occupants will be (verse 3):

   d. What level of comfort the anticipation of heaven should provide (verse 1):

3. If comfortable doing so, share with your group about a friend or family member who has yet to accept the gift of salvation. If time allows for it, pray for those mentioned that they might come to Christ.

DID YOU KNOW?

An obscure reference to the "queen of heaven" occurs five times in the book of Jeremiah (7:18; 44:17–19, 25). The "queen" is not named but was undoubtedly a female goddess in the pagan pantheon of the day (possibly Ishtar, a female Babylonian deity). Jeremiah 7:18 mentions the involvement of the whole family in worshiping the "queen of heaven": "The children gather wood, the fathers kindle the fire, and the women knead dough, to make cakes for the queen of heaven." In addition to making cakes, the Israelites burned incense and poured out drink offerings to this pagan deity (Jeremiah 44:18–19). Heaven and its occupants were a focus of speculation among ancient peoples—and even Israelites who had rejected the God of heaven.

Notes
1. "World Birth and Death Rates," *Ecology*, 2011, www.ecology.com/birth-death-rates/.
2. Cary McMullen, "Heaven: A Lot of Questions, but No One Really Knows the Answers," *The Ledger*, March 27, 2005, https://www.theledger.com/article/LK/20050327/News/608100012/LL/.

Judgment Seat of Christ

SELECTED SCRIPTURES

In this lesson we learn about the judgment that followers of Christ will face one day.

Almost everyone has at least a vague concept about a future judgment where everyone will stand before God. But few Christians realize that the Bible teaches there will be not just one but two different days of judgment! And it will be our relationship with Christ that will ultimately determine which judgment we will face.

OUTLINE

   I. The Great White Throne Judgment

  II. Judgment Seat of Christ

 III. The Judge

  IV. The Judged

   V. The Judgment
- A. The Confusion About This Judgment
- B. The Chronology of This Judgment
- C. The Courtroom of This Judgment
- D. The Criteria for This Judgment
- E. The Conclusion of This Judgment

OVERVIEW

It would be hard to ignore the fact that there is a lot of pretending going on in the world today. People pretend to be wealthier or stronger or happier or thinner than what reality testifies to be true. It is also popular to pretend to be spiritual, and some even pretend to be Christians, even though they are acutely aware that there has never been a life-changing experience of salvation in their lives.

But Christians like to play that game, too! We pretend to really love the Lord and be in fellowship with Him. We even go through the motions of serving Him, when in fact our hearts are far from that place—and we know it. So what is to become of all this pretending by us, the pretenders?

The Bible says that one day, all role-playing will finally be unmasked. All pretense will be exposed. God's Word assures us that a final judgment is coming—there is no denying that reality. Hebrews 9:27 says, "And as it is appointed for men to die once, but after this the judgment." There will actually be two judgments in the time to come, and they are very different from one another. Let's quickly look at each one.

The Great White Throne Judgment

Let's first take a look at the second judgment: the Great White Throne Judgment. At this time, all unbelievers and those who pretended to be Christians will stand before God (Revelation 20:5, 11-15). There they will face the consequences of rejecting Jesus Christ as their Savior and Lord. This is the final judgment in God's justice plan for the inhabitants of planet earth. There will be no grading on a curve, and the accused will be judged by the black-and-white standard of absolute truth and justice.

The Great White Throne Judgment is the final sentence for those who have rejected Christ—they will face an eternity without God. By the grace of God, I pray that you will not be one of those present for that judgment. Your goal in life should be to make certain that you have chosen the right path and to avoid being present at the Great White Throne. You don't want to be there, because if you are, it is too late. There is no plan for you to have a second chance after that.

Judgment Seat of Christ

But there is a judgment before that reserved just for Christians. This first judgment—the Judgment Seat of Christ—will happen 1,000 years before the Great White Throne Judgment. It occurs right after the Rapture of the Church. Second Corinthians 5:10 describes it: "For we must all appear before the judgment seat of Christ, that each one may receive the things done in the body, according to what he has done, whether good or bad."

Please note that the purpose of this judgment is not to pronounce condemnation. No one judged at this court will be condemned. All who are present at this court will already be followers of Christ. They will just have been raised in their resurrection bodies to stand at the Judgment Seat as believers before the God of heaven. The purpose of this first judgment is for Christ to assess every believer's earthly works to determine what rewards are to be received.

The expression "judgment seat" is the translation of one little Greek word: *bema*. And the word *bema* is an interesting term because it means a "raised platform." According to one historian, "In Grecian games in Athens, the old arena contained a raised platform to which the president or umpire of the arena sat. From here he rewarded all the contestants; and here he rewarded all winners. It was called the 'bema' or 'reward seat.'"[1]

From this exalted platform, the judges of the Greek Olympic games reviewed the preparation, training, and performance of each of the contestants and rewarded the winners who had kept the rules. They would be there for more than a week as the participants would come and go through all of the competitions. And the athletes would be judged not just as to whether or not they won the competition but also if they had participated according to the rules that had been set down for the competition itself.

So when Paul speaks of the Judgment Seat of Christ, the "bema seat," he is referring to the future judgment of Christians. This is not a judicial, courtroom-like event. Instead, the picture painted here is of an athletic event where the participants are being rewarded by a judge who is elevated up on a high platform, viewing everything from a broad perspective.

In this study, we are going to examine what Scripture says about the Judgment Seat of Christ. We will look at it from three perspectives. First, we will explore the Judge. Second, we will determine who the judged are. And finally, we will look at the judgment itself.

The Judge

The God of the Bible is a God who makes judgments. This first occurred in the Garden of Eden when Adam and Eve were judged for their disobedience. Judgment is a thread that runs through the whole Bible—from Genesis 3 to Revelation 22. According to Hebrews 4:13, "there is no creature hidden from His sight, but all things are naked and open to the eyes of Him to whom we must give account." The whole universe is subject to the dictates of the Judge.

On the awesome day of reckoning at the Judgment Seat, only God is qualified to make the judgment. And John 5:22 and 27 tells us that God "has committed all judgment to the Son . . .

and has given Him authority to execute judgment." Moreover, Acts 10:42 says that Jesus Christ "was ordained by God to be Judge of the living and the dead."

When you stand before the Judgment Seat of Christ, it won't be a judgment based on a group of your peers. Your wife or your husband won't be there to bring judgment against you, nor will your children or grandchildren. That judgment will be pronounced, presided over, and made by the Judge of all the earth, the Lord God of heaven, Jesus Christ. There is nothing that escapes His omniscient wisdom. He sees it all.

The Judged

Next, we need to determine who exactly are the judged who come before this Judgment Seat of Christ. If you only take away one thing from this study, let it be this point: The Judgment Seat of Christ is for believers only. No unbelievers will be present at the Judgment Seat of Christ. At this tribunal, everyone who has accepted Jesus as their personal Savior will give a personal account of themselves before the Lord. No unsaved person will appear there. The Judgment Seat of Christ is for believers only.

There are three sections of Scripture in the New Testament that give us everything that we know about the Judgment Seat: Romans 14:10–12; 2 Corinthians 5:10; and 1 Corinthians 3:11–15. In all of these passages, it is important to note that all the pronouns are personal and singular. In other words, this event is not a community affair. This is not a church gathering. This judgment is a one-on-one interview with the Son of the Living God, and each of us will have our own personal appointment.

The Judgment

I am often asked about specific details about this important event in the life of a Christian. In this section, we will review five specific areas that correlate to this event. First, let's dispel some of the misconceptions about the Judgment Seat of Christ.

The Confusion About This Judgment

There are many false ideas that have emerged about the meaning of the Judgment Seat of Christ. We don't have time to go through all of them, but I do want to scrutinize the two most commonly conveyed errors.

The first faulty idea is that the judgment that takes place at the time of death is to determine whether a person is permitted to enter heaven or not. This is the oft-portrayed picture of standing at heaven's gate where God takes all of our good works and He weighs them against our bad deeds. And based upon which side prevails, we get to go to heaven or we're kept out.

Here is some good news for you: That is not what happens. There is no such event in the future. And we should all be so grateful that such a scenario does not exist, because each and every one of us would fail such a judgment.

The truth is that the only judgment a believer in Jesus Christ will ever be subjected to is the judgment of the Cross.[2] We were judged when Jesus died on the cross. We were in Christ on the cross when the Father poured out His wrath upon Him for sin. The sin was not His, but ours. And Jesus took all of our punishment for us. When He was judged for our sin, our sin was forever and finally judged.

So if you have confessed and accepted Jesus as Lord, you will never again face the judgment for your sin from God. That judgment is past—it's history. You don't see it through the front window; you see it through the rearview mirror. It has already happened.

The second faulty idea sometimes put forth is that the Judgment Seat of Christ is a judgment of all sins that a believer commits after they become a believer. The gross error conveyed here is that the Cross takes care of all your sins up to the point of salvation. But after that, you're on your own.

Nothing could be farther from the truth. Just consider Romans 8:1, "There is therefore now no condemnation to those who are in Christ Jesus." It is ridiculous to think that somehow the salvation of a Christian is made up of everything Jesus did for you before you believed in Him. And then after you believed in Him, you have to do everything for yourself. Nonsense!

When Jesus died on the cross, how many of your sins were still in the future? All of them! So when Jesus died on the cross, what happened there was sufficient for all the sin that we would ever commit from that moment on—forevermore. Your sins have been forgiven. God has paid for all those sins through the sacrifice of His Son, Jesus Christ.

If we take our stand by the Cross, we are safe for time and eternity. The judgment has fallen, and it can never get to us again. The cross of Jesus Christ has scorched the earth for all future judgment. We will never face our sin in terms of judgment again.

The Chronology of This Judgment

So when does this all take place? The Judgment Seat of Christ is an event that is going to occur as soon as you get to heaven. As soon as you go through the pearly gates, the first agenda item will be to get your appointment with the Judge.

Revelation 22:12 says, "And behold, I am coming quickly, and My reward is with Me, to give to every one according to his work." The Bible pictures Jesus coming back to get us, bringing the rewards with Him so that as soon as we get back to heaven, He can give us our rewards at the Judgment Seat of Christ.

The Courtroom of This Judgment

The next natural question to ask is: *Where will this all take place?* Well, we've already indirectly discussed that question—it will be in heaven. So obviously whether we go to heaven or not isn't the issue—all believers will be there. You can't be at the Judgment Seat of Christ if you're not already in heaven. The Judgment Seat of Christ takes place only in heaven.

The Criteria for This Judgment

That brings us to the thing we all want to know: *What is going to happen at that moment?* What will happen when I stand before the Lord on that day? In 1 Corinthians 3:11–15, Paul gives a clear illustration of what this judgment will look like. He likens it to a building that is on fire, and after the flames extinguish, the nature of the materials that were used to build the building will be revealed.

One day at the Judgment Seat of Christ, there is going to be a fire, but the fire there will be the white-hot gaze of the eyes of the Lord Jesus Christ. In the Bible, the eyes of Christ are pictured as a blazing fire that penetrates everything (Revelation 1:14). And that fire will sort out all that we have ever done, whether it was for the right reasons or whether it was all for pretend. Fire is a well-known biblical image of testing, and fire will ultimately determine what we have done in our lives as Christians.

The Conclusion of This Judgment

The conclusion of the judgment is twofold. It encompasses both positive and negative events.

1. The Loss of Rewards

The Bible says that some people are going to stand before the Judgment Seat of Christ—where all the rewards are given—and they are not going to receive any reward. They won't have it to lose; they just will lose the opportunity to get one.

Scripture gives us some examples of how and why this happens. In Matthew 6:1, Jesus says, "Take heed that you do not do your charitable deeds before men, to be seen by them. Otherwise you have no reward from your Father in heaven." If you advertise your giving, it is of no credit to you.

Later on in the same passage, Jesus says, "And when you pray, you shall not be like the hypocrites. For they love to pray standing in the synagogues and on the corners of the streets, that they may be seen by men. Assuredly, I say to you, they have their reward" (Matthew 6:5). If you do what you do for the recognition of men and not the glory of God, you will not receive any rewards in heaven. It's that simple.

2. The Reception of Rewards

Throughout God's Word, we are told there are rewards that will be given to us in heaven and that we should endeavor to earn them by our works here on earth. We should be doing all within our ability to extend the Kingdom of God and to make a difference for Christ in our world. You shouldn't be embarrassed to be ambitious to do that, and you shouldn't be embarrassed to be ambitious in storing up for yourself treasures in heaven.

Every day, God gives us opportunities to please Him. Every day God gives us opportunities to make a difference in the Kingdom. And Scripture says that we are stewards of that which God entrusts to us—and if He has entrusted much to us, much will be required.

But whatever is given to us, God wants us to take it and use it and develop it for the Kingdom. And if we do, one day at the Judgment Seat of Christ, we will be judged, but judged for blessings and rewards. What a good and gracious God we serve!

APPLICATION

Personal Questions

1. Read 1 Corinthians 3:8–15.

   a. According to verse 8, each person's award will be given according to what?

   b. As workers of God, Paul likens believers to what two possessions of God (verse 9)?

   c. What work are all believers to take heed of doing (verse 10)?

   d. What is truly the only foundation there is (verse 11)?

   e. What will reveal the true nature of each person's work (verse 13)? How?

   f. What happens if a person's work endures the fire (verse 14)?

   g. What happens if a person's work is burned (verse 15)?

   h. Graciously, even if a person's work is lost, what will happen to them personally (verse 15)?

2. Read 2 Corinthians 5:9–11.

    a. According to verse 9, what should be our main goal in life?

    b. List some simple ways you can accomplish this aim in your own life.

    c. Where will all believers make a mandatory appearance (verse 10)?

    d. We will receive judgment for things done where? Why is this such an important distinction (verse 10)?

    e. What kind of deeds will be judged on that day (verse 10)? What is your reaction to that news?

    f. With what aspect of God are we able to persuade men (verse 11)? Do we do this today? Explain why or why not.

    g. Verse 11 says that we are "well known" to God. How can this fact make an impact on how you live your everyday life? Does it?

3. Read 1 Peter 1:17–19.

    a. Verse 17 says that God judges according to what? And in which way does He do it?

    b. Why do you think God is impartial when it comes to judging us?

    c. List the things that verse 18 states do not redeem us.

    d. In the end, what is the only thing that redeems us (verse 19)?

Group Questions

1. Read Acts 17:30–31 and discuss the following questions:

    a. God once overlooked our ignorance, but now commands us to repent in light of what?

b. Jesus will judge the world in what (verse 31)? What does that mean?

c. What did God do to ensure the fact that Jesus will indeed judge the world one day (verse 31)?

d. Discuss why Jesus' resurrection gives Him the authority to judge all living things (see John 5:22, 27; Acts 10:42).

2. Read 2 Timothy 4:1–5 and discuss the following questions:

   a. As a group, list and discuss all the commands that the Christian is to actively follow because of the reality of the coming judgment of Christ.

   b. How many of these acts does the modern church execute today? How many does it ignore? Discuss why and what steps can be taken to better live out this passage as a church and as individuals.

   c. When people turn away from sound doctrine, what do they turn to (verses 3–4)?

   d. How can keeping the coming judgment of Christ always in mind keep us from falling away?

3. Read 1 Peter 4:1–6 and discuss the following questions:

   a. Summarize the main idea of this passage of Scripture.

   b. Discuss why Christ's physical, fleshly suffering is so fundamental to not only our salvation, but also the coming judgment.

DID YOU KNOW?

The Bible tells us that at the Judgment Seat of Christ, there are five different crowns available as rewards to those who have earned them by their godly endeavors from their earthly life. The five crowns described to us in Scripture are the Victor's Crown, the Crown of Rejoicing, the Crown of Righteousness, the Crown of Glory, and the Crown of Life. But what will we do with our crowns? Revelation 4:10 gives us an idea, for as an act of worship and thanks for all that God has done, we read that the twenty-four elders continually "cast their crowns before the throne."

Notes

1. L. Sale-Harrison, *The Judgment Seat of Christ* (New York: Hephzibah House, 1938), 8.
2. J. Dwight Pentecost, *Prophecy for Today* (Grand Rapids, MI: Zondervan Publishing Company, 1961), 152.

Rewards

SELECTED SCRIPTURES

In this lesson we learn about the rewards believers will receive in heaven.

Athletes in ancient Greece practiced for years to win prizes that would soon fade away. Christians who run the spiritual race diligently will receive rewards for their faithfulness at the Judgment Seat of Christ, rewards which they will reinvest in the glory of Christ for eternity.

OUTLINE

I. **The Day of Heaven's Rewards**

II. **The Distinction of Heaven's Rewards**

III. **The Description of Heaven's Rewards**
    A. The Victor's Crown (1 Corinthians 9:25–27)
    B. The Crown of Rejoicing (1 Thessalonians 2:19)
    C. The Crown of Righteousness (2 Timothy 4:8)
    D. The Crown of Life (James 1:12; Revelation 2:10)
    E. The Crown of Glory (1 Peter 5:4)

IV. **The Difference Heaven's Rewards Can Make**
    A. Remember That the Lord Himself Is Your Chief Reward
    B. Resist Doing Works Outwardly for the Purpose of Receiving a Reward
    C. Reflect Upon the Ultimate Goal of Any Rewards We May Receive

---

OVERVIEW

To continue our theme of heaven-oriented epitaphs, here's an interesting one found on the tombstone of a woman named Samantha:

> Here lies the body of Samantha Proctor.
> She catched a cold and wouldn't doctor.
> She couldn't stay. She had to go.
> Praise God from whom all blessings flow.

I did a little research and discovered forty-two different award shows that are available to be seen each year. There are the Academy Awards, the People's Choice Awards, the Golden Globe Awards, the Screen Actors Guild Awards, the Grammy Awards, the Country Music Association Awards—and the list goes on and on. But there is an award show coming that this world knows nothing of, one that will put all other award shows to shame for its grandeur and the quality of the awards to be given. Those are the rewards given to believers prior to their permanent entrance into heaven.

Some people don't understand the rationale behind Christians getting rewards. They think it sounds like bribing children to be good by offering them candy. Doing and being good, they say, should be their own reward. But the idea of rewards is completely biblical and consistent with God's character as we will see in this lesson.

The concept of rewards is found in the Old Testament (Psalm 58:11; 62:12), and Jesus opens the New Testament era by citing rewards for those persecuted for the sake of righteousness (Matthew 5:11–12). And at the end of the Bible, in Revelation 22:12, we find Jesus saying, "And behold, I am coming quickly, and My reward is with Me." Rewards are mentioned in many other places in the New Testament (Mark 9:41; 10:29–30; Luke 18:29–30; 1 Corinthians 3:14; Colossians 3:24; Hebrews 6:10–12).

In this lesson, we'll look at the timing and the kinds of rewards God intends to give as part of our entrance into heaven.

The Day of Heaven's Rewards

Here's the big picture: The Bible says that after all believers, dead and alive, are removed from earth at the Rapture of the Church, believers will be judged individually for their works as Christians and special rewards will be handed out. Here are excerpts from several Scriptures that address this event:

- Romans 14:12: "So then each of us shall give account of himself to God."
- 2 Corinthians 5:10: "For we must all appear before the judgment seat of Christ."
- Ephesians 6:8: "Knowing that whatever good anyone does, he will receive the same from the Lord."
- 1 Corinthians 3:14: "If anyone's work which he has built on it endures, he will receive a reward."

This judgment has nothing to do with our salvation. Rather, it has to do with the kind of Christian we have been—a judgment of our faithfulness as followers of Christ. The penetrating gaze of Christ will look past all our posturing and spin and see us for what we really are. There'll be no excuses or rationalizations. We will stand silently before the Son of God and know that His judgment is wholly true. Whatever rewards we receive (or not) will be totally appropriate. There will be no need for appeals or discussions since His judgments will be perfect.

The Distinction of Heaven's Rewards

The Judgment Seat of Christ is not a final exam to determine your suitability for heaven. Because this judgment does evaluate our works, some have thought it was to determine whether we have enough good works to merit entrance into heaven. That is wrong. The Bible could not be more clear that we are saved by grace, not according to our works (Ephesians 2:8–9; see also Romans 8:1; 1 Corinthians 15:3; 1 John 2:12). If you have trusted Jesus Christ as your Savior, your sins have been forgiven, and that is what qualifies you to enter the holy presence of God in heaven. Your sins—past, present, and future—were paid for on Calvary's cross and will not be a matter of examination at the Judgment Seat of Christ regarding your salvation.

Instead, the Judgment Seat of Christ is where you will be rewarded for your service to the Lord in your Christian experience. This service is a matter of faithfulness on the part of those who are already saved, not works that bear on your salvation. These are the works described in Ephesians 2:10 that follow after our salvation by grace: "For we are His workmanship, created in Christ Jesus for good works, which God prepared beforehand that we should walk in them."

We are not saved *by* good works but are saved *for* good works. This truth has apparently not registered with much of the Christian community, since surveys indicate the lifestyles of most Christians are not significantly different from non-Christians. There will be a rude awakening at the Judgment Seat of Christ when many discover there are no rewards given to them.

Bruce Wilkinson has summarized the difference between being saved and being rewarded for service: "Our eternal destination is the consequence of what we believe on earth. Our eternal compensation is the consequence of how we behave on earth."[1]

When you stand before the Judgment Seat of Christ, it's not about getting into heaven. You'll already be there! It's about heaven's evaluation of your faithful service to Christ. The prospect of this coming judgment is what should keep us from judging one another in this life. We are not the judge—Christ is.

The Description of Heaven's Rewards

The New Testament describes five different kinds of rewards, referred to as crowns, that will be given to believers. I do not believe these are all the rewards that will be given but are representative of the whole range of crowns that will be handed out.

The Victor's Crown (1 Corinthians 9:25–27)

The Victor's Crown is called an "imperishable crown" by Paul and is compared to the perishable wreaths for which athletes competed in the Greek games. There were two athletic festivals in Greece, the Olympic Games and the Isthmian Games, the latter being held at Corinth. Contestants trained vigorously for ten months, and Paul used this training to illustrate the discipline necessary for spiritual success. Paul's point is that winning requires discipline and training. If athletes worked diligently for months to win a perishable wreath of olive branches, how much more diligently should we work to win an imperishable crown from God?

Training requires the ability to say "no" when necessary—and not just to things that are sinful. As the saying goes, "The good is the enemy of the best." In order to be and do our best for God, it may require choosing to focus only on those things with the highest value in an eternal sense. There are lots of "good" and "better" things in life that can take our focus off the "best," and it is up to us to identify them and choose accordingly. Bible study, evangelism, helping a neighbor in the name of Christ, sacrificing personal desires to free up money for God's work—all of these choices require sacrifice. And when that kind of discipline is exercised, the Victor's Crown is given.

Think of the difference between an athlete and a non-athlete, to continue Paul's illustration. An athlete makes everything subservient to his goal of winning. The non-athlete lets other desires—food, sleep, possessions—take precedence. The spiritual life is no different. Our willingness to submit to the goal of fulfilling Christ's commands will characterize us as a "victor"—one who strives to win the race. Our goal is to consider our spiritual walk like an athlete considers a race—something to make sacrifices for in order to win.

The Crown of Rejoicing (1 Thessalonians 2:19)

Paul asked the Thessalonian Christians, "For what is our hope, or joy, or crown of rejoicing?" And his answer is startling: "Is it not even you in the presence of our Lord Jesus Christ at His coming?"

This crown is given to those who are responsible for others standing before Christ at His return—often called the Soul-Winner's Crown. It's the reward given to those who reach out beyond themselves to lead others to heaven.

Christians talk about Jesus to each other often, and that's good. But when is the last time you talked about Jesus to someone who isn't a Christian? Paul's love for the Thessalonians is evident in his two letters for them—they were his hope, his joy, his Crown of Rejoicing.

The Crown of Righteousness (2 Timothy 4:8)

Paul writes the words in this verse in the last days of his life. He is a prisoner in Rome and knows his days are numbered. But he is content, knowing he has run the race with faithfulness. He looks forward to receiving the Crown of Righteousness that is given "to all who have loved His appearing"—those who have eagerly anticipated the Second Coming of Christ.

Many Christians are so caught up with all the "exciting" things they're involved in on earth that they have forgotten that earth is not their home. They love their life here and have many places to go, things to do, and people to see before going to heaven. This crown is not for those believers. It is for those who long for heaven, their true home, who long to see the face of their Savior when He comes for them in the clouds.

The Crown of Life (James 1:12; Revelation 2:10)

The recipients of this crown are those "who love Him," even, as Revelation says, in the face of death. It is a crown given to those who maintain their love for Christ while enduring and triumphing over persecution and temptation, even martyrdom. Think of the number of Christians we will see wearing this crown in heaven because they gave their life for the sake of Christ throughout the centuries of Church history.

But it's not just martyrs who will receive this crown—it's any who have suffered, endured, persevered, and encouraged others to do so as well, those who have kept the faith when it was costly to do so.

I wonder if the great hymn writer Charles Wesley had this crown in mind when he wrote these words:

> In hope of that immortal crown,
> I now the cross sustain.
> And gladly wander up and down,
> And smile at toil and pain:
> I suffer out my three-score years,
> Till my Deliverer come,

And wipe away His servant's tears,
And take His exile home.

The Crown of Life—an "immortal crown" given to those who have smiled "at toil and pain" 'til their Deliverer came.

The Crown of Glory (1 Peter 5:4)

This is a crown I get excited about because it is given to those who are faithful shepherds of the people of God. But it's not just for pastors, elders, deacons, and leaders with visibility in the church. It will be for all those who were shepherds of the sheep at some level—small groups, Sunday school classes, ministry teams, and in other places of ministry. The wounds of sheep continually need to be bound up, and they need to be guided and encouraged along the way. The Crown of Glory is for those who lay down their lives in that calling of leadership.

The Difference Heaven's Rewards Can Make

Now that we know what the five crowns are that are mentioned in the New Testament, what should we do with this knowledge? What difference should these future rewards make in our present-day relationship with the Lord?

Remember That the Lord Himself Is Your Chief Reward

In Genesis 15:1, we find God making this statement to Abram: "Do not be afraid, Abram. I am your shield, your exceedingly great reward." God was making great promises to Abram in those days about his future, and it would have been possible to be both fearful of the future and prideful about the blessings God was going to bestow. But God reminds Abram that He, God, is Abram's true reward. Land and descendants and blessing would be nothing apart from God in his life.

Resist Doing Works Outwardly for the Purpose of Receiving a Reward

There is enough of the flesh left in us to be tempted, like an immature child, to be obedient for the purpose of gaining a reward. That kind of insincere play-acting drew some strong words from Jesus when He saw it in the religious community of His day: "Take heed that you do not do your charitable deeds before men, to be seen by them. Otherwise you have no reward from your Father in heaven" (Matthew 6:1). He went on to say that our good deeds ought to be done in secret if we want God the Father to reward us for them.

If we are serving the Lord only to get a reward, we have totally misunderstood Christianity. Our motive for serving should be the same as His motive for saving: LOVE! Rewards are simply

God's expressions of joy in response to our love for Him. I have never heard anyone say that they are serving God wholeheartedly in order to get a great reward when they get to heaven. Because that is a self-serving notion, you couldn't be serving the Lord while thinking that way.

Reflect Upon the Ultimate Goal of Any Rewards We May Receive

Finally, and most important, we need to stay continually aware of what we will ultimately do with the crowns we receive in heaven. We read in Revelation 4:10–11 that the twenty-four elders, who represent the Church in heaven, "Cast their crowns before the throne, saying: 'You are worthy, O Lord, to receive glory and honor and power; for You created all things, and by Your will they exist and were created.'"

After we receive our crowns as rewards in heaven, we're going to be so excited about the privilege of having served Jesus that we're going to fall down at His feet and offer them back to Him as offerings of worship and praise. He gave His best to bring us to heaven, and we'll offer our best back to Him for the privilege of being there.

Don't miss out on that amazing experience. Live wholeheartedly for Christ for the rest of your life so you will have a crown to cast at His feet.

APPLICATION

Personal Questions

1. Read Romans 2:1–11.

   a. What is the overriding message of verses 1–3 concerning judgment? (Is there anyone who will escape God's judgment?)

   b. What does the postponement of God's judgment demonstrate about Him (verse 4)?

   c. What is the postponement of judgment supposed to accomplish in us (verse 4)?

   d. What are those who refuse to repent "treasuring up" for themselves (verse 5)?

   e. What is God's principle employed in all judgment (verse 6; see Galatians 6:7)?

   f. What will those who do good receive as a reward (verses 7, 10)?

   g. What will the disobedient receive as a reward (verses 8–9)?

   h. How do we know there is no partiality with God (verses 10–11)?

2. Turn to 1 Corinthians 9:25–27.

   a. Though all have sinned and fall short of God's glory, what will those who seek to fulfill Christ's commands on earth receive in heaven (verse 25)?

   b. Which crown will those "who love Him" receive (James 1:12)?

3. What does Matthew 6:1 advise against?

   a. Have you ever been at fault for doing this while performing a good deed?

   b. What is the ultimate reason believers will receive crowns in heaven (see Revelation 4:10–11)?

Group Questions

1. As a group, how do you reconcile Romans 2:7, 10 with Romans 3:10–18? In other words, has anyone ever performed enough good works to receive a righteous reward?

2. So, how do those who want to do good (but often fail) ever receive a righteous reward (Romans 3:22–23)?

3. The "harvest principle" of Galatians 6:7 governs our activity on earth and God's response to it. What does this principle state?

a. What is God's eternal response to man? Read Romans 6:20–23. (Those who have been set free receive _____. For the lost, the wages of sin is _____.)

b. How are those rewards experienced in this life, before eternity (Galatians 6:8)?

4. Turn to the section, "The Description of Heaven's Rewards." Discuss the reason each of these crowns will be given in heaven:

a. The Victor's Crown (1 Corinthians 9:25–27):

b. The Crown of Rejoicing (1 Thessalonians 2:19):

c. The Crown of Righteousness (2 Timothy 4:8):

d. The Crown of Life (James 1:12; Revelation 2:10):

e. The Crown of Glory (1 Peter 5:4):

5. Read 1 Corinthians 3:11–15 together.

a. Christians will be judged in spite of having received the gift of salvation freely. What will be the basis of their judgment (verses 11–13)?

b. If a Christian's work survives the judgment, what will happen (verse 14)?

c. If their work doesn't survive the judgment, what will happen to them and their work (verse 15)?

DID YOU KNOW?

The Romans used a "judgment seat" (Greek *bema*) for dispensing judgments at trials or for making o cial pronouncements. Pontius Pilate sat down on a *bema* at the trial of Jesus in Jerusalem (Matthew 27:19), and Paul was brought before the judgment seat of Gallio in Corinth (Acts 18:12). Herod delivered a speech in Caesarea from the *bema* (Acts 12:21), the same one used by Festus when he interrogated Paul years later (Acts 25:6). The idea of the *bema* as a place of judgment for Christians was used twice by Paul, calling it "the judgment seat of Christ" (see Romans 14:10).

Note
1. Bruce Wilkinson, *A Life God Rewards: Why Everything You Do Today Matters Forever* (Sisters, OR: Multnomah Press, 2002).

LESSON 17

Worship

REVELATION 4:1–11

In this lesson we discover the priority of worship in heaven.

While there is a proliferation of worship music today, some Christians see worship as optional. The apostle John looked through a doorway into heaven and saw that worship was a central activity. The Christian's life should be a dress rehearsal on earth for an eternity of worship in heaven.

OUTLINE

   I. **The Context of Worship in Heaven (Revelation 4:1)**

  II. **The Center of Worship in Heaven (Revelation 4:2–3)**

 III. **The Chorus of Worship in Heaven (Revelation 4:4, 9–11)**

 IV. **The Crescendo of Worship in Heaven**

  V. **The Contrast of Worship in Heaven**
   - A. Worship Is Not About Us—It's About Him
   - B. Worship Is Not About Here—It's About There
   - C. Worship Is Not About Now—It's About Then
   - D. Worship Is Not About One—It's About Many

Wheaton College, located in Wheaton, Illinois, outside Chicago, was for many years the bastion of Christian higher education in America. There are many fine Christian colleges now, but Wheaton was one of the first and remains one of the best.

For many years, the president of Wheaton College was Ray Edman, a godly man and great leader. In 1967, Dr. Edman was preaching a sermon to the students in the chapel at Wheaton on the subject of worship. He told the students about having met the king of Ethiopia once and how he had to conform to strict protocols when going into the presence of that earthly king. He told the students that when they came into the presence of the Lord, they needed to come in a manner worthy of the King of kings to worship.

Suddenly, in the middle of his sermon on worship, Dr. Edman collapsed and entered into the presence of the Lord whom he loved to worship. More than one writer commented after Dr. Edman's death that he would likely have had as seamless a transition from earth to heaven as anyone could imagine. He so loved and worshiped God while on earth that entering into an environment of worship in heaven would be no shock to his system at all.

Today, in worship we experience it in three parts: praise of God, prayer to God, and preaching about God. But in heaven, only one of those will remain: praise of God. There will be no need to pray, since we will be in God's presence with all our needs met. And there won't be preaching in heaven, because we will have a complete grasp of the truth about God. Therefore, praise is all that will remain. And the Bible says we will spend eternity in that activity.

Our goal on earth should be like that of Dr. Edman: to prepare ourselves for a seamless transition into the worship environment of heaven by creating that kind of environment on earth. What we learn to do in our short time on earth will prepare us for an eternity in heaven.

In this lesson we will look at Revelation 4:1–11, a central passage on the worship of God in heaven.

The Context of Worship in Heaven (Revelation 4:1)

In John's vision, he saw a door standing open, giving him a vision into heaven. Through that door he saw something no one on earth had ever seen before: worship in heaven.

John, along with Peter and James, was part of Jesus' inner circle of disciples. He was with Jesus on the Mount of Transfiguration, in the Garden of Gethsemane, at the Crucifixion, and at the Resurrection. But in addition to these high moments in his life, John had also suffered for Jesus. In fact, when he received the vision of heaven, he was on the island of Patmos in the Mediterranean where he had been exiled by the Roman emperor (Revelation 1:9). John no doubt wondered if he was going to be killed or left on Patmos to die. It was a difficult time in his life and as a disciple of Christ.

But in the midst of that difficult time, he experienced something that no one else ever had. Perhaps the vision of heaven came at a time when he was at a low point, wondering how he would survive. Suddenly a door was opened and he found himself peering through a portal into heaven itself. I simply am at a loss for words to describe what John must have thought and felt at that moment.

The Center of Worship in Heaven (Revelation 4:2–3)

The key word in these two verses is the word "throne." In fact, it might be the key word in all the book of Revelation since it occurs more than forty times. "Throne" in Revelation speaks of sovereignty, authority, rule, and control. It speaks of the fact that while on earth things may appear to be out of control, there is One in heaven who is controlling all things for His purposes.

Sometimes it appears that circumstances in our life are out of control, just as they might appear to one who lives on the earth during the Great Tribulation. But they are not. God is on His throne in heaven working out all things by His plan and for His glory.

The Bible says, "No man shall see [God], and live" (Exodus 33:20). Therefore, when John looked into heaven, he only saw the appearance of God and tried to put it into words as best he could: "like a jasper and a sardius stone in appearance; and there was a rainbow around the throne, in appearance like an emerald" (Revelation 4:3). A jasper stone is what we know as a diamond, and the sardius is our ruby. So John saw a brilliant, multifaceted stone that sparkled in the light.

Somehow, what John saw was best described in terms of brilliance, worth, beauty, and light. Who among us could have described it any better? It is hard to find words in any human language to describe the appearance of God. All John could do, and all we can do, is describe the impact of His presence, not His person. Describing God is like describing the wind—the best we can do is describe the presence or impact or appearance of the wind, not the wind itself.

The Chorus of Worship in Heaven (Revelation 4:4, 9–11)

By looking into heaven and seeing the throne of God, John became an unwitting observer of worship in heaven. It becomes apparent from his description that, where the throne of God is, there is worship.

John sees twenty-four additional thrones around the central throne of God on which were seated twenty-four elders, representatives of the Church of the living God. There were also four living creatures around the throne who continually praised God. And when the creatures praised God, the twenty-four elders fell from their thrones and cast their crowns before the throne of God and worshiped Him. I cannot even imagine what that must have sounded like—multiply the "Hallelujah Chorus" from Handel's *Messiah* by infinity, and maybe it would come close!

William Temple has defined praise like this, which must be what happens in heaven: "To worship is to quicken the conscience by the holiness of God, to feed the mind with the truth of God, to purge the imagination with the beauty of God, to open the heart to the love of God and to devote the will to the purpose of God."[1] This should be the goal of every worshiper on earth as we prepare to worship before the throne of God in heaven.

The Crescendo of Worship in Heaven

"Crescendo" basically means to start small and end big, usually applied to pieces of music. In the worship songs in Revelation, there is an obvious crescendo that grows throughout the book. In Revelation 1:6 there is a two-fold doxology; in 4:11 there is a threefold doxology; in 5:13 there is a four-fold doxology. Then, when you get to 7:12, there is a seven-fold doxology: "Amen! Blessing and glory and wisdom, thanksgiving and honor and power and might, be to our God forever and ever. Amen."

The worship grows as you move through the book—a crescendo of worship to the Lord. When church choirs do that—start soft and simple and end loud and complex—it's biblical!

There's another aspect of crescendo we should consider: It's as if the crescendo of worship for God escalates in accord with the timeline of God's purposes in the world. In other words, the farther along God's timeline of history we go, the greater becomes the praise and worship for Him. There has never been in the history of Christianity an emphasis on praise and worship like there is today. Christian radio stations can't play enough praise and worship music. Churches are incorporating more of it into their services. And CDs and DVDs of praise and worship are filling the store shelves.

If what I'm suggesting is accurate, this crescendo of praise and worship we are experiencing is in accord with His timeline because we are getting ever closer to the "grand finale" of His purposes on earth, ultimately culminating with the praise of God in heaven.

The Contrast of Worship in Heaven

In C. S. Lewis's allegory *The Great Divorce*, he tells of a man who journeys to heaven and finds it to be grander in scale and more beautiful than he could have imagined. Hell, he discovers, is the opposite, a fleck of dust by comparison with heaven. In the same way, Lewis suggests our lives in this world get smaller and smaller the more we comprehend the grandeur of heaven and eternity.[2] Seeing heaven was for John like us walking up to the edge of the Grand Canyon for the first time—speechless in wonder.

John experienced smallness and largeness at the same time on Patmos. He was probably discouraged and despairing in light of his personal circumstances. But then he was given a view of the grandeur of heaven and the majesty of heavenly worship. And he was changed. When he saw that all of heaven and earth were under the authority of God in heaven, he was able to look at his exile on Patmos in a new light. Seeing our lives against the backdrop of heaven is the best way to keep things in perspective.

By necessity, our lives are focused continually on the present—the things of this world. We face demands in life that require us to focus on the here-and-now. Yet heaven is no less real than this present world. In fact, it is even more real in an ultimate sense. This world is passing away, but heaven will last forever. When John's temporal world and circumstances were ushered into the presence of God, he was reminded that there is something bigger and more important than the day-to-day. He remembered that God is able to do above and beyond what we can ask and think or expect (Ephesians 3:20). He remembered that nothing is impossible for God (Luke 1:37).

We can be reminded of those same truths through worship. We may not see into heaven with our eyes, but we see the character of God through His Word and our songs of praise that proclaim His worthiness. We can hear Jesus remind us of the same things of which He reminded John: "John, I want you to know that things are not as they appear to be. I'm going to show you how things really are. I'm going to walk you into the throne room of heaven and show you genuine reality. Things are not out of control. Satan has not won. Evil has not triumphed. Peek through the door; get a glimpse of reality. God is on His throne, and such a sight will transform your heart and your mind forever."

Here are four things that we can learn from John's experience on the isle of Patmos.

Worship Is Not About Us—It's About Him

This is easy to forget—God is the center of our worship. It's amazing how many people in churches never get their attention centered on God because they don't like the hymns, the music, the style of worship, the personality of the worship leader, the color of the choir robes or hymn books, and a hundred other things. As a result, they make worship all about them instead of about God.

When you go into a worship service with the conscious intent to praise and worship God for who He is and what He has done, you will have blinders on that keep you from seeing all the stuff you don't like. Worship isn't about those things. It's about God.

Worship Is Not About Here—It's About There

For God, worship exalts and extols His majesty. But for us, worship gets our minds off the things of this earth and onto the realities in heaven. The only way we can live our life on earth with the values and priorities of heaven is to continually focus on heaven. If all we ever see with our spiritual eyes are the carnal and worldly affairs of this life, we will struggle. But if we are continually reminded of God's character, His purposes and plans, and His love for us, then we walk through this world with a different gait. Colossians 3:1–3 reminds us to seek and set our minds on things above. We are citizens of heaven, and that is to be the focus of our eyes and ears and the desire of our heart.

Worship Is Not About Now—It's About Then

Paul writes in 2 Corinthians 4:16–18 that we are to look not "at the things which are seen, but at the things which are not seen. For the things which are seen are temporary, but the things which are not seen are eternal." Paul is encouraging the Corinthians (and us) to leverage everything going on in their lives against the promise of the future. The contrasts he draws in these verses are powerful: The outward man is perishing, but the inward man is being renewed. The affliction of today is light, but the weight of future glory is heavy. The things that are seen are temporal, but the things that are unseen are eternal. Worship is the corridor through which we exchange the things of this world—afflication, suffering, limitations—for the reality of heaven.

Worship Is Not About One—It's About Many

We live in a day when people don't believe they need to worship in church with the Body of Christ. People claim they can worship in nature or on the golf course on Sunday morning. In the book of Revelation, what we see in heaven is corporate worship. Christianity is not an individual experience. Yes, we are saved individually, but immediately we are baptized into the Body of Christ, where we remain for eternity. I cannot encourage you enough to make sure that you learn to do on earth what you will be doing for eternity in heaven: worship with the many that God has redeemed for Himself.

Because we don't know the day or hour when we will be promoted to heaven, I encourage you to make every day a full dress rehearsal for the worship that will characterize your eternal life.

APPLICATION

Personal Questions

1. Compare the last line of Revelation 4:8 with Exodus 3:14. How is the phrase "was and is and is to come" another way of saying "I AM"?

   a. How is this confession in Revelation 4:8 a statement about the sovereignty of God throughout human history? Is there any time in which He is not "Almighty"?

   b. Write out a statement of your own, giving God "glory and honor and thanks" (Revelation 4:9).

   c. What is one reason for giving God "glory and honor and power" (Revelation 4:11)?

   d. What does that say to you about your stewardship of what God has created (Genesis 1:28)?

2. How many thrones did John see around the central throne of God (Revelation 4:4)?

   a. Who were seated on those thrones?

   b. What was their purpose (Revelation 4:9–11)?

3. In heaven there is continual praise, while on earth there is not. Are you prepared for that transition? Do you look forward to it? Explain.

   a. In what ways can you prepare for an eternity of worship in heaven, while here on earth, according to Colossians 3:1–3?

   b. In 2 Corinthians 4:16–18, what does Paul encourage believers to do in order for us not to lose heart (verse 18)?

Group Questions

Read Revelation 4:8–11 and discuss the following questions:

a. Note the similarities in appearance between the four creatures John saw and the seraphim Isaiah saw in their visions of God on His throne (Isaiah 6:2). What were the seraphim in Isaiah's vision doing with their six wings?

b. What reasons can you suggest for the seraphs covering their faces and feet? Of what might these acts be symbols?

c. Why do you think the creatures in John's vision had so many eyes (Revelation 4:8)?

d. What is the significance of their continual (day and night) praise to God (verse 8)?

e. How do their words provide continuity with the seraphim in Isaiah's vision (Isaiah 6:3; Revelation 4:8)?

f. What significance do you find in the seraphim calling to one another instead of directing their praise to God (Isaiah 6:3)?

g. What practical example do you find in this? What value is there in confessing our beliefs about the character of God to one another?

h. Is the earth "full of His glory" at present, or are these merely prophetic words of the seraphim (Isaiah 6:3)?

i. What value do you see in confessing what you know the future holds, even though it has not yet appeared?

DID YOU KNOW?

The creatures seen by Isaiah are called "seraphim" by the prophet (Isaiah 6:2; "seraph" is singular, "seraphim" is plural, *-im* being the plural ending in Hebrew). Isaiah's vision is the only place in Scripture where heavenly creatures are called seraphim. The Hebrew root *srp*, from which seraph likely comes, means to burn. It also is the basis for the word "serpent," as in the bronze serpent Moses mounted on a pole in Numbers 21:8–9 to save Israel from the bites of the "fiery [*srp*] serpents" among them (Numbers 21:6). Were the seraphim in Isaiah's vision serpentine-shaped creatures? Images of winged serpents have been uncovered by archaeologists from the Old Testament era, but it is impossible to tell if Isaiah's seraphim had that shape.

Notes
1. William Temple, cited in Erwin Lutzer, *Pastor to Pastor* (Grand Rapids, MI: Kregel Inc., 1998), 79.
2. C. S. Lewis, *The Great Divorce* (London, UK: Geoffrey Bles, 1945).

PART 4

TRIBULATION
SIGNS

Four Riders

REVELATION 6:1–8

*In this lesson we learn how a fourth of the world's population
will be destroyed in the Tribulation.*

A cursory look around our globe reveals some terrifying realities—war, starvation, diseases with no cure, uncontrollable dictators, biological terrorism. Some might think the Tribulation has already begun. In reality, these are just birth pangs of something much worse to come.

OUTLINE

I. The First Seal Opened: The White Horse

II. The Second Seal Opened: The Red Horse

III. The Third Seal Opened: The Black Horse

IV. The Fourth Seal Opened: The Pale Horse

V. Conclusion
    A. The Response of Praise
    B. The Response of Passion
    C. The Response of Personal Evaluation

OVERVIEW

We have arrived in our study at Revelation 6—the place where the real action of the Great Tribulation begins. Chapter 1 contained the things John saw, chapters 2–3 the things which are, and chapters 4–5 the setting of the throne of God in heaven from which the judgments of the Tribulation will proceed. Held in the hand of the One on the throne is a scroll which is taken by the Lamb who was slain (5:7). That scroll contains seven seals, the seventh of which contains seven trumpets, the seventh of which contains seven bowls—judgments all, about to fall upon the earth.

In this lesson, we will cover Revelation 6:1-8 and discover the content of the first four seals that are opened by Christ. The first four seals consist of four horsemen who are released to ride upon the earth, carrying various forms of judgment. In our day, the relevance of the horse as a metaphor for judgment is unfamiliar. But in the biblical world, the horse would have been readily understood. For example, Job 39:19-25 is an extended reference to the esteem in which horses were held in the ancient world. In battle, the strength and fearlessness of the horse was respected. The horse was primarily thought of as a weapon of war more than as an agricultural asset or mode of transportation. So the image of four horsemen would bring to mind immediately the idea of warfare and battle to the ancient reader of Revelation.

Four times (6:1, 3, 5, 7) we read the word, "Come!" Most translations have this command directed to John—but he is already there. It seems better to read the word with its alternate meaning, "go" or "proceed," and have it directed to the four horsemen. Therefore, the living creature issuing the command sends each of the four horsemen out of heaven to their mission on earth—"Go!"

The First Seal Opened: The White Horse

The white horse (verse 2) in oriental imagery was the picture of a conqueror. Since it is the first horse sent out at the beginning of the Tribulation period, we must discover the purpose and meaning of this first horseman. Because there is a reference to Christ riding a white horse in Revelation 19:11, some believe that Christ Himself must be the rider on this white horse. But there are some differences which make that conclusion strained, at best. Consider the differences:

- In chapter 19, Christ's weapon is a sword; in chapter 6, the rider's weapon is a bow with no arrows.

- In chapter 19, Christ wears a crown (a diadem, or kingly crown); in chapter 6, the rider wears a *stephanzos*, a victor's crown of one going forth to conquer. It could be worn by anyone, whereas the diadem can only be worn by Christ.
- In chapter 19, the white horse signals the end of judgment; in chapter 6, the white horse signals the beginning of judgment. It isn't likely that Christ would appear in both places, especially since His Second Coming is the more logical place for Him to appear to put an end to judgment.

These and other disparities between the two riders lead me to believe that the rider of the white horse in Revelation 6 is not Christ but the Antichrist. He carries no arrows because we know he conquers in the name of false peace. He is the prince mentioned in Daniel 9:26 who makes a covenant with Israel to protect the Jews from their enemies. This treaty marks the beginning of the Great Tribulation. The next horseman (verse 4) is allowed to "take peace from the earth"—the peace which the first horseman, the Antichrist, has established.

The person represented by the rider on the white horse could be alive in our world today since he will appear at the beginning of the Tribulation as a full-grown man. That means he would have been born thirty to fifty years prior to his appearance at the beginning of the Tribulation. Many believe the world stage is set for the appearance of such a person, meaning he could be alive at this moment.

The Second Seal Opened: The Red Horse

It is very clear that the rider on the second horse personifies war; its red color (verses 3–4) speaks clearly of the shedding of blood. War is nothing new to the human race; thousands and thousands of conflicts fill the pages of recorded human history. In the last 100 years alone, two world wars claimed the lives of forty-two million people, with fifty million more being wounded. Millions more civilians were killed or died in concentration camps. But the wars yet to be fought on planet earth, and the suffering which attends war, will be more devastating than anything in history. The "great sword" the rider holds in his hand is the large sword used by Roman soldiers going into battle—used when nations rise against nations.

You may ask why it is important to know about these four horsemen if, as a Christian, you are going to be absent from the earth during the period of the Tribulation. The reason is that every event casts its shadow before it. That which will take place in the future has its portents in the present. The "wars and rumors of wars" (Matthew 24:6) we hear of today are the foretastes of that which is yet to come—and those foretastes are part of the diet of the world each of us lives in today.

As wars and conflicts increase, the world will become restless for someone to bring peace and unity to our divided and embattled world. And it is in that context that the Antichrist will arise. There will be a thin dividing line between the signs of the appearing of the Antichrist and his actual inauguration as a world leader. Between those two events, the Rapture of the Church will occur. But the Church may be on earth during a significant part of the turmoil leading up to the revealing of the Antichrist. That is why it is important to know the stages of judgment represented by the four horsemen.

The Third Seal Opened: The Black Horse

The color black is often connected with death and starvation, and famine often occurs as a result of war. Scarcity of food and other resources often result in an increase in prices so that enough food to subsist on can consume all of one's daily wages. Verse 6 indicates that a quart of wheat, or three quarts of barley (enough for one day), would cost a denarius (penny), which constituted a day's wage in biblical times. In the Tribulation period, along with the appearance of the Antichrist followed by war, famine will appear, and the globe will be wrenched with hunger because of the inability to secure food. All but the rich will suffer, for their staples, oil and wine, will not be harmed. But the average person will border on starvation.

This setting also plays directly into the hands of the Antichrist. Revelation 13:17 says that "no one may buy or sell except one who has the mark or the name of the Beast, or the number of his name." The Beast will control the world through the world's own hunger. Men and nations will do unusual and unplanned things in order to get food—and unfortunately, individuals will as well. Hunger is a basic human motivation, and the Antichrist will use it to his advantage as a means of moving people to give him allegiance.

We see evidences of the politicization of food distribution in some African countries today. The pathetic and heart-wrenching photos we see of starving children and adults (many of them Christians) make us think in terms of food shortages. In reality, what has sometimes happened is that food supplies have been cut off by warring political factions. As the African proverb has stated for generations, "When elephants battle, the ants get trampled." Using starvation as a means of genocide is a twenty-first century reality in our world. If it is happening today, how much more might it continue at the hand of an evil world ruler?

The Fourth Seal Opened: The Pale Horse

The three previous horses each had one rider only. Now John looks and sees that the fourth horse has a rider with another person following (verses 7–8). Death is the rider with Hades following close behind. Death and Hades are mentioned three times in Revelation. Christ has the keys to Death and Hades in 1:18, and 20:14 says that Death and Hades will be cast into hell. But 20:13 tells us a little more about them. They will be judged one day, following the Tribulation during which they have reigned. They will be judged, "each one according to his works." Found guilty, they will be cast into hell.

After the Antichrist's brief treaty of peace comes war, and after war comes famine, and after famine comes death and Hades. They are armed with the sword, hunger, pestilence (plagues), and wild beasts. These are the four judgments the Lord said he would send in Ezekiel 14:21. In our day, we have seen war and famine wreak havoc on our world, and we are now in the process of seeing pestilence and beasts and plague do the same.

"Pestilence" is a word for "epidemic." The epidemic, or pandemic, that affected millions of people globally is the HIV/AIDS virus. Since its inception, more than thirty-five million people have died from AIDS. The incubation period of the HIV virus can be from six months up to ten years, so many people who were infected (HIV-positive) did not know it—and unknowingly transmitted the disease—if they had not been tested. As a result, the disease continued to spread. It is estimated that about 5,753 people become infected with HIV each day. While new antiviral treatments are being successful in many cases, there is no cure for AIDS. When HIV advances to AIDS, the life expectancy without treatment is about three years. This is a pestilence like we read about in Revelation.

Diseases are also spread by "beasts" of the earth—which could be anything from rats, which can carry as many as thirty-five known diseases, to disease-resistant microorganisms spread by birds and animals that are shipped or that migrate from one country to another. In past decades and centuries, diseases could be contained in their country of origin fairly easily. But today, a person can contract an animal-borne disease in one country (for example, AIDS or the Ebola virus, which both originated in animal populations in Africa) and arrive by airplane in another country in a matter of hours—and be "lost" among the population.

It is not difficult to imagine that "Death" and "Hades" will account for twenty-five percent of the world's population being killed during the Tribulation (6:8).

Conclusion

The Response of Praise

Neither is it difficult to see why praise and worship are the central focus of chapters 4 and 5 of Revelation. Why? Because those who know the Lord Jesus Christ as Savior and Lord will be worshiping Him in heaven while the events of Revelation 6–19 are unfolding on the earth.

If being excluded from the fourth of the world's population killed by war, hunger, disease, and the beasts of the earth isn't a reason to praise, I don't know what is.

The Response of Passion

But there is another response we should have. It would be selfish and self-centered for us to be concerned only about saving ourselves. If there is any "neighbor" whom we are to love as we love ourselves, we must warn them of what is coming upon the earth. If we really believe the messages of the four horsemen, we will tell anyone and everyone how they can be spared from the torment of the Tribulation.

The Response of Personal Evaluation

Which brings us to the necessary question, *where will you be when Revelation 6 begins to unfold on the earth?* Don't wait another minute before making sure that when the trumpet of the Lord sounds, you will leave this earth at the Rapture. After that trumpet—after the Church is gone—it will be too late to reconsider.

APPLICATION

Personal Questions

1. Read Matthew 24:3–15.

   a. What question do the disciples have for Jesus (verse 3)?

   b. How does verse 5 parallel the notion of an Antichrist coming into the world?

   c. Which of the four horsemen in Revelation 6:1–8 could fulfill the sign Jesus mentions in verses 6–7?

   d. What is the parallel between verse 7 and the horseman in Revelation 6:5–6?

   e. What does verse 9 suggest about when these events will begin—that is, the relation of these events to the Rapture of believers?

f. What is characteristic of birth pangs? That is, do they begin slowly and gradually increase or arrive suddenly with full intensity? What does this suggest as to the timing of these events in relationship to the Rapture?

2. Read Matthew 24:32–35.

   a. What sign is evident on a fig tree with regard to the approach of summer (verse 32)?

   b. What should the disciples of Jesus learn from this parable with regard to the end of the age (verse 33)?

   c. What generation did Jesus refer to in verse 34—the generation to which He was speaking or the generation that sees the beginning of the signs He has described?

   d. How certain can we be that the signs (including the four horsemen of Revelation 6) will come to pass (verse 35)?

Group Questions

1. Read Revelation 6:1–8 and discuss (1) what each of the horses and riders personify, and (2) what event each brings to the world. Explain your reasoning for each answer:

   a. The rider on the white horse (verse 2):

   b. The rider on the red horse (verse 4):

   c. The rider on the black horse (verses 5–6):

   d. The rider on the pale horse (verse 8):

2. What did horses signify in the ancient world? Using that definition, what would the image of four horsemen bring to mind?

3. What evidence do you see in our world today that might be signs of the presence of these four horsemen?

   a. The rider on the white horse (verse 2):

   b. The rider on the red horse (verse 4):

   c. The rider on the black horse (verses 5–6):

   d. The rider on the pale horse (verse 8):

4. Why is it important to study the four horsemen when, as Christians, we will not be present for the Great Tribulation?

5. What is our calling as we await the Great Tribulation?

DID YOU KNOW?

The four horsemen of the Apocalypse, described in Revelation 6:1–8, have become cultural icons and models through the centuries. Their title has been applied to characters in computer games, rock bands, rock songs, NASA scientists during the Apollo era, Supreme Court justices during the New Deal era of Franklin Roosevelt, a group of atheist scientists, professional wrestlers, and a group of computer scientists. The most well-known group were the four members of the backfield on the Notre Dame University football team, coached by the legendary Knute Rockne, in 1924. All are examples of how the truth of Scripture can be diluted by cultural misuse.

Antichrist

In this lesson we learn about the character and future activities of the coming Antichrist.

History is full of the accounts of presumptuous leaders who perpetrated "crimes against humanity" for the sake of their own agendas. But no prior leader will compare, in arrogance or evil, with the soon to come Antichrist who will eventually rule the world with an iron fist.

OUTLINE

   I. **His Preparation**

  II. **His Presentation**

 III. **His Personality**

 IV. **His Plan**

  V. **His Pride**

 VI. **His Peace Treaty**

VII. **His Persecutions**

VIII. **His Power**

IX. His Profaneness

X. His Punishment

OVERVIEW

It is reported that the former prime minister of Belgium, P. H. Spaak, made the following statement:

> The truth is that the method of international committees has failed. What we need is a person, someone of the highest order, of great experience, of great authority, of wide influence, of great energy. Let him come and let him come quickly. Either a civilian or a military man, no matter what his nationality, who will cut all the red tape, shove out of the way all the committees, wake up all the people and galvanize all governments into action. Let him come quickly. This man we need and for whom we wait will take charge of the defense of the West. Once more I say, it is not too late, but it is high time.[1]

Sentiments like that will make the rise of the Antichrist a welcome event to many when it happens.

While the Antichrist is described in more than one hundred passages of Scripture, the word "Antichrist" itself occurs in only four verses, each time in the writings of the apostle John. Most of those mentions involve people in John's day who were anti-Christ—they were opposed to Christ and His Gospel (see 1 John 2:18, 22; 4:3; 2 John 7). Only once did John apply the term to *the* Antichrist, the person described in Revelation 13:1–10: "Little children, it is the last hour; and as you have heard that the Antichrist is coming, even now many antichrists have come, by which we know that it is the last hour" (1 John 2:18). There is an anti-Christ spirit at work in the world today that will be manifested fully in *the* Antichrist who will come at the end of the age.

While we cannot know the identity of the Antichrist before he appears, we can know much about him based on more than twenty-five titles given to him and the hundred-plus times he is mentioned. Underlying everything is this: He is a man empowered and controlled by Satan.

His Preparation

Daniel 8:23–24 describes him as "a king" having "fierce features," employing "sinister schemes," having power that is not his own, and who prospers, thrives, and destroys. He will come at "the time of the end in the latter time of indignation" (see Daniel 8:17, 19). That last phrase—"the latter time of indignation"—refers to the seven-year period called the Tribulation.

The Antichrist will rise out of the mass of humanity: "And I saw a beast rising up out of the sea" (Revelation 13:1). "Sea" doesn't refer to the ocean but to humanity—specifically, the Gentile nations of the world. This is confirmed in Revelation 17:15 with the phrase, "peoples, multitudes, nations, and tongues."

There are at least four reasons the Antichrist will not be a Jew:

- Daniel indicates that the Antichrist ("prince") will be from the people that would destroy Jerusalem and the temple (Daniel 9:26). Those people were the Romans under Titus in AD 70. Therefore, the Antichrist will be a "Roman," or Gentile.

- Daniel also saw the Antichrist as the little horn that arose out of ten horns on the head of the fourth beast that represented the Roman Empire (Daniel 7:7–8, 19–26).

- John describes the Antichrist as "a beast rising up out of the sea" (Revelation 13:1). In prophecy, the "sea" represents the vast multitudes of Gentile people.

- He is described as history's most vicious and wicked persecutor of the Jewish people. Gentiles, not Jews, persecute Jews.

His Presentation

Second Thessalonians 2:3–4, 7 describes a "falling away" that will take place before the appearing of "the man of sin" (the Antichrist). The word for "falling away" is the word from which we get "apostasy." Before the Antichrist will be revealed and the Tribulation begins, there will be a falling away from the faith by true believers. The falling away is more than just a few people; it is a major departure from the faith by a large segment of believing Christianity.

Jesus Himself predicted such a time: "And then many will be offended, will betray one another, and will hate one another. Then many false prophets will rise up and deceive many. And because lawlessness will abound, the love of many will grow cold" (Matthew 24:10–12). And Paul wrote to Timothy about the same occurrence: "in latter times some will depart from the faith." They will "not endure sound doctrine"; they will "turn their ears away from the truth, and be turned aside to fables" (1 Timothy 4:1; 2 Timothy 4:3–4). The present age will not end in a great revival but a great falling away and apostasy.

Nor can the Antichrist appear before "He who now restrains . . . is taken out of the way" (2 Thessalonians 2:7). The restrainer is the Holy Spirit who, by virtue of the Rapture of true believers, will be removed from earth. The Holy Spirit presently restrains sin in the world and the Antichrist, the embodiment of sin. But when the Spirit is removed, all hell—literally speaking—will break loose on earth.

His Personality

According to Daniel, the Antichrist will have a "mouth speaking pompous words . . . against the Most High" (Daniel 7:8, 25). He will "exalt and magnify himself above every god, [and] shall speak blasphemies against the God of gods" (Daniel 11:36). He will be a powerful and charismatic speaker, boasting of his stature above God.

A. W. Pink describes the Antichrist in these terms:

> He will have a mouth speaking very great things. He will have a perfect command and flow of language. His oratory will not only gain attention but respect. Revelation 13:2 declares that his mouth is "as the mouth of a lion" which is a symbolic expression telling of the majesty and awe-producing effects of his voice.[2]

He will be attractive (Daniel 7:20) and of great intellect (Daniel 8:23, 25). He will possess a stature and magnetism that will draw the world's population to him as a leader when things turn bad during the Tribulation period. People will look to him as their only hope.

His Plan

In short, the Antichrist will "seize the kingdom by intrigue" (Daniel 8:25; 11:21). In his dream recorded in Daniel 7, Daniel saw "a little [horn], coming up among them, before whom three of the first horns were plucked out by the roots" (Daniel 7:8). "Plucked out" refers to "push out" or "cleverly replace." The Antichrist is the little horn who arises among ten others and who subdues three of the ten. The ten are kings—a confederation in the Last Days—among whom the Antichrist will gain prominence (Daniel 7:24). By political intrigue and manipulation, he will eliminate three kingdoms, gathering their power to himself. This is not a sudden coup but a gradual shifting of power. He arises as a minor player among major players and eliminates three of the existing kingdoms in his march to power.

His Pride

"Then he opened his mouth in blasphemy against God, to blaspheme His name, His tabernacle, and those who dwell in heaven" (Revelation 13:6; see also Daniel 11:36–39).

Dr. Henry Morris describes what will motivate the Antichrist's actions:

> Not content to rail against God, the dragon-inspired beast must utter diatribes and obscenities against all [God] stands for (His name), defaming His holiness, His love, His law, His grace. He curses the heavens (the dragon has recently been expelled from heaven) where God dwells. Those who dwell with God in heaven, including not only the holy angels but also all the raptured saints, share in his vilifications. This continual barrage of slander must now take place on earth, since the Devil no longer has access to heaven where he used to accuse the brethren.[3]

The Antichrist will acknowledge no religion at all other than the worship of himself and Satan. In his attempt to wipe the thought of God from the world's collective mind, he will try to change the moral and natural laws of the universe: "And shall intend to change times and law" (Daniel 7:25). He will do whatever he can to remove the notion of God from the world.

His Peace Treaty

Daniel 9:27 says the Antichrist will "confirm a covenant with many for one week." This will be a covenant—a peace treaty—with Israel, guaranteeing her protection at the beginning of the Tribulation. Israel will trust in this treaty as a defense from attack by her hostile neighbor nations. He will be seen as the one to finally resolve the Middle East peace problem with this covenant. He will probably be hailed around the world as an international hero, a diplomat of peace.

However, in the middle of the seven-year Tribulation period, the Antichrist will break his covenant and turn against Israel: "But in the middle of the week [after three and one-half years], He shall bring an end to sacrifice and offering. And on the wing of abominations shall be one who makes desolate, even until the consummation, which is determined, is poured out on the desolate" (Daniel 9:27). The Antichrist will turn from being Israel's protector to her persecutor.

His Persecutions

After breaking the treaty he brokered with Israel, the Antichrist will install himself and his image in the Jewish temple. This act of sacrilege marks the beginning of the second half of the

Tribulation, often referred to as "The Great Tribulation" (see Matthew 24:21). He unleashes his fury upon any who have become Christians during the first half of the Tribulation (remember: the Church was removed from earth before the start of the seven-year period) (Daniel 7:21, 24–25; Revelation 13:7, 16–17).

The word "persecute" literally means "to wear out." The Antichrist's constant persecution and pressure on those who profess faith in God will serve to wear them down. They will be unable to buy food or other necessities because of having refused the mark of the Antichrist. No doubt many will starve to death. Jesus said this period of time will be like nothing in world history (Matthew 24:21-22). John tells us that the Antichrist will be "given authority to continue for forty-two months"—that is, for three-and-one-half years, the second half of the Tribulation period (Revelation 13:5).

Antiochus Epiphanes, a Greek king who ruled the Seleucid Empire in the Middle East from 175-164 BC, prefigured the behavior of the Antichrist in the way he treated Jews of that period. On one occasion he discovered a number of Jews hiding in a cave, so he lit fires in the cave and sealed the entrance and suffocated all those within. He was a cruel and barbaric ruler, just as the Antichrist will be.

His Power

Paul wrote that the "coming of the lawless one [the Antichrist] is according to the working of Satan, with all power, signs, and lying wonders" (2 Thessalonians 2:9). "Signs and wonders" describes the miraculous works of God throughout Scripture—to include the works of God through Moses (Exodus 7:3), Jesus (Acts 2:22), and the apostles (Acts 2:43). But they are also present in the activity of false prophets (Mark 13:22); thus, the phrase "lying wonders" used by Paul. The purpose of the Antichrist's signs and wonders is to delude people into believing in him. And many will (2 Thessalonians 2:10-12).

When the Antichrist breaks his treaty with Israel, almost simultaneously he will kill God's two true witnesses (Revelation 11:7-8). Also, it will appear as if the Antichrist is killed, but he will come back to life, astonishing the whole world. This will be a gross imitation and counterfeit of the resurrection of Jesus Christ, again in an attempt to establish his credibility (Revelation 13:13). Just as Christ's resurrection caused many to believe, many will give their allegiance to the Antichrist when they see him appear to come back to life.

Remember Paul's description of the Antichrist's work—"according to the work of Satan." The day is coming when God will bring the dead back to life (John 5:28-29) by His divine power. But the Antichrist's return to life will be "according to the work of Satan."

His Profaneness

The result of all the Antichrist's tricks and persecution is that the people worship him: "And they worshiped the beast, saying, 'Who is like the beast? Who is able to make war with him?'" (Revelation 13:4).

The Jews will have rebuilt the temple in Jerusalem by this time, and the Antichrist will have allowed the Jewish worship system to be restarted. But then when he breaks the covenant with Israel, he will surround Jerusalem with his armies and seize control of the city and the temple. And as a final act of presumption, the Antichrist will establish himself as God in the temple: "All who dwell on the earth will worship him, whose names have not been written in the Book of Life of the Lamb slain from the foundation of the world" (Revelation 13:8).

The False Prophet will erect a giant image, or statue, of the Antichrist and command everyone to worship it. He will even cause the image to speak (Revelation 13:14–15)! These events are the "abomination of desolation" spoken of by Daniel the prophet (Daniel 11:31; 12:11; Mark 13:14; see also Matthew 24:15).

His Punishment

It is reasonable to ask, *What kind of punishment does a man such as the Antichrist deserve?* His punishment will come after defying the return of Jesus Christ Himself to earth: "He shall even rise against the Prince of princes, but he shall be broken without human means" (Daniel 8:25).

The Antichrist will gather all the kings of the earth and their armies together to make war against Israel—and then against the returning Christ and His armies from heaven when He appears in the sky (Revelation 19:19; see also Zechariah 12:1–22; 14:1–3; Revelation 16:16). But Christ will be victorious over them all and "consume [them] with the breath of His mouth and . . . the brightness of His coming" (2 Thessalonians 2:8).

The Antichrist will not be annihilated, but he, along with the False Prophet, will be judged and consigned for all eternity to the lake of fire (Revelation 19:20). A thousand years later, at the end of the Millennium, the Antichrist and False Prophet will still be alive, at which time they will be joined by their mastermind, Satan. "And they will be tormented day and night forever and ever" (Revelation 20:10).

We are surely living in a time when signs are pointing to the events described in this lesson. When world leaders begin to publicly voice a desire for one leader to become a savior for a broken and conflicted world, we know the end is drawing nigh. Every Christian must live daily in preparation for these events, anchoring themselves in a faith that cannot be shaken.

APPLICATION

Personal Questions

1. Make a note of how the Antichrist is described in each of the following verses and what you think the description conveys about his character or activity:

   a. Daniel 7:8:

   b. Daniel 8:23:

   c. Daniel 9:26:

   d. Daniel 9:27:

   e. Daniel 11:36:

   f. 2 Thessalonians 2:3:

   g. 2 Thessalonians 2:9:

   h. Revelation 6:2:

   i. Revelation 13:1:

2. Who are the "antichrists" John refers to in 1 John 2:18?

   a. Define the standard John used in 1 John 2:22 to refer to anyone as an antichrist.

   b. What guideline is given in 1 John 4:3?

   c. Based on John's words in 1 John 2:18 and 4:3, what can you assume about the presence of antichrists in the world today?

d. How should the subject of antichrists impact the Christian today? Where should we look for them? How should we measure their words and works (1 John 4:1)?

Group Questions

1. Discuss what two things must happen before the Antichrist is revealed according to 2 Thessalonians 2:3–8:

   a. Event 1 (verse 3):

   b. Event 2 (verse 7):

2. Why should we not expect a massive revival in the Church of Jesus Christ near the end times (see also Matthew 24:10–12; 1 Timothy 4:1; 2 Timothy 4:3–4)?

   a. Who is the "restrainer" that now keeps sin and the Antichrist in check?

   b. If your faith ever begins to grow cold, how should these teachings serve as a warning to you?

3. Why is outward appearance not always a good indication of character (1 Samuel 9:1–2)?

   a. What kind of person can easily be drawn to a charismatic, beautiful leader?

   b. Compare the appearance and demeanor of the Christ (Isaiah 53:2) with that of the Antichrist (Daniel 7:20; 8:23, 25).

   c. Discuss why many will give their allegiance to the Antichrist halfway through the Tribulation.

DID YOU KNOW?

The prophet Daniel spoke of the coming Antichrist changing "times and law" as the ruler of the world (Daniel 7:25). Such a radical transformation of societies and commerce would be an attempt to break any and all connections with religious, commercial, and legal precedents, all to be replaced by the Antichrist's rule. This was tried during the French Revolution when, from 1793 to 1805, the French Republican (or Revolutionary) Calendar was instituted. There were still twelve months, but the weeks were changed from seven days to ten days. These and many other societal and economic changes were a revolutionary attempt to cut all ties to the previous government and way of life.

Notes
1. Quoted by Robert Glenn Gromacki, *Are These The Last Days?* (Old Tappan, NJ: Fleming H. Revell Company, 1970), 110.
2. A. W. Pink, *The Antichrist* (Grand Rapids, MI: Kregel Publications, reprinted in 1988 from original in 1923), 9.
3. Henry M. Morris, *The Revelation Record* (Wheaton, IL: Tyndale House Publishers, Inc., 1983), 241.

False Prophet

REVELATION 13:11-18

In this lesson we learn about the satanically inspired man known as the False Prophet.

No one should doubt the power of religion in human life. Throughout history it has been used to inspire and unite populations. And so it will be during the Tribulation when the Antichrist's spiritual assistant will use his satanic power to promote the worship of the world leader.

OUTLINE

I. **His Profile**

II. **His Purpose**

III. **His Power**
   A. Calling Down Fire from Heaven
   B. Commanding That an Image Be Built
   C. Causing the Image to Breathe and Speak

IV. **His Program**

V. **His Punishment**

OVERVIEW

It is impossible for us today to know exactly how the False Prophet will rise to power as the spiritual leader and assistant to the Antichrist. But this we know: The book of Revelation makes it abundantly clear that the world will come under the influence, actually the domination, of this satanic duo. The Antichrist will be the supreme ruler of the world, focusing on political and economic unity. The False Prophet will promote spirituality based on the acknowledgement of the "deity" of the Antichrist. The fact that Revelation describes them both as beasts—the Antichrist as a beast from the sea, the False Prophet as a beast from the earth—is all we need to know to imagine their destructive powers.

Today in history no one knows the identity of the two figures, whether they are alive today or not. But the more we know of their future activities, the more readily we will detect the signs of their appearing. In this lesson, we will study the profile, purpose, power, program, and punishment of the False Prophet.

His Profile

John introduces the False Prophet this way: "Then I saw another beast coming up out of the earth, and he had two horns like a lamb and spoke like a dragon" (Revelation 13:11). This person, referred to as a "beast" here, is referred to as the "false prophet" three times in Revelation (16:13; 19:20; 20:10).

John saw two different dimensions of the beast's character: He was both a lamb and a dragon (Revelation 13:11). As a lamb, he was the counterfeit of the Lamb of God who takes away the sins of the world (John 1:29). Jesus warned His disciples about "false prophets, who come to you in sheep's clothing, but inwardly they are ravenous wolves" (Matthew 7:15; see also Matthew 24:11, 24; Mark 13:22; 1 John 4:1).

As a dragon, the False Prophet will be powerful, as described by John Phillips:

> The dynamic appeal of the false prophet will lie in his skill in combining political expediency with religious passion, self-interest with benevolent philanthropy, lofty sentiment with blatant sophistry, moral platitude with unbridled self-indulgence. His arguments will be subtle, convincing, and appealing. His oratory will be hypnotic, for he will be able to move the masses to tears or whip them into a frenzy. . . . His deadly appeal will lie in the fact that what he says will sound so right, so sensible, so exactly what unregenerate men have always wanted to hear.[1]

The term "beast" is applied to Satan, the Antichrist, and the False Prophet in Revelation—a label that binds them together in their destructive aims. These three represent an unholy Trinity—a counterfeit to God the Father, Son, and Holy Spirit. Donald Grey Barnhouse has said: "The devil is making his last and greatest effort, a furious effort, to gain power and establish his kingdom upon the earth. He knows nothing better than to imitate God. Since God has succeeded by means of an incarnation and then by means of the work of the Holy Spirit, the devil will work by means of an incarnation in Antichrist and by the unholy spirit."[2]

His Purpose

Just as the Holy Spirit's purpose is to exalt the Lord Jesus Christ, so the False Prophet's purpose is to exalt the Antichrist: "And he exercises all the authority of the first beast in his presence, and causes the earth and those who dwell in it to worship the first beast, whose deadly wound was healed" (Revelation 13:12). "As Christ received authority from the Father (Matthew 11:27), so Antichrist receives authority from the dragon (Revelation 13:4), and as the Holy Spirit glorifies Christ (John 16:14), so the false prophet glorifies the Antichrist (Revelation 13:12)."[3]

The False Prophet's goal is to unite the world in a religious spirit to support the Antichrist. Religious leaders have played a major role in the rise and fall of powers throughout world history. W. A. Criswell has written:

> I do not suppose that in the history of mankind, it has ever been possible to rule without religious approbation and devotion. . . . In the days of Pharaoh, when Moses and Aaron stood before the sovereign of Egypt, he called in Jannis and Jambres, the magicians, the religionists of his day, to oppose Jehovah. When Balak, the king of Moab, sought to destroy Israel, he hired the services of Baalim to curse Israel. When Absalom entered his revolutionary scheme to destroy his own father, David, he did so by the wisdom and advice of Ahithophel. . . . Ahab and Jezebel were able to do what they did in Israel, in the debauchery of the kingdom, because they were abetted and assisted by the prophets of Baal.[4]

Satan does not love Christianity, but he loves religion and will use it to inspire the world to worship the Antichrist under the leadership of the False Prophet.

His Power

Satan will empower the Antichrist, and the Antichrist will empower the False Prophet to do the following: "He performs great signs . . . in the sight of men. And he deceives those who dwell on the earth by those signs which he was granted to do in the sight of the beast" (Revelation 13:13–14).

Five times in Revelation 13:2–8 we are told the devil gives power to the Antichrist; and three times in Revelation 13:12–15 we learn that the Antichrist gives power to the False Prophet. All the power of the two future leaders originates with Satan. Jesus foretold a day when false prophets would arise and demonstrate great power (Matthew 24:24–25). And *the* False Prophet is the one in whom Jesus' predictions culminate and are fully expressed.

Just as Satan's goal has been to counterfeit the words and works of the true God (Genesis 3:4–5; 2 Corinthians 11:13–15), so will his chief emissaries on earth seek to counterfeit God on the world stage. The False Prophet will display his counterfeit power in three ways.

Calling Down Fire from Heaven

"He performs great signs, so that he even makes fire come down from heaven on the earth in the sight of men" (Revelation 13:13). This counterfeits the work of God, who often displayed His own power with fire from heaven: Fire rained down on Sodom and Gomorrah (Genesis 19:24), fire consumed Nadab and Abihu (Leviticus 10:1–2), and fire will one day destroy Satan's army on earth (Revelation 20:9).

It is also possible that the False Prophet will try to falsely fulfill the prophecy of Malachi 4:5 concerning the coming of Elijah before the day of the Lord. And it was Elijah who called down fire from heaven to consume the prophets of Baal on Mount Carmel (1 Kings 18:38). The False Prophet will try to convince people he is the fulfillment of the Elijah prophecy spoken through Malachi. Scholar Craig S. Keener reminds us that in Scripture prophets are known "by their message and their fruit, not by their gifts [of power] (Deuteronomy 13:1–5; Matthew 7:15–23)."[5]

Commanding That an Image Be Built

The second display of the False Prophet will come by his building "an image to the beast who was wounded by the sword and lived" (Revelation 13:14). This will be a giant statue in honor of the Antichrist—the focal point of false worship on the earth during the seven-year Tribulation (Revelation 13:14, 15; 14:9, 11; 15:2; 16:2; 19:20; 20:4).

This image is likely the object of Jesus' words concerning an "abomination of desolation" in the last days (Matthew 24:15–16, 21). Paul wrote about "the man of sin" exalting himself above God "so that he sits as God in the temple of God, showing himself that he is God" (2 Thessalonians 2:3–4). The image is the public manifestation of the self-exaltation of the Antichrist under the leadership of the False Prophet. The world will be commanded to worship the image much as Nebuchadnezzar commanded in Babylon (Daniel 3).

Causing the Image to Breathe and Speak

One of the most earth-shaking events that will happen is when the False Prophet animates the image set up in honor of the Antichrist. He will "give breath to the image . . . that the image of the beast should . . . speak" (Revelation 13:15). I do not believe this will be done through ventriloquism or animatronics as used at modern theme parks to make "animals" speak. I believe Dr. Henry Morris's explanation is more likely correct:

> The false prophet is enabled (by his own master, Satan) to impart a spirit to the image, but that spirit is one of Satan's unclean spirits, probably a highly placed demon in the satanic hierarchy. This is a striking case of demon possession, with the demon possessing the body of the image rather than that of a man or woman.[6]

Through Satan, the False Prophet will cause an inanimate object to appear to come to life. This is a radical example of the dark spiritual power that will be active during the Tribulation. The image will command the entire world to worship it—that is, to worship the Antichrist—upon pain of death for refusal.

His Program

The False Prophet will tell the world that a mark of obedience to the Antichrist will be necessary to buy or sell in the marketplace: "He causes all, both great and small, rich and poor, free and slave, to receive a mark on their right hand or on their foreheads, and that no one may buy or sell except one who has the mark or the name of the beast, or the number of his name" (Revelation 13:16–17).

In Revelation 7:3, God's 144,000 Jewish witnesses are sealed on their foreheads as belonging to God, so the Antichrist demands that everyone else in the world display a seal of allegiance to him—on their forehead or their right hand. The mark of the Antichrist will be needed to buy the necessities of life. Often in the Roman Empire a seal of the emperor would be used to stamp official documents and grant the right to conduct commerce.

The cooperation between government and religion will leave no place of refuge for any who rebel. Frederick Tatford says:

> What is portrayed is a tremendous union in which capital and labor are both subject to the control and direction of one man. Anyone who is outside that vast combination will be ruthlessly boycotted; no one will work for him or employ him; no one will purchase his produce or sell goods to him. Bankruptcy and starvation face such a man.[7]

Many are alive in America today who remember the rationing that was in place during World War II. Ration tickets were necessary to buy basic commodities because the War effort greatly reduced the availability of goods. It will be similar in the Tribulation; but instead of being able to buy only a little, people will be able to buy nothing without the mark of the Antichrist showing on forehead or hand.

There is a clue to what the mark will be in Revelation 13:18: "Here is wisdom. Let him who has understanding calculate the number of the beast, for it is the number of a man: His number is 666." In spite of many fanciful suggestions through the ages, no one knows what "666" stands for in terms of the mark of the Antichrist.

The number 6 is associated with man throughout Scripture, and the number 7 is associated with God. In Revelation, the number 7 occurs more than fifty times. Six is the number of man, as Revelation 13:18 says, while 7 is the number of God. Six is the number of incompleteness, while 7 is the number of completeness. Perhaps 666 is a symbol of the incompleteness of man's efforts to bring about righteousness and perfection on earth, which is what the Antichrist will try to do. Man always falls short of the glory of God (Romans 3:23).

Donald Grey Barnhouse illustrated why the mark of the Antichrist should create a desire for God, not for man, in us:

> The children of the great composer, Bach, found that the easiest method of awakening their father was to play a few lines of music and leave off the last note. The musician would arise immediately and go to the piano to strike the final chord.
>
> I awoke early one morning in our home and played the well-known carol "Silent Night." I purposely stopped before playing the last note. I walked out into the hallway and listened to the sounds that came from upstairs. My eight-year-old son had stopped reading and was trying to sound the final note on his harmonica. Another child was singing the last note. An adult called down, "Did you do that purposely? What is the matter?" Our very nature demands the completion of the octave.[8]

As a human man, the Antichrist will never satisfy the world's need for the perfection and completion only God can provide.

His Punishment

We have to skip ahead to the end of Revelation to discover the fate of the False Prophet: "The beast was captured, and with him the false prophet who worked signs in his presence, by which he deceived those who received the mark of the Beast and those who worshiped his image. These two were cast alive into the lake of fire burning with brimstone" (Revelation 19:20).

Being cast alive into the lake of fire is quite a contrast to the role of power and dominion the False Prophet and Antichrist enjoyed during the Tribulation. As Judge of all the earth, the Lord Jesus Christ consigns them to their fate when He returns to earth at the end of the Tribulation period. The devil, after being bound for a thousand years during the Millennium, will then join them in the lake of fire (Revelation 20:10).

It is not just the False Prophet who is judged—all those who took the mark of the Antichrist upon their bodies will suffer a similar judgment (Revelation 14:9–11; 16:1–2). Revelation makes clear that those who refuse the mark will be honored with eternal life (Revelation 20:4). Jesus' words in Matthew 10:28 will prove to be true: "And do not fear those who kill the body but cannot kill the soul. But rather fear Him who is able to destroy both soul and body in hell."

APPLICATION

Personal Questions

1. In Revelation 16:13, why is it fair to refer to the three figures mentioned as an "unholy trinity"?

   a. Moving from left to right, draw lines connecting the members of the unholy trinity to their biblical identities and to their parallel figures in the Holy Trinity:

Biblical Names of the:

Unholy Trinity		Holy Trinity
the dragon	the False Prophet	God the Father
the beast	Satan	God the Holy Spirit
the false prophet	the Antichrist	God the Son

b. What does Leviticus 11:10, 41 say about the clean or unclean nature of frogs?

c. What is the point of unclean creatures coming out of the mouth in Revelation 16:13? (What is the mouth's primary function?) What will the world hear from these three creatures when they speak?

d. In John's vision of Christ returning, what is coming out of Christ's mouth (Revelation 19:15)? What is meant by a sword coming from the mouth of Christ instead of the sword being in His hand?

e. How does the Word of God "judge" us if we are sensitive to it (Hebrews 4:12)?

2. What outward demeanor is suggested by the vision of the False Prophet as a lamb (Revelation 13:11)?

a. Why is this "gentle" image appropriate for one who will pose as a spiritual leader?

b. What is the ultimate goal of a false prophet (Matthew 24:11)?

Group Questions

1. Why is the False Prophet pictured as a lamb if he is actually a deceiver (Matthew 7:15)?

a. What will the False Prophet use to deceive people into believing he is from God (Matthew 24:24)?

b. What does that say about "power" as a sign of spiritual authenticity? Why is character more important than power? (What determines how power will be used?)

c. How does John say Christians should respond to demonstrations of power (1 John 4:1)?

d. What kind of tests would reveal the nature of someone demonstrating spiritual power or authority (see, for example, 1 John 4:2–3)?

e. Why is a spiritual leader's opinion of Christ always the definitive test?

2. What should you do when encountering a seemingly powerful spiritual leader about whom you have doubts?

DID YOU KNOW?

Throughout history people have sought to connect the number 666 by *gematria*—assigning numerical value to letters, words, or phrases. Using this and related methods, the number 666 has been linked to historical figures such as the Roman Emperor Nero, Muhammad, Hitler, some American politicians, and various Popes through the ages. Obviously, all those connections have proved to be false. A parallel to 666 on the hand and forehead may be the Jewish custom of binding the Word of God in small packets on the back of the hand and the forehead to honor the Word of God (Deuteronomy 6:8). The mark of the Antichrist on hand and forehead would be in direct contrast—honoring the commands of man rather than of God.

Notes
1. John Phillips, *Exploring Revelation: An Expository Commentary* (Grand Rapids, MI: Kregel Publications, 1987), 171.
2. Donald Grey Barnhouse, *Revelation: An Expository Commentary* (Grand Rapids, MI: Zondervan, 1971), 240.
3. Robert H. Mounce, *The New International Commentary on the New Testament: The Book of Revelation* (Grand Rapids, MI: Wm. B. Eerdmans Publishing Co., 1998), 255.
4. W. A. Criswell, *Expository Sermons on Revelation, Vol. 4* (Grand Rapids, MI: Zondervan, 1965), 115–116.
5. Craig S. Keener, *The NIV Application Commentary: Revelation* (Grand Rapids, MI: Zondervan, 2009), 357.
6. Henry Morris, *The Revelation Record* (Wheaton, IL: Tyndale House Publishers, 1963), 251.
7. Fredrick A. Tatford, *Prophecy's Last Word: An Exposition of the Revelation* (London, UK: Pickering & Ingles Ltd., 1947), 154.
8. Donald Grey Barnhouse, *Revelation: An Expository Commentary* (Grand Rapids, MI: Zondervan Publishing House, 1978), 250.

Martyrs

REVELATION 6:9–11

*In this lesson we discover the fate of those who embrace Christ
during the Tribulation and are martyred for their faith.*

Throughout history there have been many who gave up their lives rather than deny their faith
in God. And there will be many more. During the seven-year Tribulation, there will be many
who are killed because of their allegiance to Christ, for which they will be eternally rewarded.

OUTLINE

I. **The Context of Their Martyrdom**

II. **The Cause of Their Martyrdom**

III. **The Consequence of Their Martyrdom**

IV. **The Cry of Their Martyrdom**

V. **The Comfort of Their Martyrdom**
   A. They Are Given a Refuge
   B. They Are Given a Robe
   C. They Are Given a Rest
   D. They Are Given Retribution
   E. They Are Given a Reward

VI. **The Courage of Martyrdom**

OVERVIEW

The third-century Church father Tertullian wrote, "The blood of the martyrs is the seed [of the church]." By that, he meant that the more the Church is persecuted and Christians are killed, the more the Church grows. In spite of all the attempts throughout history to persecute the people of God, more and more are added.

The Pharaoh of Egypt tried to kill all male babies when they were born to keep the Hebrew slaves from multiplying. The wicked Persian official, Haman, devised a plan to exterminate all the Jews in Persia (following the Babylonian captivity). In the second century before Christ, Antiochus Epiphanes, a Seleucid king in the Middle East, persecuted the Jews who had returned from Babylon. Herod tried to kill Christ by murdering Jewish males under two years of age. John the Baptist was beheaded. The apostle James was beheaded. Following Pentecost, Jewish officials put many Jewish Christians to death. Many other Christians were persecuted and killed all over the Roman Empire for their faith. Many post-Reformation Christians in Europe were persecuted for breaking from the Catholic Church. Untold numbers of Christians have died in the modern era in China and Russia.

So intense was Hitler's persecution of the Jews in Europe that the Jewish population of the world was reduced to probably less than the number of Jews who left Egypt under Moses. In Germany, in 1938, almost 600 synagogues were destroyed within a few days. The windows of every Jewish establishment had been shattered. In the Buchenwald concentration camp, the death rate was thirty percent of the inmates. Similar conditions prevailed in concentration camps in Sachsenhausen and Dachau. The Auschwitz camp was equipped to execute 10,000 Jews per day. In Treblinka, another of Hitler's torture camps, 25,000 per day could be destroyed. The infamous Adolf Eichmann expressed Nazi hatred for the Jews: "I shall leap into my grave, for the thought that I have five million lives on my conscience is to me a source of inordinate satisfaction."[1]

The prediction of Moses concerning the Jews has literally been fulfilled throughout Jewish history:

> Then the LORD will scatter you among all peoples, from one end of the earth to the other, and there you shall serve other gods, which neither you nor your fathers have known—wood and stone. And among those nations you shall find no rest, nor shall the sole of your foot have a resting place; but there the LORD will give you a trembling heart, failing eyes, and anguish of soul. Your life shall hang in doubt before you; you shall fear day and night, and have no assurance of life. In the morning you shall say,

"Oh, that it were evening!" And at evening you shall say, "Oh, that it were morning!" because of the fear which terrifies your heart, and because of the sight which your eyes see (Deuteronomy 28:64–67).

In spite of all that, the number of Jews and Christians continues to increase. But the apostle John tells us that suffering and martyrdom has not ended; there will be more martyrs in the future during the Tribulation. From what John saw in his revelation from Jesus Christ, we can know who they are, how they will suffer, and how they will be preserved and rewarded by God.

The Context of Their Martyrdom

The most important contextual fact is that the Church of Jesus Christ has been removed from earth; after the Rapture, there will be no Christians on planet earth. So the martyrs are non-Christians at the beginning of the Tribulation who hear the Gospel and believe—and are subsequently martyred for their faith.

John sees the martyrs in heaven calling out for judgment on those who had killed them on earth, so their persecutors were still alive (Revelation 6:10). These saints were martyred in the early part of the Tribulation (included among those seen in Revelation 15:2).

During the Tribulation, God will deal once again with Israel, and many Jews will turn to Him. Paul writes in Romans 11:25–26 that after "the fullness of the Gentiles has come in . . . all Israel will be saved." Paul anticipates the fulfillment of the prophecy in Isaiah 59:20, which is echoed in Romans 11:26: "The Deliverer will come out of Zion, and He will turn away ungodliness from Jacob." God will remove the blindness from Israel's eyes (Isaiah 6:9–10; Matthew 13:13–15), and she will recognize Christ as her Messiah and believe. But the price for that faith will be high; the Antichrist will murder many.

People will be saved during the Tribulation through various means: the two witnesses (Revelation 11:3), the 144,000 Jewish evangelists (Revelation 7:4), and by reading copies of the Word of God and other Christian books that they will find all over the world. Dr. Henry M. Morris has written:

Millions upon millions of copies of the Bible and Bible portions have been published in all major languages, and distributed throughout the world through the dedicated ministries of the Gideons, the Wycliffe Bible Translators, and other such Christian organizations. Removal of believers from the world at the rapture will not remove the Scriptures, and multitudes will no doubt be constrained to read the Bible in those days. . . . Thus, multitudes will turn to their Creator and Savior in those days, and will be willing to give their testimony for the Word of God and even to give their lives as they seek to persuade the world that the calamities it is suffering are judgments from the Lord.[2]

Many will be called upon during the Tribulation to love God more than their very lives (Revelation 12:11; see also Psalm 44:22). They will be called to emulate the commitment of Shadrach, Meshach, and Abed-Nego—the young Hebrew men in Babylon who refused to bow down to the king's idol: "Let it be known to you, O king, that we do not serve your gods, nor will we worship the gold image which you have set up" (Daniel 3:17–18). And the commitment of New Testament martyrs as well: John the Baptist (Mark 6:14–29), Stephen (Acts 7), those killed by Saul of Tarsus (Acts 8:3; 9:1), James (Acts 12:1–2), and Antipas (Revelation 2:13).

Jesus warned His followers of the possibility of death (Matthew 24:9; Luke 21:12–19). The prophet Zechariah wrote that a day was coming when two-thirds of the population of Israel would be "cut off." The remaining third would be brought through the fire and refined (Zechariah 13:8–9). And Jesus described this coming bloodshed in His sermon on the Mount of Olives: "Then they will deliver you up to tribulation and kill you, and you will be hated by all nations for My name's sake" (Matthew 24:8–10).

Scholar Richard Bauckham has clarified: The book of Revelation doesn't say every living Christian on earth will be killed in the Tribulation. "But [Revelation] does require that every faithful Christian must be prepared to die."[3]

The Cause of Their Martyrdom

The martyrs are killed "for the word of God and for the testimony which they held" (Revelation 6:9)—the same reasons John himself was exiled to Patmos (Revelation 1:9). Their "testimony" is likely the message of coming judgment that they preach, warning others to repent and be saved. In spreading such a message, these Tribulation saints will join other biblical heroes who preached the same message: Samuel, Isaiah, Jeremiah, Jonah, and the rest of the prophets.

The word "slain" (Revelation 6:9), used to describe the killing of the martyrs, is always used by the apostle John to refer to the killing of Christ or His followers (one exception: Revelation 13:3). It could easily be translated "slaughtered," "butchered," or "murdered," as when it was used in the context of sacrificial animals. John means to emphasize the brutal nature of these martyrs' deaths.

The Consequence of Their Martyrdom

The fact that John saw the souls of the martyrs "under the altar" (Revelation 6:9) is a reference to their blood being spilled as a sacrifice for the cause of Christ. This calls to mind the practice of the priests in the Old Testament who would pour some sacrificial blood *on* the altar and pour the remainder *under* (at the base of) the altar: "You shall take some of the blood of the bull and put it on the horns of the altar with your finger, and pour all the blood beside the base of the altar" (Exodus 29:12). Being under the altar of God pictures the martyrs as having sacrificed their blood (their life) for Christ.

The Cry of Their Martyrdom

The martyrs cry out, "How long, O Lord, holy and true, until You judge and avenge our blood on those who dwell on the earth?" (Revelation 6:10). This is another piece of evidence that these martyrs are not from the Church Age, where calling for vengeance on one's enemies would be improper (Romans 12:17-19). Instead, the correct response toward one's murderers would be that of Stephen: "Lord, do not charge them with this sin" (Acts 7:60; see also Romans 12:20–21).

The martyrs of the Tribulation period are not living in the age of grace; they were living in a period of judgment by God upon His enemies on earth. An imprecatory prayer will be highly appropriate in that day. Louis T. Talbot has said this about the martyrs' cry for vengeance:

> A man prays according to the attitude God is taking toward the world in the dispensation in which he lives. This present age is the age of grace. God is showing grace and mercy to the worst of men, and we are told to pray for them that despitefully use us. But in the tribulation period God will be meting out judgment upon the earth.[4]

The Comfort of Their Martyrdom

"Then a white robe was given to each of them; and it was said to them that they should rest a little while longer, until both the number of their fellow servants and their brethren, who would be killed as they were, was completed" (Revelation 6:11). It is amazing to think about "resting" while waiting for other martyrs on earth to be "killed as they were." But that is the rest that accompanies being secure in the will of a sovereign God.

They Are Given a Refuge

"Under the altar" (Revelation 6:9) serves as an image of safety and protection. It conveys the idea that the redeemed, regardless of what their earthly experience has been, are safe in the presence of God.

Dr. Donald Grey Barnhouse reminds us:

> We are not to think that John had a vision of an altar with souls peeping out from underneath. The whole teaching of the Old Testament is that the altar was the place of the sacrifice of blood. To be "under the altar" is to be covered in the sight of God by that merit which Jesus Christ provided in dying on the cross. It is a figure that speaks of justification. . . . These martyred witnesses are covered by the work of the Lord Jesus Christ.[5]

They Are Given a Robe

Each of the Jewish martyrs "under the altar" was given a white robe to wear (Revelation 6:11). Generally speaking, the white robe is a sign of righteousness (Revelation 19:8). But the very notion of a robe, being a garment, raises this question: *What kind of a body do the martyrs have in heaven?* They will not receive their own resurrection bodies until the end of the Tribulation. So what is their form until then?

Dr. John Walvoord addresses this question:

> The martyred dead here pictured have not been raised from the dead and have not received their resurrection bodies. Yet it is declared that they are given robes. This would almost demand that they have a body of some kind. A robe could not hang upon an immaterial soul or spirit. It is not the kind of body that Christians now have, that is the body of the earth, nor is it the resurrection body of flesh and bones of which Christ spoke after His own resurrection. It is a temporary body suited for their presence in heaven but replaced in turn by their everlasting resurrection body given at the time of Christ's return.[6]

They Are Given a Rest

When the martyrs ask how long it will be until they are avenged for their death, they are told to rest for a little while "until both the number of their fellow servants and their brethren, who would be killed as they were, was completed" (Revelation 6:11). That is, God's judgment would be forestalled "a little while longer" before it could be fully realized.

There are two primary times of Jewish martyrdom during the Tribulation—here, under the fifth seal judgment (Revelation 6:9), and a second period yet to come. Until the second period of persecution and martyrdom is complete, God will withhold His judgment. In the interim, the martyrs are told to rest: "Write: 'Blessed are the dead who die in the Lord from now on.' 'Yes,' says the Spirit, 'that they may rest from their labors, and their works follow them'" (Revelation 14:13).

They Are Given Retribution

Finally, retribution is realized:

> Then another angel came out of the temple which is in heaven, he also having a sharp sickle. And another angel came out from the altar, who had power over fire, and he cried with a loud cry to him who had the sharp sickle, saying, "Thrust in your sharp sickle and gather the clusters of the vine of the earth, for her grapes are fully ripe." So the angel thrust his sickle into the earth and gathered the vine of the earth, and threw it into the great winepress of the wrath of God. And the winepress was trampled outside the city, and blood came out of the winepress, up to the horses' bridles, for one thousand six hundred furlongs (Revelation 14:17–20).

The martyrs cried out to be avenged from the altar in heaven. From that same altar the angel of judgment is sent to avenge them in judgment.

They Are Given a Reward

For being faithful through a brief time of persecution and pain on earth, the martyrs are rewarded with a thousand years of reigning with Christ on earth:

> And I saw thrones, and they sat on them, and judgment was committed to them. Then I saw the souls of those who had been beheaded for their witness to Jesus and for the word of God, who had not worshiped the beast or his image, and had not received his mark on their foreheads or on their hands. And they lived and reigned with Christ for a thousand years (Revelation 20:4).

The martyred saints will be honored in heaven forever; but even before that, they will be honored on earth as they live and reign with Christ during His Millennial reign.

All who pay the ultimate price for faithfulness to Christ throughout history will gain the everlasting reward of righteousness and fellowship with Him forever.

The Courage of Martyrdom

When we think of Christian martyrdom, we tend to think of the many stories of ancient witnesses who sacrificed their lives for their beliefs. But martyrdom isn't just in ancient history; Christians around the world today are still suffering martyrdom as well.

In the summer of 2005, two young Bangladeshi men showed the *Jesus* film to guests in their home. They were threatened with death if they did not cease the showings. When they did not comply, they were attacked in the dead of night and killed. Stories like this are not rare. Around the world today, Christians are experiencing persecution and death for their faith.

As we can see from history and current events today, persecution and martyrdom are the norm for the Christian. These martyrs—past, present, and future—provide ample examples of courage that should inspire us to a deeper commitment to Christ and a determination to stand strong for Him, no matter the cost.

APPLICATION

Personal Questions

1. God told Israel they would endure times of persecution and trouble (Deuteronomy 28:64–67). But what would be the cause of that trouble (Deuteronomy 28:58)?

   a. So at least one reason for persecution can be _____.

   b. How would you explain the persecution and martyrdom of those mentioned in Hebrews 11:35–38?

   c. So another reason for persecution can be _____.

   d. Into which of those two categories do the Tribulation martyrs fall?

e. Compare Hebrews 11:39–40 with Revelation 2:17. What is the end result for those who suffer for their faith?

2. What is the primary reason a Christian would be martyred (Revelation 6:9)?

Group Questions

Read Luke 14:25–35 and discuss the following questions:

a. What serious condition does Jesus establish for any who want to follow Him (Luke 14:27)?

b. Compare verse 27 with verse 33. In addition to material things, what else is included in the "all" in verse 33 (in light of "cross" in verse 27)?

c. What is Jesus' point in verses 28–33? Why should martyrdom be considered a possible cost for following Christ?

d. What do Jesus' final words (last words of verse 35) suggest about taking up one's cross and counting the cost? Why might some Christians not "hear" this message (see, for example, John 6:66)?

e. Why is risking martyrdom for Christ's sake still a good idea (John 6:67–68)?

f. How long were you a Christian before you realized the implications of taking up your "cross"? How many new Christians are encouraged to "count the cost" of following Jesus?

g. How do you think you would respond to the threat of martyrdom for your faith?

h. How does John 15:13 fit into the martyrdom equation? Is Jesus our "friend" (see verse 14)? What would be the greatest act of love for Jesus we could show?

DID YOU KNOW?

Technically, an imprecation is a spoken curse. An imprecation can be issued in the form of a request when one prays that God would curse, or judge, His enemies (the enemies of His people). Revelation 6:10 contains an imprecatory prayer offered by the Tribulation martyrs: "How long . . . until You judge . . . those who dwell on the earth?" Imprecatory prayers were common in the Old Testament, specifically in the Psalms (35; 40; 69; 79; 83; 109; 139; 143). Imprecatory prayers were not personal; the prayer was not offered out of frustration or a desire for personal revenge or vengeance. They were based on a desire for God's honor to be defended and restored; for His name to be vindicated. Vengeance and justice are always God's to pursue, not ours, as the New Testament teaches (Romans 12:17–21).

Notes
1. Jacob Presser, *The Destruction of the Dutch Jews* (New York: Dutton, 1969), 336.
2. Henry M. Morris, *The Revelation Record* (Wheaton, IL: Tyndale House Publishers, Inc., 1983), 119.
3. Richard Bauckham, *Climax of Prophecy—Studies in the Book of Revelation* (Edinburgh: T. & Agents of the Apocalypse Study Guide, Lesson 2, "The Martyrs," T. Clark, 1993), 424–425.
4. Louis T. Talbot, *The Revelation of Jesus Christ* (Grand Rapids, MI: Wm. B. Eerdman's, 1937), 99.
5. Donald Grey Barnhouse, *Revelation: An Expository Commentary* (Grand Rapids, MI: Zondervan, 1971), 134.
6. John F. Walvoord, *The Revelation of Jesus Christ* (Chicago, IL: Moody Press, 1966), 134–135.

144,000

REVELATION 7:1–8; 14:1–5

In this lesson we discover the traits of the coming 144,000 Jewish evangelists who will preach to the world during the Tribulation.

The world has never seen a massive league of Christians—especially Jewish Christians—wholly set apart to God, in purity and practice, to represent Him as preachers of the Gospel. But during the coming Tribulation, it will. Millions will turn to Christ as 144,000 Jews evangelize the world.

OUTLINE

I. They Are Selected from the Twelve Tribes of Israel

II. They Are Sealed on Their Foreheads

III. They Are Servants of the Living God

IV. They Are Separated unto God

V. They Are Strong in Their Faith

VI. They Are Spared from Coming Judgment

VII. They Are Secure in the Midst of the Tribulation

  VIII. **They Are Successful in Their Ministry**

   IX. **They Are Set Apart for the Kingdom**

    X. **They Are Singing a New Song in Heaven**

OVERVIEW

While the Antichrist is consolidating his power and exalting himself in the Holy of Holies in Jerusalem, crushing those who refuse to bow before his statue, the greatest spiritual awakening of all time will take place through the ministry of 144,000 set-apart Jewish evangelists. Their story is another dramatic demonstration of God taking care of His people during an hour of trial and tribulation—a reminder that "God has not cast away His people whom He foreknew" (Romans 11:2).

In Revelation 7:1–8 and 14:1–5, we learn ten important truths about this special group of Jewish witnesses for Jesus who will preach to the world during the Tribulation.

They Are Selected from the Twelve Tribes of Israel

In Revelation 7:4 we learn their number and legacy: "One hundred and forty-four thousand of all the tribes of the children of Israel were sealed." In spite of this clear statement, some scholars see the 144,000 as representing the Church. But that is impossible since the Church is now in heaven, having been removed from earth at the Rapture just before the beginning of the Tribulation (between the events of Revelation 3 and 4).

The great Bible commentator J. A. Seiss has written:

> Nor is there a vice or device of sacred hermeneutics, which so beclouds the Scriptures, and so unsettles the faith of men, as this constant attempt to read Church for Israel, and Christian peoples for Jewish tribes. As I read the Bible, when God says "children of Israel," I do not understand Him to mean any but people of Jewish blood, be they Christians or not; and when He speaks of the twelve tribes of the sons of Jacob, and gives the names of the tribes, it is impossible for me to believe that He means the Gentiles, in any sense or degree, whether they be believers or not.[1]

Their identity is confirmed by a list of the twelve tribes of Israel, noting that 12,000 are taken from each tribe (Revelation 7:5–8; 12 x 12,000 = 144,000).

The number twelve in Scripture has always been associated with Israel: twelve sons of Jacob, twelve tribes, twelve stones on the High Priest's breastplate, twelve loaves on the table of showbread, twelve gates in the heavenly city of God, and twelve future thrones on which the twelve apostles will sit to judge the twelve tribes of Israel (Matthew 19:28).

They Are Sealed on Their Foreheads

God commanded an angel to seal the 144,000 (protect them from harm) before releasing judgments on the earth (Revelation 7:2–3). The seal is the "Father's name written on their foreheads" (Revelation 14:1). We are told nothing more about the seal except that its purpose will be to protect God's witnesses until their mission is complete.

God protected Noah and his family from the Flood and offered protection for Lot and his family from the judgment on Sodom. Rahab was protected from the destruction of Jericho. God sealed 7,000 prophets in Elijah's day who did not submit to Baal. And God protected the Israelite families in Egypt who put the blood of the Passover lamb on their doorpost.

The Antichrist will also use a seal during the Tribulation—the number 666 on the forehead or hand to signify allegiance to him. Without that seal, it will be impossible for people to buy or sell or do business. Those who refuse the seal will be persecuted and eventually killed.

They Are Servants of the Living God

God's original instruction to the angel about the 144,000 refers to them as "the servants of our God" (Revelation 7:3). They will be sealed and protected because they have been given a mission by God.

The combination of being sealed and receiving a mission from God is also found in Jesus Christ (John 6:27). He was referring to the seal of the Holy Spirit who descended upon Him (Matthew 3:16) and empowered Him to do His work. Paul wrote also about the Holy Spirit as a seal in the life of the Christian (2 Corinthians 1:22; Ephesians 1:13; 4:30). When the Holy Spirit was poured out upon the Church at Pentecost in Jerusalem, Peter connected the event to the prophecies of Joel concerning the Holy Spirit (Joel 2:28–32; Acts 2:14–21).

Wherever there is work for God to be done, the Holy Spirit will be there to provide power and guidance.

They Are Separated unto God

A further characteristic of the 144,000 has caused confusion among Bible students: "These are the ones who were not defiled with women, for they are virgins" (Revelation 14:4). Some have wrongly suggested that this is a reference to *spiritual* purity rather than physical purity (2 Corinthians 11:2; James 4:4). While that is a possibility, it is better to take the text literally and assume that these are celibate males who, due to the pressures of the Tribulation period, will not have married. Paul suggests the reasonableness of forgoing marriage for ministry in 1 Corinthians 7:29, 32–33, 35). The Tribulation will be a time when single-minded focus on serving God will be required.

They Are Strong in Their Faith

The 144,000 will be men of faith: "These are the ones who follow the Lamb . . . for they are without fault before the throne of God" (Revelation 14:4–5). Because of their unique character and strong faith, millions will respond to their preaching during the Tribulation. The world will have never seen this kind of spiritual witness and impact. Such mobilized godliness will produce a strong result.

They Are Spared From Coming Judgment

When the angels of God prepare the judgments to come upon the earth during the Tribulation, they will be delayed until the 144,000 are sealed, guaranteeing their immunity from the judgments (Revelation 7:1–3). This sealing of the 144,000 answers the question posed in the last verse of Revelation 6: "For the great day of His wrath has come, and who is able to stand?" (Revelation 6:17). God's sealed witnesses will be able to stand!

They Are Secure in the Midst of the Tribulation

Everyone who does not "have the seal of God on their foreheads" will suffer the judgments of the Tribulation (Revelation 9:4). The 144,000, having God's seal, will be secure in the midst of the judgments of God. When the 144,000 are seen in Revelation 14:1–5, it is not 143,999. Not one has been lost.[2]

They Are Successful in Their Ministry

When John sees a vision of those "who come out of the great tribulation," he sees they are from "all nations, tribes, peoples, and tongues, standing before the throne and before the Lamb"

(Revelation 7:9, 14). John Walvoord has written about those who respond to the Gospel during the Tribulation:

> The majority of the saints in the tribulation will die as martyrs. Many will be killed by earthquakes, war, and pestilence. Others will be the objects of special persecution by the world ruler. They will be hounded to death much as the Jews were in World War II. Because they will not worship the beast, they will be under a death sentence (Revelation 13:15). Those who accept Christ in that time may be faced with the solemn alternative of either renouncing their faith in Christ or worshiping the beast or being slain. The result will be multiplied thousands of martyrs.[3]

There will be a great revival *during* the Tribulation, but not before. Before the Rapture, there will be a great "falling away" from the faith (2 Thessalonians 2:3). During the Tribulation, the revival will be led by the 144,000 Jewish evangelists with help from the two witnesses of Revelation 11. Because of the great travail that will come upon the earth, many will turn to Christ. Though many will be saved spiritually, not all will be saved physically. The universality of those saved is referenced several times in the book of Revelation: 5:9; 11:9; 13:7; 14:6; 17:5. As Jesus Himself said, "And this gospel of the kingdom will be preached in all the world as a witness to all the nations, and then the end will come" (Matthew 24:14).

They Are Set Apart for the Kingdom

These 144,000 will be kept alive through the Tribulation in order to enter the Millennium with Christ and reign with Him. Remember: At the end of the Tribulation, Christ will return to earth to judge the Antichrist and False Prophet and establish His thousand-year reign of righteousness over earth. According to Ezekiel 48, each of the twelve tribes will have their own geographical boundaries assigned in the Millennium. And the 144,000 will help to populate those tribal regions in Israel under Christ's authority. There will be peace, finally, in Israel (Zephaniah 3:13).

They Are Singing a New Song in Heaven

John also saw a vision of the 144,000 worshiping God before the throne, singing a song that only they could sing (Revelation 14:2).

Singing after a great victory is what Moses and the Hebrew slaves did following the defeat of the Egyptian army at the Red Sea:

> I will sing to the LORD,
> For He has triumphed gloriously!
> The horse and its rider
> He has thrown into the sea! (Exodus 15:1).

We also find the song of Deborah in Judges 5 and King David's song of victory in 2 Samuel 22 (and Psalm 18). These songs are always in praise of God's victory over His enemies. New Testament scholar N.T. Wright has said, "You could summarize the whole of Christian discipleship [as a] summons . . . to sing!"

Earlier, John had seen a great choir made up of "ten thousand times ten thousand, and thousands of thousands" (Revelation 5:11) praising God. But now he sees a relatively smaller choir made up of the 144,000 singing a song that no one else can learn. They alone could learn the song because they were the only ones who had walked through the fiery judgments. They had experienced the carnage and destruction during the Tribulation, the shedding of the blood of many martyrs who had come to faith through their own preaching. Because of what they had seen and experienced, they had a song of praise that no one else knew. But John has given us the lyrics: "Salvation belongs to our God who sits on the throne, and to the Lamb!" (Revelation 7:10).

One of my fondest memories as a student at Dallas Theological Seminary is of my first day attending chapel. The seminary chaplain asked the students (all men at that time) to stand and sing. And the powerful sound of 500 men singing praises to God brought tears to my eyes. If 500 voices uniting in praise to God is enough to create an emotional response, what would the sound of 144,000, or "ten thousand times ten thousand," sound like?

As for instruments, the 144,000 are accompanied by harps, an instrument mentioned more than forty times in the Old Testament—and always in a context of joy and praise. Harps were never used in a setting of mourning or sadness. Psalm 137 says that the captives in Babylon hung up their harps while they mourned their captivity (see Isaiah 24:8). Psalm 144:9–10 talks about singing a "new song . . . on a harp of ten strings."

The closest thing I know to imagining the sounds of voices from every nation on the earth is the work of Eric Whitacre, a Grammy Award-winning composer. He found fame first with what he called the Virtual Choir. He wrote a song, and then asked people from all over the world to sing the various parts and upload their audio-video files to YouTube. Hundreds and hundreds of people from around the world participated. He selected the best videos and merged them together into a giant Virtual Choir—images of individuals singing alone in their homes, yet now blended together into a beautiful four-part "choir."

The Virtual Choir 1.0 featured 185 singers from twelve different countries; 2.0 involved 2,000 voices from fifty-eight countries; 3.0 combined 3,746 submissions from seventy-three countries and was released in April 2012. Whitacre has received international recognition for this project—deservedly so. As fantastic as the Virtual Choirs have been, the apostle John saw choirs in heaven that will dwarf them in size and complexity—tens of thousands of voices from different ethnicities and languages uniting in praise to God.

Singing in worship has always had a profound impact. Historian Mark Noll cites the words of Jonathan Edwards in the early eighteenth century in America:

> One of the most notable, but least studied, aspects of the 18th century revivals that led to the rise of modern evangelicalism was the disputed place of hymn singing. In his very first report on the unusual religious stirrings in Northampton, Massachusetts from 1736, Jonathan Edwards noted that . . . the revival had worked an extraordinary musical effect: "Our public praises were greatly enlivened, and God was served in our psalmnody as in the beauties of holiness. There was scarce any part of divine worship wherein God's saints among us had grace so drawn forth and their hearts lifted up, as in singing the praises of God."[4]

One commentator summarizes the truth of the verses we have studied in this lesson with these words of encouragement:

> So what threatens you? The loss of a job? Betrayal of a spouse? Children in danger? The economic downturn? Socialized medicine? Murderous unbelievers? The temptations of the world? The main point of the book of Revelation is for Christians to see God in his glory, and that glory is on display as God shows justice and mercy. The awesome glory of God in mercy is what we see in chapter 7. He seals the saints, and the saints praise him. Do you know what this means for you? It means you are invincible. It means your faith is unassailable—not because of the strength of your faith—salvation belongs to God! Your faith is unassailable because God has sealed his people.[5]

In other words, we have every reason to praise the God who has saved us and will save us to the uttermost. And worship with songs of praise is the time-honored way people have expressed their love for who God is and what He has done.

Professor Jeremy Begbie tells about attending a church service in a poor South African township after a string of disasters had struck the congregation:

> The pastor began his opening prayer: "Lord, you are the Creator and the Sovereign, but why did the wind come like a snake and tear our roofs off? Why did a mob cut short the

life of one of our own children, when he had everything to live for? Over and over again, Lord, we are in the midst of death."

As he spoke, the congregation responded with a dreadful sighing and groaning. And then, once he finished his prayer, very slowly, the whole congregation began to sing, at first very quietly, then louder. They sang and they sang, song after song of praise—praise to a God who in Jesus had plunged into the very worst to give us a promise of an ending beyond all imagining. The singing gave the congregation a foretaste of the end.[6]

APPLICATION

Personal Questions

Read Revelation 14:1–5.

a. Who is with the Lamb in verse 1? What is written on their foreheads, and what is the significance of what is written there?

b. In verse 2 there are the sounds of "harpists" playing. What type of event do they convey?

c. Explain the meaning of the "new song" in verse 3. Why was this song unique?

d. Describe the characteristics of the 144,000 in verse 4.

e. List the ten truths about these Jewish witnesses for Christ that were found in this lesson.

f. What differences can you suggest between the 144,000, their righteousness, and their mission to preach the Gospel—and the Church at large as suggested by Matthew 28:19–20?

Group Questions

Read Revelation 14:4–5 and discuss the following questions:

a. How is the phrase "follow the Lamb" (Revelation 14:4) similar to the call given by Jesus in Luke 14:27?

b. What differences will there be between following Christ today and following Christ during the Tribulation?

c. What does the phrase "wherever He goes" suggest about the necessity for faith (verse 4; see also 2 Corinthians 5:7)? How might the "cross" become a very important issue for a follower of Christ during the Tribulation?

d. Why are the 144,000 called the "firstfruits to God and to the Lamb" (Revelation 14:4)? How does this relate to the Rapture having already occurred?

e. What does "firstfruits" suggest about the likelihood of more fruit to follow during the Tribulation (see Romans 8:29)?

f. Since the 144,000 will be young adults when called by God near the beginning of the Tribulation, they will be natural-born sinners. How should we then interpret verse 5 concerning their standing before God?

g. How are the 144,000 like all redeemed sinners? How should we be like them?

DID YOU KNOW?

The earliest examples of seals in the ancient world were small, carved designs pressed into soft clay. When the clay hardened, the letters, name, or image in the seal conveyed ownership, authority, blessing, or warning. The most common use of seals was similar to the stamp of a modern notary—to give a document official status. Official clay tablets might be impressed with a king's seal. Centuries later, rolled-up vellum or parchment scrolls might be fastened with wax that bore a king's seal. The seal was to say, "Violation of this document is an act against the king." References to seals occur more than fifty times in Scripture.

Notes
1. J. A. Seiss, *The Apocalypse* (Grand Rapids, MI: Zondervan Publishing House, 1865), 161.
2. Mark Hitchcock, *The End* (Carol Stream, IL: Tyndale House Publishers, Inc., 2012), 291.
3. John Walvoord, *The Revelation of Jesus Christ* (Chicago, IL: Moody Bible Institute, 1966), 146.
4. Mark Noll, "Singing the Lord's Song," Books & Culture, *Christianity Today,* January/February 2004, https://www.booksand-culture.com/articles/2004/janfeb/6.15.html.
5. James M. Hamilton Jr., *Revelation: The Spirit Speaks to the Churches* (Wheaton, IL: Crossway Books, 2008), 196.
6. Quoted in Dallas Willard, ed., *A Place for Truth* (Downers Grove, IL: InterVarsity Press, 2010), www.PreachingToday.com; story told by Jeremy Begbie in his talk titled "The Sense of an Ending."

Two Witnesses

*In this lesson we learn about the two prophets who warn Jerusalem
and the world during the first half of the Tribulation.*

God always sends forerunners to warn of judgments on sin. For the first three-and-one-half years of the Tribulation, two prophets of God will call Israel and the world to repent of ungodliness. Their ministry miracles will be surpassed only by the miracle of their resurrection and ascension.

OUTLINE

I. Their Personalities

II. Their Prophecies

III. Their Power
    A. The Power of Their Preaching
    B. The Power of Their Plagues

IV. Their Persecution
    A. The Death of the Witnesses
    B. The Display of Their Bodies
    C. The Delight of Their Enemies

V. **Their Preservation**
   A. Their Resurrection
   B. Their Rapture
   C. Their Revenge

OVERVIEW

After the Rapture of the Church—the removal of all true believers and the Holy Spirit from earth—there will no longer be any witness for Jesus Christ at a time when the world is filled with non-believers. To provide an initial testimony in Jerusalem—and via technology to the rest of the world—God will provide two witnesses to speak for Him. Just as Satan will have two witnesses during the Tribulation (the Antichrist and False Prophet), so God will send two witnesses of His own. Through their personalities, prophecies, power, persecution, and ultimate preservation, these two men will call the world to repent.

Their Personalities

"And I will give power to my two witnesses, and they will prophesy one thousand two hundred and sixty days, clothed in sackcloth" (Revelation 11:3).

These two witnesses are not metaphorical—they do not stand for "Law and Gospel" or "Old and New Testaments." They are literal men like the prophets of old. They do have a symbolic purpose, however. Revelation 11:4 calls them "the two olive trees and the two lampstands standing before the God of the earth." These are references to the prophet Zechariah who saw a golden candlestick with seven lamps flanked by two olive trees that provided oil for the lamps (Zechariah 4:11–13). Zechariah saw the olive trees as "two anointed ones" (Zechariah 4:14) who lived in his day and were witnesses for the Lord—most likely Joshua, the high priest, and Zerubbabel, the governor who rebuilt the temple. These two were illustrations of the truth in Zechariah 4:6: God does His work "not by might nor by power, but by [the Holy] Spirit."

John saw them as two witnesses empowered by the Holy Spirit (olive oil being a symbol of the Spirit) whose ministry in the Tribulation will be by God's power, not by man's. The witnesses being like lampstands is an image of their testimony of light in the dark days of the coming Tribulation. Their power will be a clear testimony to the power of the Holy Spirit.

The question that has created debate among prophecy students for years is centered on the identity of these two witnesses in Revelation 11. Most students agree that one of the witnesses is the prophet Elijah for the following six reasons:

- It is predicted by Malachi that the prophet Elijah would appear before the Second Coming to prepare the way for the Messiah: "Behold, I will send you Elijah the prophet before the coming of the great and dreadful day of the LORD. And he will turn the hearts of the fathers to the children, and the hearts of the children to their fathers, lest I come and strike the earth with a curse" (Malachi 4:5–6). John the Baptist came in the spirit and power of Elijah (Luke 1:17), but he was not Elijah the prophet as he himself emphatically stated in John 1:21. Therefore, Malachi's prophecy remains unfulfilled at present.

- Elijah did not experience physical death (2 Kings 2:9, 11) and thus could return and experience death as the witnesses do.

- The witnesses have the same sign as was given to Elijah—the absence of rain for an extended period of time (1 Kings 17:1; Revelation 11:6).

- Elijah called down fire from heaven, which is consistent with the two witnesses' miraculous powers (2 Kings 1:10).

- The period of drought in Elijah's day (1 Kings 17:1) was the same duration as the time of the ministry of the witnesses (Luke 4:25; James 5:17–18; Revelation 11:3).

- Elijah was one of the two who appeared at the transfiguration (Matthew 17:3).

While there is general agreement that one of the witnesses will be Elijah, there is a diversity of opinion concerning the identity of the other witness. Some think that the second witness is Enoch (who did not experience physical death—Genesis 5:24); but I believe that the other witness is Moses, for the following reasons:

- Moses appeared with Elijah at the transfiguration when the death of Christ was discussed (Matthew 17:3).

- The miracle of Moses turning the waters into blood is the same sign performed by the witnesses (Exodus 7:19, 20; Revelation 11:6).

- God preserved the body of Moses so that he might be restored (Deuteronomy 34:5–6).

- Satan contended with Michael for the body of Moses, as Jude tells us: "Yet Michael the archangel, in contending with the devil, when he disputed about the body of Moses" (Jude 9), suggesting Satan's desire to hinder God's future plan for Moses.

- Moses and Elijah stand for the Law and Prophets. For a period of time that is distinctly Jewish, as the Great Tribulation will be, it makes sense for representatives of the Law and Prophets to appear to the Jews.

John Whitcomb explains why Elijah and Moses make the most sense as the witnesses of Revelation 11:

> No two men in Israel's entire history would receive greater respect and appreciation than Moses and Elijah. Moses was God's great deliverer and lawgiver for Israel (see Deuteronomy 34:10–12). First-century Jews actually thought that Moses had given them the manna in the wilderness (John 6:32). And God raised up Elijah to confront Israel in a time of great national apostasy. God vindicated him by sending fire from heaven and "a chariot of fire and horses of fire" to escort him out of this world. So highly did the Jews of Jesus' day think of Elijah that when they saw Jesus' miracles, some people concluded that Elijah had returned (Matthew 16:14).[1]

Their Prophecies

"And I will give power to my two witnesses, and they will prophesy one thousand two hundred and sixty days, clothed in sackcloth" (Revelation 11:3).

The two witnesses are given power and authority to prophesy to the inhabitants of planet earth for three-and-one-half years (42 months of 30 days each = 1,260 days). The nature of their prophecies is indicated by their dress: "clothed in sackcloth" (verse 3). In Scripture, such apparel is always a sign of mourning or repentance (2 Samuel 3:31; Psalm 35:13; Matthew 11:21).

The content of their prophecy is judgment—first on the Jews, then on the Gentiles. Every day for three-and-one-half years the two witnesses speak out against ungodliness and the judgment to come. The fact that there are two witnesses qualifies their judgment according to Deuteronomy 17:6—testimony of sin had to be corroborated by "two or three witnesses." God often used "twos" to accomplish His work: Moses and Aaron, Joshua and Caleb, Zerubbabel and Joshua, Peter and John, Paul and Silas, Timothy and Titus, and the disciples whom Jesus sent out in pairs (Luke 10:1).

Their Power

The power of the two witnesses will be demonstrated in two ways: their preaching and the plagues they call down upon the earth.

The Power of Their Preaching

The great commentator William R. Newell has captured the essence of the witnesses' preaching agenda in Jerusalem:

> Day after day the excitement will increase as these witnesses give their testimony. And what will that testimony be?
>
> • They will say that the Lord Jesus Christ, who has been rejected, is the Lord of all the earth. They will say, "As Jehovah the God of Israel, liveth, before whom I stand, there shall not be dew nor rain these years but according to my word."
>
> • They testify unsparingly of human wickedness to men's very faces. You have probably never heard a preacher tell you to your face just how bad you were. . . . These witnesses will tell to the teeth of a horrid godlessness which is ready to worship the Devil, just what they are before God!
>
> • They will testify of the character of the judgments just past as having been directly from God, and they will warn of coming judgments infinitely more terrible.
>
> • They will decry the blasphemous claims the wild Beast will shortly be making (chapter 13), that man is to be deified! They will denounce all the goodness of man as a lie!
>
> • They will testify that Jerusalem, although the holy city in God's purposes, is spiritually Sodom and Egypt, and will announce the coming judgments upon the city and the people. They will tell the Jews that they killed the Lord Jesus (1 Thessalonians 2:15–16) and that He will yet be the King over all the earth.
>
> Now such witnessing as this brings out men's wickedness. People fairly rave to destroy these witnesses![2]

The Power of Their Plagues

Though only three in number, the plagues called down by the two witnesses resemble some of Moses' plagues upon Egypt.

1. The Plague of Death
The witnesses will be protected from harm during the time of their ministry, not least by the fire that "proceeds from their mouth and devours their enemies" (Revelation 11:5). Elijah called down fire from heaven (1 Kings 18:37–38; 2 Kings 1:10, 12), but the witnesses' fire will come straight from their mouths. They will be protected until their work is finished.

2. The Plague of Drought
They will also have power to close the windows of heaven "so that no rain falls in the days of their prophecy" (Revelation 11:6). For three-and-one-half years it will not rain on earth, apparently coinciding with the first half of the seven-year Tribulation. Again, this miracle parallels that of Elijah (James 5:17; see also 1 Kings 17–19).

3. The Plague of Disease
The last of the three specific plagues involves turning the water "to blood, and to strike the earth with all plagues, as often as they desire" (Revelation 11:6). This plague mirrors that of Moses turning the Nile to blood in Egypt and corresponds to the second trumpet judgment of Revelation 8 when "a third of the sea became blood" (verses 8–9).

Their Persecution
The two witnesses are ultimately killed in order that an even greater miracle—their resurrection and ascension into heaven—can occur as a final testimony.

The Death of the Witnesses
The Antichrist will "make war" against the two witnesses and "overcome them, and kill them" (Revelation 11:7). This is the first of thirty-six references to "the beast" (the Antichrist) in Revelation. But he will have been active prior to killing the two witnesses, creating a geo-political alliance among nations during the first half of the Tribulation. Most importantly, he will have created a treaty of protection for Israel that he will break midway through the seven-year period. His breaking of the peace treaty will coincide with the killing of the two witnesses—the first dramatic event he will use to consolidate power and allegiance.

The Display of Their Bodies
The witnesses' lifeless bodies will lie untouched in the streets of Jerusalem as a form of public mockery of their supposed power (Revelation 11:8). The Antichrist has supposedly negated their powers and brought them into submission.

John calls Jerusalem "Sodom and Egypt" (verse 8) as an indication of the spiritual and moral apostasy of God's earthly capital city. The Jews in Jerusalem will not respond to the witnesses' warnings and will rejoice in their death. Sodom was a morally perverted city and Egypt was famous for persecuting the people of God. And now Jerusalem has fulfilled both likenesses. Outwardly, things in Jerusalem will be good—the city will be at peace, the temple will be in place, and the ancient sacrifices restored. But inwardly, there will be only corruption.

Via modern technology (television, Internet video), "peoples, tribes, tongues, and nations will see [the witnesses'] dead bodies" (Revelation 11:9). The world will celebrate their death.

The Delight of Their Enemies

The death of the witnesses will be treated like a holiday around the world: "And those who dwell on the earth will rejoice over them, make merry, and send gifts to one another, because these two prophets tormented those who dwell on the earth" (Revelation 11:10).

William R. Newell suggests this description of that day:

> Now comes the real revelation of the heart of man: glee, horrid, insane, inhuman, hellish, ghoulish glee! There is actual delight at the death of God's witnesses, utter unbounded delight. Newspapers have whole front pages of jubilation. Excursions are run into Jerusalem to see the unburied corpses of these prophets of God . . . peoples, tribes, tongues and nations look upon their bodies three days and a half, and suffer not their corpses to be laid in a tomb. . . . A regular Christmastime-of-Hell ensues.[3]

This is the only mention of any kind of rejoicing or celebrating on earth during the entire Tribulation Period.

Their Preservation

Like Christ, the death of the two witnesses will only be temporary. In a startling display of God's vindication, the two witnesses will be raised from the dead and taken into heaven.

Their Resurrection

"Now after the three-and-a-half days the breath of life from God entered them, and they stood on their feet, and great fear fell on those who saw them" (Revelation 11:11).

There will be no question that the witnesses are brought back to life since they will have lain, unmoving, for three-and-one-half days in the streets of Jerusalem. Not surprisingly, great fear will descend upon the world, and the Antichrist will not be able to explain this miracle.

Their Rapture

"And they heard a loud voice from heaven saying to them, 'Come up here.' And they ascended to heaven in a cloud, and their enemies saw them" (Revelation 11:12).

The same thing that will happen to the Church that marks the beginning of the Tribulation—being caught up into the clouds (1 Thessalonians 4:16–17)—will happen to the two witnesses. There is one difference: The Rapture of the Church will take place "in a moment, in the twinkling of an eye" (1 Corinthians 15:52), whereas the rapture of the two witnesses will be observed by all the world (Revelation 11:12).

Dr. Henry Morris has written:

> The ascent of the prophets into heaven was a dire prediction that even greater judgments were about to descend from heaven. The three-and-a-half-day festivities were about to be followed by another three-and-a-half years of judgments more severe than ever.[4]

Their Revenge

"In the same hour there was a great earthquake, and a tenth of the city fell. In the earthquake seven thousand people were killed, and the rest were afraid and gave glory to the God of heaven" (Revelation 11:13).

Coinciding with the ascension of the two witnesses is the destruction of a tenth of Jerusalem by an earthquake, and the death of 7,000 people.

Better to fear God now than then by obeying His call to repent and believe on the Lord Jesus Christ (Philippians 2:10).

APPLICATION

Personal Questions

Read Revelation 11:1–14.

a. Who does God send to Jerusalem in verse 3?

b. Do we know who the two witnesses are?

c. Evidence indicates that at least one of the witnesses is Elijah. List the reasons why this is believed to be true.

d. What are the five points in their testimony?

e. Why wouldn't God just send miraculous messages of warning to Jerusalem during the Tribulation instead of using two human witnesses? What is God's purpose in using human means to accomplish His ends?

f. How will people respond to the preaching of the witnesses?

g. What will happen to the witnesses "when they finish their testimony" (Revelation 11:7–13)?

Group Questions

1. Read Revelation 11:3. What power was given to the two witnesses?

2. How long are the witnesses given to proclaim God's Truth?

3. What is the connection between how one dresses and acts (for example, wearing sackcloth) and one's spiritual condition (2 Samuel 3:31; Psalm 35:13; Matthew 11:21)?

4. What connection do you see between Job's spiritual state and his actions (Job 2:7–8)?

5. Should there be outward signs of grieving over sin or calamity among Christians today?

6. What does it say about the future citizens of Jerusalem and the world that they would harden their hearts against the clear divine origin of the two witnesses?

   a. What connection do you see between that future reality and Exodus 9:12 and Romans 1:24, 26, and 28? Do you see evidence that God's patience is limited?

   b. When is the best time to repent of sin (Hebrews 3:7–12)?

   c. What role do we play in each other's lives to encourage repentance and obedience (Hebrews 3:13–15)?

DID YOU KNOW?

Sackcloth was a coarse cloth woven from goat or camel hair. Our English word is based on the Hebrew *saq* and Greek *sakkos*—hence, "sackcloth." Because it was an uncomfortable and coarse fabric, it was worn to signify uncomfortable moments in life such as grieving, distress, mourning, sorrow, or repentance—especially when it was worn next to the skin instead of over another garment. Sackcloth could be worn for personal reasons or national reasons. When the prophet Jonah preached to the city of Nineveh and the city repented, even the animals in Nineveh were covered with sackcloth (Jonah 3:8). Sackcloth was not just for garments of grieving; it was also used to make items where a strong cloth was needed, like tents or floor coverings.

Notes
1. Timothy J. Demy and John C. Whitcomb, "Witnesses, Two," in *The Popular Encyclopedia of Bible Prophecy*, Ed Hindson and Tim LaHaye, eds. (Eugene, OR: Harvest House Publishers, 2004), 402–403.
2. Quoted in William R. Newell, *Revelation: Chapter-by-Chapter* (Chicago, IL: Moody Press, 1935), 152–153.
3. Ibid., 155.
4. Henry Morris, *The Revelation Record* (Wheaton, IL: Tyndale House Publishers, 1963), 204.

Dragon

REVELATION 12:1-17

*In this lesson we get an overview of Satan's age-old strategy
against Israel and her Messiah.*

Since the Garden of Eden, Satan has had a strategy: stop the mission of the Son of God. And since God's Son was to come to earth through Israel, Satan has worked tirelessly to attack the nation and her coming Messiah. The victory of the Messiah means defeat for the enemy of God.

OUTLINE

I. **The Great Sign of a Woman**

II. **The Great Dragon**
   A. Satan's Power
   B. Satan's Partners
   C. Satan's Purpose

III. **The Great War**

IV. **The Great Wrath**
   A. An Aggravated Assault
   B. An Anti-Semitic Assault
   C. An Angry Assault

V. **The Great Wings**

OVERVIEW

Satan appears throughout the Bible, beginning with Genesis 3 and concluding with his being cast into the lake of fire in Revelation 20. In between Genesis and Revelation, his attempts to oppose, obstruct, and counterfeit the work of God are well documented. But when it comes to his specific activity during the end times, one chapter is where we must look: Revelation 12.

Revelation 12 is a book of four "greats," which form the outline of this lesson on Satan during the Tribulation: a great sign—a woman (Revelation 12:1–2), a great and fiery dragon (Revelation 12:3), a great wrath (Revelation 12:12), and two wings of a great eagle (Revelation 12:14).

First, the great sign of the woman who represents the nation of Israel.

The Great Sign of a Woman

"Now a great sign appeared in heaven: a woman clothed with the sun, with the moon under her feet, and on her head a garland of twelve stars. Then being with child, she cried out in labor and in pain to give birth. . . . She bore a male Child who was to rule all nations with a rod of iron. And her Child was caught up to God and His throne" (Revelation 12:1–2, 5).

Many ideas as to the identity of the woman have been offered, but only one fits with the teaching of the Bible: the woman can be none other than Israel. This view is consistent with what Isaiah saw—a woman in labor who "delivered a male child" (Isaiah 66:7–8). The Child whom John saw "was to rule all nations with a rod of iron. And her Child was caught up to God and His throne." Israel brought forth Jesus Christ, destined by God to rule the earth, and now seated at the right hand of God in heaven.

John's vision was also consistent with the Messianic prophecy in Psalm 2, where the Messiah is promised the nations as an inheritance, which He will rule "with a rod of iron" (Psalm 2:8–9). And the vision was completed in Revelation 19:15, where John saw Christ returning to "rule [the nations] with a rod of iron."

So the first "great" in Revelation 12 is a great sign—a woman representing the nation of Israel who will bring forth the Jewish Messiah.

The Great Dragon

"And another sign appeared in heaven: behold, a great, fiery red dragon having seven heads and ten horns, and seven diadems on his heads. His tail drew a third of the stars of heaven and threw them to the earth. And the dragon stood before the woman who was ready to give birth, to devour her Child as soon as it was born. . . . So the great dragon was cast out, that serpent of old, called the Devil and Satan, who deceives the whole world; he was cast to the earth, and his angels were cast out with him" (Revelation 12:3-4, 9).

Revelation 12 gives us a glimpse into heaven, where we see Satan being expelled from heaven: "For the accuser of our brethren, who accused them before our God day and night, has been cast down" (Revelation 12:10). The description of Satan in verse 9 is perhaps the most complete description of him anywhere in Scripture. He is called the great dragon, the serpent of old (a reference to Genesis 3), the devil, Satan, and deceiver of the whole world.

The Old Testament word for "Satan" means "adversary"—the adversary of God and all of God's children, pictured in the New Testament seeking to devour whomever he can like a roaring lion (1 Peter 5:8). Jesus summed up Satan well by saying, "He was a murderer from the beginning" (John 8:44). The following chart illustrates Satan's counterfeit strategies:

SATAN'S COUNTERFEIT STRATEGY

JESUS CHRIST	SATAN
The Light of the World (John 9:5)	Transformed into an angel of light (2 Corinthians 11:14)
King of kings (1 Timothy 6:15)	King over the children of pride (Job 41:34)
Prince of Peace (Isaiah 9:6)	Prince of the world (John 12:31; 14:30; 16:11; Ephesians 2:2)
The Lord my God (Zechariah 14:5)	The god of this age (2 Corinthians 4:4)
Lion of the tribe of Judah (Revelation 5:5)	Roaring lion, seeking whom he may devour (1 Peter 5:8)

The Greek (New Testament) word for *devil* is *diabolos*. Literally, the term means "slanderer." He is so labeled in Revelation 12:10: "the accuser of our brethren." In the New Testament the devil is the seducer of men; he is presented as the one who tempts men into actions that defy God.

The final phrase that Revelation 12 uses to describe the devil is deceiver. The great purpose of the devil in the past was to keep Christ away from the world. Having failed in that attempt, the only option left to him is to keep the world away from Christ. Paul wrote about this strategy in his letter to the Corinthians: "Whose minds the god of this age has blinded, who do not believe, lest the light of the gospel of the glory of Christ, who is the image of God, should shine on them" (2 Corinthians 4:4).

In Revelation 12 we also get a glimpse of Satan's power, partners, and purpose.

Satan's Power

The power of Satan to conduct his strategies is indicated by John's description: "a great, fiery red dragon having seven heads and ten horns, and seven diadems on his heads" (Revelation 12:3). In Scripture, seven is the number of completeness or perfection, and "heads" is a reference to intelligence. So the seven heads present an image of extreme intelligence and cunning. Not omniscience or infinite intelligence like God, but sufficient and universal intelligence to carry out Satan's plans on earth (1 John 5:19). And what is his plan? To blind the minds of humanity to "the glory of Christ, who is the image of God" (2 Corinthians 4:3–4).

The image of Satan as a dragon (and a serpent elsewhere) speaks of his power, cunning, and cruelty. At the core of his being is murder and death. The "seven diadems" (Revelation 12:3) on his head speak of a king and a kingdom, something supported by Jesus (Matthew 23:25–26), John (John 12:31; 14:30; 16:11), and Paul (2 Corinthians 4:4; Ephesians 2:2). John also tells us that "the whole world lies under the sway of the wicked one" (1 John 5:19). No one should forget that Satan has power and authority.

Satan's Partners

"Lucifer" means "star of the morning" in Hebrew (Isaiah 14:12), which helps us understand the reference in Revelation 12:4 to him drawing "a third of the stars of heaven and [throwing] them to the earth." The point is this: When Satan rebelled against God in heaven and was expelled, he took a third of the angels with him. (Angels are referred to as "morning stars" in Job 38:7.)

Those fallen angels are what the New Testament calls demons—lesser angels who are Satan's army in his service. Some have been imprisoned (2 Peter 2:4; Jude 6), but the rest have free course to move about. Satan appears on earth (in the Garden of Eden) and in heaven, accusing Job of unfaithfulness before God (Job 1–2). They have access to the earth and its population as they oppose the work of God.

Satan's Purpose

From the beginning, Satan has had a mission to destroy the Child of the woman in John's vision (Revelation 12:1–5). The Child in John's vision is the "seed of the woman" who would ultimately "bruise [Satan's] head" (Genesis 3:15). So Satan set about to keep that Seed from ever coming to life through the line of promise—Abraham and his descendants. Esau attempted to kill Jacob (also named "Israel"), Pharaoh tried to destroy the nation through slavery and by killing the male babies.

At one point, the line of promise came down to one child, as W. A. Criswell explains:

> After Jehoshaphat the wicked King of Judah died, his son Jehoram had all the children of David's family killed, saving alive his own children. The Arabians then attacked the family of Jehoram and killed all of his children except Ahaziah. When Jehu later killed Ahaziah, Athaliah, the queen-mother, usurped the crown. She was the daughter of Ahab and Jezebel, and she killed all of the royal seed except a little boy named Joash. Joash's aunt, who was also the wife of the high priest, took the infant prince and hid him away for six years.[1]

Joash survived, and the line of promise continued. But Haman, the wicked Persian official, planned to exterminate the Jews—and would have if not for Esther. King Herod tried to kill the newborn Jesus by murdering all the infant boys in Judea. Three decades later, Satan confronted Jesus in the wilderness in a direct offer to give up His loyalty to God, but Jesus resisted (Matthew 4; Luke 4). Satan later tried to move the crowds to throw Jesus off a cliff (Luke 4:29). And when Jesus hung on a cross, it looked as if Satan had won—except for His glorious resurrection from the dead.

So Satan's purpose to kill the Child of the woman, Israel, was defeated. Yet he continues his attacks. The war between Satan and God continues.

The Great War

Revelation 12:7-8 pictures the cosmic and ongoing struggle between Satan and his angels on one side and God—represented by Michael the archangel—and His angels on the other side. The Bible tells us that this battle of the ages will culminate in a final conflict. There are only a few places in Scripture where we get a glimpse into the present, ongoing nature of this conflict (see Ephesians 6:12 for a mention of Satan's angelic hierarchies).

Daniel 10 presents the most detailed window into heavenly, spiritual combat. Daniel had been praying for twenty-one days without an answer from God when an angel (probably Gabriel; see Daniel 8:16; 9:21) appeared to him. He told Daniel that he had been dispatched with an answer for Daniel the first day he began praying, but he was delayed because of a conflict with the "prince of Persia" (Daniel 10:20). Only assistance from the angel Michael allowed Gabriel to resume his mission to answer Daniel's prayer.

The "prince of Persia" is an obvious reference to a Satanic angel who tried to thwart God's plans. This appears to be an example of the hierarchies referred to by Paul (Ephesians 6:12)—Satanic angels assigned to influence the rulers of nations. And since Daniel was in Persia at the time of his prayer, it is consistent that the "prince of Persia" would attempt to stop God's help from reaching Daniel and the Jews in Persia.

Yes, Satan was defeated at the cross (John 16:8, 11; Hebrews 2:14). But the legal action of the cross has not been fully executed. Satan has been judged and sentenced, but his "execution" awaits. It will be accomplished at the end of the Millennium (Revelation 20:10).

Earthly victories depend on heavenly victories. Prayer, that God would defend us against Satan's tactics, is our chief weapon against him now. Paul recommended as much in Ephesians 6:18 at the end of his discussion of the Christian's spiritual armor. Prayer, based on God's truths, is our spiritual strategy (2 Corinthians 10:5). Someone has said, "It's not the mayors that make the world go 'round; it's the prayers."

The Great Wrath

Satan has been judged, but he will unleash all his fury against God and His people at the end of the age.

An Aggravated Assault

The vision presents a warning: "Woe to the inhabitants of the earth and the sea! For the devil has come down to you, having great wrath, because he knows that he has a short time" (Revelation 12:12). Satan knows the future; he knows that his days are numbered, and he is not happy about it. Like a caged lion—caged by the limits God allows (Job 1:12; 2:6)—Satan is ready to attack.

An Anti-Semitic Assault

Satan will continue his attack upon the woman, Israel, in a final attempt to destroy God's work through His chosen people (Revelation 12:13, 15). Satan hates Israel, because through Israel the Messiah came. As the time for Christ's return to earth gets closer, Satan's persecution against Israel will increase. That was true in Nazi Germany prior to World War II and remains true today as Israel is threatened by her Arab and Muslim neighbors.

Satan's attack comes as water spewed "out of his mouth like a flood," directed at Israel. It is difficult to know exactly what that flood represents—perhaps a literal flood in Israel or a flood of words (a flood coming from the mouth, the source of speech) and propaganda against Israel. Whatever its form, the attempt will be to do what floods do—sweep away everything in its path.

An Angry Assault

Revelation 12:17 says, "And the dragon was enraged with the woman, and he went to make war with the rest of her offspring, who keep the commandments of God and have the testimony of

Jesus Christ." Jewish believers in Christ will be the focus of Satan's attack. I believe this refers specifically to the 144,000 Jewish witnesses who will be active during the Tribulation (Revelation 7).

The Great Wings

Israel will not be left at the mercy of Satan. She is given "two wings of a great eagle" by which she is protected "for a time and times and half a time" from Satan. And the earth "opened its mouth and swallowed up the flood" that Satan will have let loose (Revelation 12:14, 16). This vision calls to mind the "eagles' wings" on which God brought Israel up and out of Egypt (Exodus 19:4; Deuteronomy 32:11–12).

The image is one of divine protection for Israel in "the wilderness"—supernatural protection and provision as Israel experienced in the wilderness. Wherever that place of refuge is, a godly remnant of Jews will be preserved. Once again Satan will fail in his attempt to eradicate the people of God before they can be united with their coming Messiah.

Just as a large, dangerous snake will continue to thrash and struggle after being decapitated, so Satan is continuing to thrash and cause trouble even though he was "decapitated" by the cross and the resurrection of Jesus. The Garden serpent was promised that the seed of the woman would crush him, and so it will come to pass. But in the meantime, God's people must be on the alert for the one who, despite his death sentence, can still cause them harm.

The key phrase is "God's people." Make sure that you are among the spiritual descendants of Abraham, through faith in Christ, and thus secure forever from the present and future assaults of God's arch-enemy.

APPLICATION

Personal Questions

1. What promise did God make to the serpent in the Garden of Eden (Genesis 3:15)?

   a. How did the serpent bruise the heel of the Seed of the woman?

   b. What is the difference between a bruise on the head versus a bruise on the heel? (Which is temporary?)

c. How will Satan ultimately experience a bruise on his head (Revelation 20:10)?

2. How many people did God keep alive to continue the promise of defeating the serpent when the earth became totally wicked (Genesis 6:10, 18)?

   a. How did Abraham and Sarah become the new "parents" through whom God would give a Seed to bless the world (Genesis 12:1–6)?

   b. What was the line of promise that God established through Abraham (Genesis 50:24)?

   c. What did Jacob's name become (Genesis 32:28)? ("The children of Israel" is another way of saying "the children of _____.")

   d. How were the descendants of Israel almost wiped out (Exodus 1:8–19)?

   e. Through which tribe of Israel's sons would the promise continue (Genesis 49:8–12)?

   f. Of which tribe was King David (1 Samuel 17:12)? Of which tribe was Joseph, the earthly father of Jesus (Luke 1:26–27)?

Group Questions

1. How did Satan attempt to snuff out the life of Jesus at the very beginning (Matthew 2:16)? How was this prevented (Matthew 2:13–15)?

2. When did Satan launch his next major attack on Jesus (Matthew 4:1–11; Luke 4:1–13)?

   a. What indication of Satan's relentless strategy do you find in Luke 4:13?

   b. What was the final "opportune time" in which Satan tempted Jesus (Luke 22:41–44)?

   c. Why does Paul focus on the resurrection of Christ as the key element in Christian faith (1 Corinthians 15:14, 17)?

   d. Why did the death of Christ look like a victory for Satan at first?

3. Why is the story of the disciples on the Emmaus road a good illustration of the difference the resurrection makes between defeat and victory (Luke 24:17, 33–35)?

4. Why should victory in the Christian life never be decided on the basis of temporary circumstances (1 Corinthians 15:57)?

DID YOU KNOW?

The Swiss theologian Oscar Cullman, who lived during World War II, has pointed out that every great war has had a decisive battle. For the French against the British-led coalition, it was Waterloo. For the American Civil War, it was Gettysburg. And in World War II, it was the Normandy invasion that began on D-Day, June 6, 1944. The successful invasion that began on D-Day marked the turning point in the war and the ultimate defeat of the Axis forces built around Nazi Germany. Even though World War II did not end until September 1945, its outcome turned on D-Day. Similarly, Satan's outcome was sealed over the three days of Christ's death and resurrection. The battles and skirmishes rage on, but the outcome is already determined.

Note
1. W. A. Criswell, *Expository Sermons on Revelation, Volume 4: Revelation 11 through 17* (Grand Rapids, MI: Zondervan Publishing House, 1966), 85–87.

Mark of the Beast

REVELATION 13:1–18

*In this lesson we learn about the satanic activity of the Antichrist
and the False Prophet during the Tribulation.*

If a well-known political leader today suddenly began manifesting miraculous powers—
signs and wonders—he would receive instant acclaim. During the Tribulation, Satan will
give such power to the Antichrist and False Prophet to induce the world to worship them
instead of God.

OUTLINE

  I. **The Mark Is Originated by Satan**

 II. **The Mark Is Ordered by the Antichrist**

III. **The Mark Is Orchestrated by the False Prophet**
    A. The Description of the False Prophet
    B. The Deeds of the False Prophet
    C. The Deception of the False Prophet
    D. The Demand of the False Prophet
    E. The Doom of the False Prophet and His Followers

OVERVIEW

October 7, 2009, marked the fifty-seventh anniversary of the barcode—that rectangular set of black lines on a white background that appears on everything we purchase today. Officially known as a UPC—Universal Product Code—the barcode was invented by two American graduate students and first used at a supermarket in Troy, Ohio, in 1974.

While the barcode is not going away, a new identification system—RFID (Radio Frequency IDentification)—is becoming even more widespread. It is a tiny microchip that is used to keep track of products in shipment, the movement of people (via a chip on a name or ID tag), even animals. RFID chips are everywhere—and usually unseen because of their tiny size. And the technology is now available to implant the chips, about the size of a grain of rice, under human skin. Their first use is to implant them under the skin of emergency workers, soldiers, and others to make identification possible as a last resort.

While fascinating, this technology is frightening at the same time, especially to those who have read Revelation 13—a chapter detailing some of the policies of the Antichrist during the Tribulation. We are already seeing a gradual erosion of privacy in our day, and during the Tribulation citizens will have none. When we look at where technology is taking us, we can only stand in awe of the biblical prophecies made 1,900 years ago depicting these same events. God knows the beginning and the end, seeing past, present, and future as one (Isaiah 46:9–10). The mark of the Beast, the subject of this lesson, is a prime example of how biblical prophecy will be fulfilled with today's technology.

I am often asked whether Christians, who will be raptured from the earth before the Tribulation, need to be concerned about these developments. We know the events of Revelation 13 take place in the second half of the seven-year Tribulation, or three-and-one-half years after the Rapture of the Church. We also know that the Rapture is imminent—that it could happen at any moment. No other biblical prophecy needs to be fulfilled before the Rapture can occur. So if the Rapture could happen today, then we could be just three or four years away from the events described in Revelation 13. But those events will not happen suddenly. There will be a gradual buildup to those events. And we are living in a time when the technology is developing and the sweeping power of government is growing to the extent that we could begin to see signs of the nearness of the Tribulation events taking place. I truly believe we are living in the shadows of Tribulation events.

Revelation 13 introduces us to the methods for population control the Antichrist will use in the second half of the Tribulation, one of them being a "mark" affixed to the hand or forehead of every individual on earth.

The Mark Is Originated by Satan

We are told in Revelation 13:2 that it is "the dragon" which gives "the beast" (the Antichrist) his power. The reference to Satan as "the dragon" comes from the previous chapter, Revelation 12:9, which depicts "the great dragon" being cast out of heaven along with the rebellious angels who were allied with him. It is obvious in Revelation 12 that the Dragon is Satan. And in Revelation 13, John continues by saying it is the Dragon who empowers the Beast (the Antichrist).

It is Satan's desire to be worshiped that we see also in the Antichrist. In Isaiah 14:12–14 we find Satan saying, "I will be like the Most High" (verse 14). And when Satan tempted Jesus in the wilderness, he offered Jesus "all the kingdoms of the world" if Jesus would "fall down and worship [him]" (Matthew 4:8–9). It is Satan's long-standing desire to be worshiped "like the Most High," and it is no surprise that we have seen an increase in Satanic worship in our day. And his primary goal during the Tribulation will be to deflect worship away from the true and living God to his (Satan's) representative on earth, the Antichrist.

Satan is a counterfeiter; a copycat. We'll see that just as God is a Trinity, Satan has his own trinity: himself, the Antichrist, and the False Prophet. Just as the Holy Spirit brings glory to Jesus Christ, so the False Prophet will bring glory to the Antichrist. The mark of the Beast is a way to force people to worship someone out of fear.

The Mark Is Ordered by the Antichrist

John saw the Beast rising up out of the sea. The Beast is a composite of the four animals seen by Daniel in his prophecy of the end times. They represented Babylon, Medo-Persia, Greece, and Rome. The Beast has seven heads and ten horns and represents the ruler of the revived Roman Empire, the Antichrist himself. He will be an international leader, uniting people from all races and all regions of the world. No human could do that alone, but with Satan working behind the scenes, it will happen.

The Antichrist's activities are detailed in Revelation 13:3–10, activities that are consistent with Satan's career—especially the Antichrist's blasphemous words against God. Satan's main mission in life is to make God look bad so people will not worship Him. And the Antichrist will take up that blasphemous task during his time on earth with the intent to turn people away from God to worship him.

He also makes war against the saints—those who profess faith in Christ during the Tribulation. He exercises power over "every tribe, tongue, and nation" (verse 7). And he is successful: "All who dwell on the earth will worship him"—all, that is, "whose names have not been written in the Book of Life of the Lamb slain from the foundation of the world" (verse 8). A frightening world is coming shortly.

The Mark Is Orchestrated by the False Prophet

The mark is originated with Satan and ordered by the Antichrist, but it is orchestrated by the False Prophet—the second beast of Revelation 13. He is the one who executes the plan to put the mark of the Beast on the population of planet earth.

The Description of the False Prophet

John notes that this second beast looks like a lamb but speaks like a dragon. That is, he appears meek and mild but, in reality, is bent on destruction. Again, Satan is all about counterfeiting. Jesus was "the Lamb of God who takes away the sin of the world" (John 1:29), so Satan makes the False Prophet into a false lamb. But this lamb is really a wolf in sheep's clothing; a demonized man exercising authority and power in the name of the Antichrist. He has miraculous powers by which he amazes and deceives the residents of planet earth (Revelation 13:13–14).

Though Christians will not be around to witness these miracles, we must beware of false prophets today who are "ravenous wolves" in sheep's clothing (Matthew 7:15). Many could be named, but people like Jim Jones (The Peoples Temple) is a good example—a preacher who began his ministry based on Scripture but ultimately led hundreds of people to their deaths by suicide in Guyana. A tragic case of satanic deception that ended in the deaths of hundreds of hopeful, but deceived, people.

The Deeds of the False Prophet

I fear some Christians underestimate the power of our enemy. He gives the False Prophet power to work miracles—"great signs"—like making "fire come down from heaven on the earth in the sight of men." Satan is not God's peer or equal. But he is definitely powerful and can create "signs" that look equivalent to what God has done. Again, his expertise is counterfeiting.

The reason the False Prophet calls down fire from heaven is probably a reference to Malachi 4:5-6, which says that before the coming of the Messiah, Elijah will appear. And Elijah is the only Old Testament prophet to have called down fire from heaven. The False Prophet will be attempting to convince people he is Elijah—the forerunner of the Lord who will return. It is a deceitful attempt to give an air of legitimacy to his presence.

The Deception of the False Prophet

The False Prophet's miracles have their intended effect: He convinces people to build "an image to the beast"—a giant image in honor of the Antichrist (Revelation 13:14). I believe the Antichrist then sets this image in the rebuilt Jewish temple in Jerusalem, in the Holy of Holies, thus fulfilling the prophecy of Daniel 12:11 (also in Daniel 9:27 and 11:31) concerning "the abomination of desolation." This prophecy of Daniel was fulfilled as a foreshadowing by Antiochus

Epiphanes who set up a statue of the Greek god Zeus in the Holy of Holies and sacrificed a pig on the temple altar. These acts would have indeed been an abomination to any God-fearing Jew of the day. And the Antichrist will perform similar acts with the help of the False Prophet.

Jesus also made reference to this coming abomination in Matthew 24:15–16, 21. This act marks the beginning of the second half of the Tribulation (the 1,290 days, or three-and-one-half years, mentioned in Daniel 12:11). Following this event, Jesus said, "there will be great tribulation, such as has not been since the beginning of the world until this time" (Matthew 24:21).

At the beginning of the Tribulation, the Antichrist will make a covenant with Israel to protect her against her enemies. But he breaks the covenant at the midpoint of the Tribulation and turns against Israel by desecrating her temple and Holy of Holies. He defiles everything the Jews hold holy and turns his full fury upon Israel to destroy her. Paul says that the Antichrist will sit "as God in the temple of God, showing himself that he is God" (2 Thessalonians 2:4). At that moment, the diabolical trinity of Satan, the Antichrist, and the False Prophet will have fulfilled their desire of receiving worship as God.

And here is a truly diabolical part: The False Prophet is able to cause the image of the Antichrist to speak (Revelation 13:15). There is no magic or deceit here. It is pure demonic power at work according to the testimony of 2 Thessalonians 2:9: "The coming of the lawless one is according to the working of Satan, with all power, signs, and lying wonders." Satan has the power to make an inanimate object like an image appear to come to life. It is another example of the dark power that will characterize the Tribulation period—especially the second half.

The Demand of the False Prophet

Once the Antichrist's and False Prophet's power has been displayed, they are ready to demand the acceptance of the mark of the Beast "on their right hand or on their foreheads" (Revelation 13:16).

Again, counterfeiting is seen. In Revelation 7:3, the servants of God are sealed on their foreheads to set them apart from those not belonging to Him. These are the 144,000 Jewish witnesses who serve as evangelists during the Tribulation period. The seal is to protect them before certain judgments are released on the earth. The Antichrist's seal is for the same purpose—protection. By receiving his mark, people will be able to buy and sell and engage in commerce. Without it, they will become targets of the Antichrist. The RFID microchip already mentioned is a possible way for this to take place.

The Doom of the False Prophet and His Followers

In spite of the power and control the Antichrist exercises during the Tribulation, his doom is sealed. We turn forward in Revelation to chapter 19 for the details. There we find that "these two [the Antichrist and the False Prophet] were cast alive into the lake of fire burning with brimstone" (verse 20).

And those who took the mark of the Beast and worshiped his image did not fare well either. Revelation 16:1–2 details "a foul and loathsome sore" that came upon them. Revelation 14:9–11 says they will "drink of the wine of the wrath of God" and "shall be tormented with fire and brimstone in the presence of the holy angels and in the presence of the Lamb . . . forever and ever." While it may appear that those who take the mark of the Beast are simply doing what they have to do to protect themselves and their families, they are judged for identifying with the satanic evil of the Antichrist.

What is the mark of the Beast? Revelation 13:18 says, "Let him who has understanding calculate the number of the beast, for it is the number of a man: His number is 666." For two thousand years people have wanted to know what 666 represents, who it points to. People are afraid of the number—to have it in their address or their phone number. The first mark in the Bible was put on Cain after he killed Abel (Genesis 4:15).

There have been numerous attempts through the years to come up with a mathematical formula for equating letters with numbers in order to arrive at 666 and thus the identity of the Antichrist. But all those attempts have failed. Perhaps the best thing to remember is that the number seven in Scripture is the number of completeness—the divine number. Six, therefore, is an incomplete number, a number that falls short of God's completeness. And human beings certainly fall short of God's completeness due to sin. That may be what 666 represents: incomplete man in rebellion against God.

What about those who refuse to take the mark of the Beast? Revelation 20:4 identifies them as having been "beheaded for their witness to Jesus and for the word of God," for not worshiping the Beast or his image and not receiving the mark of the Beast. "And they lived and reigned with Christ for a thousand years." They are resurrected and rule with Christ during the Millennium.

If you are a Christian today, you will never face the decision of whether to receive the mark of the Beast or not. You will be in heaven with Christ during the Tribulation. But what would you do if you were faced with such a decision—a decision to swear allegiance to a godless ruler or maintain your allegiance to Christ? We have examples in Scripture of people faced with that choice: Daniel's three friends, Shadrach, Meshach, and Abed-Nego. They refused to worship the king of Babylon and were sorely tested—but God preserved them. They didn't know He would. They were willing to die as faithful Jews (Daniel 3).

That should be our stance today as well. Whether we are tested with ridicule, embarrassment, financial reversal, or even the threat of death—may God give us grace to stay true to the One who has given His all to save us for all eternity.

APPLICATION

Personal Questions

1. Read Isaiah 14:12–14.

   a. Where was Satan (Lucifer) before being consigned to earth (verse 12a)?

   b. Describe the five prideful assertions Lucifer made that resulted in his downfall (verses 13–14):

      1) I will _____.

      2) I will _____.

      3) I will _____.

      4) I will _____.

      5) I will _____.

   c. Which of the five eventually most clearly parallels the intention of the Antichrist during the Tribulation?

2. Read Matthew 7:15–20.

   a. What does Jesus warn His followers about in this passage (verse 15)?

b. Why does Jesus make this warning? (Is it possible that something can appear legitimate to us when it really isn't?)

c. How does Paul affirm this possibility in 2 Corinthians 11:13–15?

d. How do the men in Paul's day parallel the activity of the False Prophet during the Tribulation?

e. What does the term "ravenous wolves" in Matthew 7:15 signify to you? (How serious is the intent of false prophets?)

Group Questions

1. Read Matthew 7:15–20 and discuss the following questions:

   a. How does Jesus say a false prophet can be detected (verse 16)?

   b. Why are miracles not always the only "fruit" that must be checked (Revelation 13:13–14)?

   c. What other kinds of "fruit" should one look for (Galatians 5:22–23)?

   d. What is the ultimate determinant of whether a New Testament "prophet" is true or false (1 John 2:22)?

   e. If a tree ("prophet") bears some good fruit and some bad fruit, what determination must be made about him (verses 17–18)?

f. What must be done with trees that bear bad fruit (verse 19)? How would you translate this metaphor into practical terms for the Church today?

2. Read Daniel 3:16–18 and discuss the following questions:

a. What were the three Hebrew men convinced God was able to do (verse 17)?

b. But what did they know might actually happen (verse 18a)?

c. What difference did it make to them what God chose to do (verse 18)?

d. Why is it important to decide on our convictions before pressure arises in our life?

DID YOU KNOW?

RFID (Radio Frequency IDentification) tags require, like a barcode, a reader to pull data stored on the RFID microchip. Because the information is transmitted wirelessly, RFID chips have an advantage over barcodes in that they can be read at a distance. RFID tags are currently used to track livestock (chips in ear tags), monitor individuals coming in and out of facilities (employees wearing ID badges with embedded chips), inventory control (chips embedded in clothing and on pallets of products in shipment), transportation payments (cars going through toll booths, passengers boarding buses, subways, and trains), timing of individuals and vehicles in sport races, tracking international travel via passport chips, and many other uses. Human implants of RFID chips have been in progress since 1998.

LESSON 26

Armageddon

REVELATION 16:13-16; DANIEL 11:36-45

In this lesson we learn about earth's final war—and how it ends.

The word "Armageddon" is used in modern cultures to describe doomsday-type events—or even a "meeting with the boss." Many people don't know it is the biblical name for earth's final great battle—when Israel is saved from annihilation and the rebellious nations of earth are defeated.

OUTLINE

I. The Preparation for the Battle of Armageddon

II. The Place of the Battle of Armageddon

III. The Purpose of the Battle of Armageddon
   A. To Finish His Judgment upon Israel
   B. To Finalize His Judgment upon the Nations That Have Persecuted Israel
   C. To Formally Judge All the Nations That Have Rejected Him

IV. The Perspective of the Battle of Armageddon

V. The Participants in the Battle of Armageddon
   A. The Deal Between Israel and the Antichrist
   B. The Demand That Everyone Worship the Antichrist
   C. The Decision to Fight Against the Antichrist
   D. The Disturbing News From the East
   E. The Descending Lord from the Heavens

OVERVIEW

America is no stranger to war. Since the beginning of our nation, we have experienced a major war about every twenty-five years beginning with the Revolutionary War, the War of 1812, the Civil War, The Spanish-American War, World Wars I and II, the Korean War, the Vietnam War, the Persian Gulf War, and the wars in Afghanistan and Iraq. Hardly any generation has been able to live their whole life without sending their young to war.

The Bible says there is going to be a final war one day on this earth. That war, called Armageddon, will signal the coming down of the curtain on modern civilization. And preparation for that war is under way in our world at this very moment. The only thing blocking the players in that war from moving onto the stage of battle is the Rapture—the transfer of the Church of Jesus Christ to heaven. Following that event, the final war—the Battle of Armageddon—will take place.

The Preparation for the Battle of Armageddon

The Battle of Armageddon begins in heaven and descends to earth with the casting out of Satan (Revelation 12:9–13). Satan is the "prince of the power of the air" (Ephesians 2:2)—his dominion is the heavenly region surrounding planet earth. But during the seven-year Tribulation, he will be cast out of that domain to earth where he will begin to persecute "the woman who gave birth to the male Child" (Revelation 12:13). The "woman" is not Mary, Jesus' mother, but Israel—the one through whom Jesus Christ came into this world. Satan's goal will be to destroy Israel before the return of Christ to establish His kingdom on earth.

Satan will have two human helpers: the Beast and the False Prophet (Revelation 16:13). These three form an unholy trinity of persecution against God's chosen people during the Tribulation. And it is that reign of terror against Israel that will lead the world to the Battle of Armageddon.

The Place of the Battle of Armageddon

Revelation 16:16 identifies Armageddon as a place in the Holy Land. "Armageddon" is a Hebrew word made up of two smaller words: *Har* (mount) and *Megiddo* (slaughter). So Armageddon is "mount of slaughter." I once stood on a hill overlooking the vast Plain of Megiddo in northern Israel—about eighteen miles southeast of Haifa and over fifty miles north of Jerusalem. In 1799 the French conqueror Napoleon stood at Megiddo and declared, "All the armies of the world could maneuver their forces on this vast plain. There is no place in the whole world more suited for war than this. [It is] the most natural battleground on the whole earth."[1]

The Battle of Armageddon will not be fought only at Megiddo—it will spill over into all of Israel and even other parts of the world. Joel says there will be fighting in "the Valley of Jehoshaphat" which is east of Jerusalem (Joel 3:2). Isaiah says the sword will fall on Edom, which was south of the Dead Sea (Isaiah 34:5). And Zechariah refers to Jerusalem as being part of the stage of battle (Zechariah 12:2).

Revelation 14:20 says blood will flow "up to the horses' bridles, for one thousand six hundred furlongs." That distance in furlongs is about 200 miles—about the distance from one end of Israel to the other. The "horses' bridles" reference is an ancient one, probably referring to quantity. In other words, a great deal of blood is going to be spilled in the Battle of Armageddon.

The Purpose of the Battle of Armageddon

Why would God allow such a blood-bath to take place on earth? There are three biblical reasons.

To Finish His Judgment upon Israel

For all the sympathy it is easy to feel toward Israel during this period when she is being attacked by others, we have to remember that she is still living in rebellion toward God. Even the reestablishment of the nation in 1948 was more a Zionist cultural, political movement than a spiritual one. Israel to this day has not embraced her Messiah, and judgment will fall upon her for that reason. It is that judgment that will cause many Jews during the Tribulation to turn to God and accept the Messiah they rejected (Zechariah 12:10).

To Finalize His Judgment upon the Nations That Have Persecuted Israel

As God allows the nations of the world to inflict judgment upon Israel, He will be inflicting judgment on them: "I will also gather all nations, and bring them down to the Valley of Jehoshaphat; and I will enter into judgment with them there" (Joel 3:2).

God promised to "curse him who curses [Abraham and his descendants]" (Genesis 12:3). And that is why these nations of the world will be judged during the wars that make up Armageddon.

To Formally Judge All the Nations That Have Rejected Him

Revelation 19:15 says that God will "[tread] the winepress of the fierceness and wrath of Almighty God." Not only will the nations be judged because they have attacked Israel but also because they have rejected God and His Son, the Lord Jesus Christ. Psalm 2 pictures the Lord in heaven laughing at the "kings of the earth" who "take counsel together" against God and His Anointed. But they will be judged for their rejection of Him.

The Perspective of the Battle of Armageddon

Let's reset the stage for this end-time conflagration: The Church of Jesus Christ is raptured to heaven which marks the beginning of the seven-year Tribulation period. The ruler of the European nations, the Antichrist, makes a peace treaty with Israel, ensuring her safety from the surrounding Arab nations—a time when Israel is living in "unwalled villages" (Ezekiel 38:11). During this time the coalition of nations from "the north" (Russia, Iran, and others) attack Israel but is stopped and defeated by God: the Battle of Gog and Magog. This is not the Battle of Armageddon—these two battles need to be kept separate:

GOG AND MAGOG	ARMAGEDDON
Russian-led coalition of nations	All the nations of the world
Invaders come from the north	Invaders come from all directions
Purpose is to take Israel's wealth and land	Purpose is to annihilate the Jews and fight against Christ and His armies as they return to earth
Russia will be the leader	The Antichrist will be the leader
Invaders are defeated by earthquake and disease	Invaders are defeated by Christ
Those killed limited to land of Israel	Armies killed all over the earth
The dead will be buried	Dead will be consumed by birds
Not the final battle on earth	The final war before the Millennium begins[2]

The Participants in the Battle of Armageddon

There are five major stages in the Battle of Armageddon—beginning with the treaty between Israel and the Antichrist.

The Deal Between Israel and the Antichrist

Daniel 9:27 is the verse that tells us about the "covenant" (treaty) the Antichrist makes with Israel—a seven-year peace-protection pledge. From his position of power in the revived Roman Empire (Europe)—and his apparent resurrection from an assassination—he begins to accumulate power and "speak blasphemies against the God of gods" (Daniel 11:36). The "god" of his own strength and power is the only god he worships (Daniel 11:37–39).

With this power, he convinces Israel to enter into a treaty that will protect Israel from the growing storm of threats against her in the world—specifically from her Arab neighbors.

The Demand That Everyone Worship the Antichrist

If you think the world is looking for answers today to problems like global climate change, food shortages, gas prices, and warring nations, it is only going to be worse in the future. Life in the future is not going to get easier; it's going to get harder. When the Antichrist rises to the stage of power, people will be eager to submit to him. His seeming supernatural abilities will cause people to see him as the savior of mankind.

But after signing the peace treaty with Israel, the Antichrist makes a mistake: he demands that people worship him under threat of death (Revelation 13:15). Some of the earth's peoples rebel at this extension of the Antichrist's power, which sets the stage for the next movement.

The Decision to Fight Against the Antichrist

Daniel 11:40 says that the "king of the South" and "the king of the North" will attack the Antichrist. If you consider that many nations of the world have strong religious heritages—especially Muslim nations—it's not difficult to see how some would resist, even refuse, the idea of worshiping the Antichrist as a god. So they decide to move against him and remove him from power.

Daniel's prophecy describes a great army from Africa, including not only Egypt but also other countries of the continent. The army, probably numbering in the millions, will attack the Middle East from the south. And at the same time, Russia and other armies from the north will mobilize another powerful military force. Even though Russia may have lost a lot of its people and military earlier in the Battle of Gog and Magog, they will apparently have recovered enough to begin to recoup their losses and get involved in this battle again. And so what happens at the beginning is the Antichrist is all puffed up with his power, demanding the worship of the world, and here are the armies of the north and the south coming and saying, "We're going to take this guy out. We'll not have him do this to us."[3]

The Disturbing News from the East

As the Antichrist is resisting the armies from the south and the north, "news from the east and the north shall trouble him; therefore he shall go out with great fury to destroy and annihilate many" (Daniel 11:44). Suddenly, the Antichrist is being attacked from all different directions. Revelation 16:12 pictures a great army coming from the east over a dried-up Euphrates River. The number of that army coming from the east is 200 million (Revelation 9:16). Many Bible students stumble at the thought of an army that large, but it would not be difficult, given the population of China alone, for a coalition of countries from the east (Asia) to field an army of 200 million soldiers.

So the Antichrist is facing armies coming at him from all directions. But there is a supernatural component to this: "For they are the spirits of demons, performing signs, which go out to the kings of the earth of the whole world, to gather them to the battle of that great day of God Almighty" (Revelation 16:14).

The Descending Lord from the Heavens

These armies are moving toward Israel under the inspiration of Satan himself. Satan's goal, of course, is to gather all the armies of the world to attack Israel and destroy her for good. The problem is that while everyone has been checking north, south, east and west, they have forgotten to check "up." If they had, they would have seen the Lord Jesus Christ Himself descending with His armies from heaven:

> Now I saw heaven opened, and behold, a white horse. And He who sat on him was called Faithful and True, and in righteousness He judges and makes war. His eyes were like a flame of fire, and on His head were many crowns. He had a name written that no one knew except himself. He was clothed with a robe dipped in blood, and His name is called The Word of God. And the armies in heaven, clothed in fine linen, white and clean, followed Him on white horses. Now out of His mouth goes a sharp sword, that with it He should strike the nations. And He himself will rule them with a rod of iron. He himself treads the winepress of the fierceness and wrath of Almighty God. And He has on His robe and on His thigh a name written: KING OF KINGS AND LORD OF LORDS (Revelation 19:11–16).

Israel suddenly gets reinforcements from the sky—reinforcements no one had anticipated. And it changes the entire battle scene. The armies that return with Jesus Christ are made up of saints—all true believers who were raptured off the earth prior to the Tribulation—and angels. If you are a Christian, you will be part of this army that descends from heaven with Christ.

Descending with All His Saints

Several verses in Scripture refer to the appearance of God with His saints at the end of time (Zechariah 14:5; 1 Thessalonians 3:13; 2 Thessalonians 1:10; Jude 1:14). Think of the number of saints this represents—all the faithful from the beginning of time who were resurrected at the Rapture—and those who were alive on earth at the Rapture!

It is a finite number, but one that is too large to consider estimating. At the least, it is a number that will make the gathered armies of earth look puny in scope. The column of saints coming behind Christ on His white horse (Revelation 19:11) will be the most awe-inspiring sight in all of human history and will no doubt strike fear in the hearts of all on earth.

Descending with All His Angels

Along with the saints from the ages will come the heavenly hosts—the angels of heaven: "When the Son of Man comes in His glory, and all the holy angels with Him, then He will sit on the throne of His glory" (Matthew 25:31; see also 2 Thessalonians 1:7).

Christians are going to fight side-by-side with angels! But wait—there is no record in Scripture of us lifting a single finger in the fight. Rather, it is the "sharp sword" going "out of [Christ's] mouth" with which He "strike[s] the nations" (Revelation 19:15). That "sharp sword" is not a literal sword. Because it comes out of His mouth, it is a metaphor for the words of judgment He will speak; words that will signal the end of the rebellious armies of earth. He will speak, and it will be over.

So what is our purpose on that day? It is the same as we have seen in other settings where God intervenes: so that His glory might be revealed to us. Second Thessalonians 1:10 says that on that day He will be "glorified in His saints and . . . admired among all those who believe." All the saints of the ages—that great "cloud of witnesses" (Hebrews 12:1)—will witness Christ in all His glory pronounce judgment on those who oppose God and His people, the Jews.

In a day when Israel has no earthly allies by her side, the only true ally she has ever had, her own Messiah, saves her from destruction. If you want to see the greatest battle in history ended with a word, make sure you are among the armies of heaven who return with Christ and witness His judgment.

APPLICATION

Personal Questions

From your study of Revelation 16, describe the events that take place prior to and at Armageddon.

a. By whose authority are the events leading to Armageddon ordered (verse 1)?

b. What do the seven bowls in verse 1 represent?

c. What did the first angel pour out on those worshiping the Antichrist (verse 2)?

d. What happened to the oceans as a result of the second angel's bowl (verse 3)?

e. What ironic interpretation did the third angel give to the effects of the third bowl judgment (verses 4–6)?

f. Who does the voice of the "altar" represent in verse 7 (see Revelation 6:9)? Why would this group agree with the angel's statement in verses 5–6?

g. What was the content of the fourth bowl judgment (verse 8)?

h. What occurred when the angel poured out the contents in the fifth bowl (verse 10)?

i. What did the sixth angel's bowl accomplish (verse 12)?

Group Questions

Read Revelation 16 and discuss the following questions:

a. How do we know that the Antichrist and his False Prophet will be demonically possessed (verses 13–14)?

b. Discuss the climactic events that occur when the seventh angel pours out his bowl (verses 17–21).

c. Compare the words coming from the temple (verse 17) with the words spoken in John 19:30. How are they two different aspects of the same conclusion?

d. What is the only way to avoid the calamitous events described in Revelation 16?

DID YOU KNOW?

We speak of the "battle" of Armageddon as if it was a one-time event—a single battle. In reality, it is more of a war or a campaign. The Greek word translated "battle" in the book of Revelation and other places in the New Testament occurs a total of eighteen times and is translated "wars" or "war" as often as battle. A war or military campaign is made up of many battles, and such will be the Battle of Armageddon. It will involve many battles fought throughout the land of Israel over a three-and-one-half year period of time. *The* Battle of Armageddon usually refers to the culminating event in which Christ defeats the gathered foes of God—the last battle in the lengthy war.

Notes
1. J. Vernon McGee, *Through the Bible, Vol. 3* (Nashville, TN: Thomas Nelson, 1982), 513.
2. Adapted from Carl G. Johnson, *Prophecy Made Plain for Times Like This* (Chicago, IL: Moody Press, 1972), 169–170.
3. John Walvoord with Mark Hitchcock, *Armageddon, Oil and Terror* (Carol Stream, IL: Tyndale House, 2007), 174.

PART 5

END

SIGNS

Return of the King

REVELATION 19:11–21

In this lesson we study the details of Christ's victory in earth's greatest battle.

Planet earth's most amazing day is yet to come: The largest amassing of armies in world history will turn their faces skyward to see Jesus Christ descending from the clouds with His own armies. By the word of His mouth, He will pronounce judgment upon all who rebel against God.

OUTLINE

I. **The Anticipation of Christ**

II. **The Advent of Christ**
   A. The Designation of Christ
   B. The Description of Christ

III. **The Armies of Christ**

IV. **The Authority of Christ**

V. **The Avenging of Christ**
   A. The Fowls of Heaven
   B. The Foes of Heaven

VI. The Application of Christ's Second Coming
  A. We Should Refrain from Judging Others
  B. We Should Remember the Lord's Table
  C. We Can Relate to One Another in Love
  D. We Can Recommit Ourselves to Ministry
  E. We Must Refuse to Neglect the Church
  F. We Must Reach the Lost for Jesus Christ

OVERVIEW

The first and second comings of Christ are both important—but they are very different. Note the following comparisons:

CHRIST'S FIRST COMING	CHRIST'S SECOND COMING
Clothed in swaddling clothes	Clothed in a robe dipped in blood
Surrounded by cattle and common people	Surrounded by armies of saints and angels
The door of the inn was closed to Him	The door of heaven is opened for Him
His voice was the cry of a baby	His voice is like the sound of many waters
The Lamb of God for salvation	The Lion of the Tribe of Judah for judgment

In this lesson, we examine the climax of all prophetic Scriptures: the return of Jesus Christ to earth to reign as King of kings and Lord of lords.

The Anticipation of Christ

Next to faith, the Second Coming of Christ is the most dominant subject in the New Testament. For every time the first advent of Christ is mentioned, the Second Coming is mentioned eight times. Jesus Himself is recorded as mentioning His Second Coming twenty-one times. There are 333 prophecies about Christ in the Bible, but only 109 were fulfilled at His first coming, leaving 224 to be fulfilled at the Second Coming.

Christ's Second Coming is mentioned throughout the Bible. Zechariah the prophet mentions it (Zechariah 14:4), angels mention it (Acts 1:11), Jesus declared He would return (Matthew 24:17, 29), the apostle John confirmed it (Revelation 1:7)—just to mention a few.

Never let anyone tell you that the Second Coming of Christ is immaterial to the message of the Bible. It is a central doctrine and must be taught as part of the whole counsel of God.

The Advent of Christ

Revelation 19 is the central prophetic passage in Scripture on the actual return of Jesus Christ to earth. When He returns, it will be to the same place from which He ascended: the Mount of Olives in Jerusalem (Acts 1:10–12).

The Designation of Christ

There are three names given to Christ in Revelation 19: "Faithful and True" (verse 11), "The Word of God" (verse 13), and "King of kings and Lord of lords" (verse 16). Those names represent Him and His ministry: His unchanging nature from eternity past (Hebrews 13:8), His incarnation as the living Word (John 1:14), and His future role as ruler of God's kingdom (Luke 1:32).

The Description of Christ

Revelation 19:12–13 gives a magnificent description of Christ: eyes like flaming fire and a head on which were many crowns, clothed in a robe dipped in blood. Eyes of fire mean there will be no posturing or pretending in His presence. His eyes will burn away all pretense and see men's hearts as they really are. The multiple crowns speak of His ultimate kingship over all the so-called kings of the earth, making Him worthy for every knee to bow before Him (Philippians 2:10). The robe dipped in blood reminds us that He is the Lamb who was "slain from the foundation of the world" (Revelation 13:8).

I believe throughout eternity the representation of the Lord Jesus Christ we will see is as the Lamb of God. We will see His nail-scarred palms and His spear-wounded side and be reminded for all eternity that He is the only reason we are there. We will have the same response that the apostle John had when he said, "Behold! The Lamb of God who takes away the sin of the world!" (John 1:29)

The Armies of Christ

In a previous lesson we noted that the armies who return with Christ are all the saints of the ages—having been in heaven since the Rapture, seven years prior—and the angels. In Revelation

19:14 we learn how we will appear: "clothed in fine linen, white and clean, [following] Him on white horses." Soldiers normally don't wear white into battle, but in this case it's okay because we are not actually going to enter into combat. It is the word of His judgment (the "sharp sword" going out of His mouth) that carries the day. Jude 14–15 gives the most detailed explanation of the reasons for this judgment: "to convict all who are ungodly among them of their ungodly deeds . . . and of all the harsh things which ungodly sinners have spoken against Him."

When Christ returns, it is primarily for judgment. Remember that most of the people on the earth at this time have rejected the 144,000 evangelists (Revelation 14:1) and the two witnesses (Revelation 11:3–14) that God sends during the Tribulation. In other words, they are deserving of judgment. God never sends judgment without first having sent a warning or an opportunity to believe. But a time will come when judgment is no longer delayed.

The Authority of Christ

When Christ returns, the parts of Isaiah 9:6–7 that were not fulfilled in His first coming will be fulfilled: He will assume His place on the throne of His forefather David and "of the increase of His government and peace there will be no end." There was never a time in His first coming that "the government [was] upon His shoulder." The Old Testament prophets saw truth in their prophetic vision—in this case, the complete picture of God's Messiah—but they did not always see the timing. They did not see the gap of time between His first and second coming.

When He returns, He will rule with the authority given to the throne of David in Israel. He will "strike the nations" and "rule them with a rod of iron" (Revelation 19:15). And there will be no end to His authority, government, and the resulting peace.

The Avenging of Christ

The Battle of Armageddon is where justice is meted out upon the ungodly on this earth (verses 17–21).

The Fowls of Heaven

An angel in heaven calls to "all the birds that fly in the midst of heaven" for them to "gather together for the supper of the great God"—meaning for them to consume the flesh of the armies killed in the last battle when Christ returns (verses 17–18). These are essentially vultures that come to pick over the bones of the dead after the massive destruction of humanity.

This supper to which the vultures are called is the second supper described in Revelation 19, the first being the Marriage Supper of the Lamb (verse 9)—the celebration of the union between Christ and His Church in heaven. I strongly suggest making reservations now for the Marriage Supper of the Lamb rather than "the supper of the great God."

The Foes of Heaven

Even though the Antichrist's doom is sealed, he still gathers the armies of earth to fight against the returning Christ.

1. The Futility of Fighting Against God

Verse 19 presents something almost unbelievable: "And I saw the beast, the kings of the earth, and their armies, gathered together to make war against Him who sat on the horse and against His army." The Antichrist is obviously a very intelligent human being, but this is not a smart move on his part—going up against the Son of God in battle. This is the ultimate act of rebellion of Satan, the one inspiring the Antichrist—a last-ditch effort to inspire humanity to shake its collective fist in the face of God. This attempt, like all others, will be futile.

2. The Fatality of the Beast and the False Prophet

The Beast and the False Prophet were captured and "were cast alive into the lake of fire burning with brimstone" (verse 20). The "lake of fire" is, of course, eternal hell. Satan, the one who inspired them, will end up there as well, but a thousand years later (Revelation 20:7-10). During the Millennium, Satan is confined but is set free near the end. He foments a rebellion against Christ but is judged and confined to the lake of fire along with the Beast and the False Prophet, where they will be "tormented day and night forever and ever" (Revelation 20:10).

It's a sad fact that nobody talks about hell anymore—especially preachers. But there's more in the Bible about hell than about heaven. It will be a shame someday for people to be facing an eternity in hell because the reality of that place was never mentioned in the churches they attended for years. Preachers shouldn't preach on hell every Sunday, but they definitely should preach on it when and where it occurs in the biblical text. To avoid it is to deny people the truth. The fact that Satan, the Antichrist, and the False Prophet all spend eternity there makes it an unsavory place for people to go. We ought to be honest about the reality of hell so at least people know what their future holds if they choose to reject Jesus Christ.

3. The Finality of Christ's Victory over Rebellion

With Satan bound for a thousand years, Christ will rule an earthly kingdom of peace, righteousness, and justice. He will sit on the throne and oversee the turning of implements of war into implements of agriculture and peace (Isaiah 2:4; Micah 4:3). There will be no war during the Millennium and only a short rebellion at the end when Satan is loosed from his chains in preparation for his judgment. Mankind will experience for the first time what it means to live under the rule and reign of God Himself.

The Application of Christ's Second Coming

Because of what is going on in the world—and will be going on in the future, I have six observations on how we should live in light of the coming end-time events.

We Should Refrain from Judging Others

In 1 Corinthians 4:5, the apostle Paul wrote, "Therefore judge nothing before the time, until the Lord comes, who will both bring to light the hidden things of darkness and reveal the counsels of the hearts. Then each one's praise will come from God."

In other words, when Christ returns, He will set all the accounts right; He will judge what needs to be judged—for believers before the Millennium (1 Corinthians 3:11–15) and unbelievers at the end of the Millennium (Revelation 20:11–15). But don't misunderstand this point: "Don't judge" doesn't mean we don't call "sin" sin. It doesn't mean we don't identify evil and wickedness and immorality where we see it and take a stand against it. It means we should not jump to conclusions and condemn people when we ourselves might be guilty of the same things (Matthew 7:3–5).

We Should Remember the Lord's Table

Second, we should be faithful in "[proclaiming] the Lord's death till He comes" (1 Corinthians 11:26) by participation in the Lord's Table. When we gather as a corporate body for Communion, we look back at the death of Christ and remind ourselves of why He died. But we do that knowing it is a temporary remembrance: We do it "until He comes." The Lord's Table keeps us mindful of Christ's death and His Second Coming at the same time.

We Can Relate to One Another in Love

First Thessalonians 3:12–13 says we should "increase and abound in love to one another and to all" so that our hearts might be "blameless . . . at the coming of our Lord Jesus Christ with all His saints."

All the saints of God will be united together in the army of Christ when we return with Him at the end of the Tribulation period when He executes judgment upon the ungodly nations of the earth. Since we are going to be united then, shouldn't we live united today? That is, shouldn't we be exercising love toward one another ("and to all") in all we do now? Since we are going to spend eternity together, it behooves us to begin to live that way in our earthly relationships. There is no convincing argument for why we shouldn't.

We Can Recommit Ourselves to Ministry

This next one is primarily an exhortation to preachers and teachers: "I charge you . . . preach the word! Be ready in season and out of season. Convince, rebuke, exhort, with all long-suffering and teaching" (2 Timothy 4:1–2). Preachers of the Word are to be faithful, saying exactly what God says—especially as the time nears for the return of Christ. And that applies to any who minister the Word in Christ's stead until He returns—Bible study leaders, Sunday school teachers, personal counselors, campus ministry discipleship leaders, and Bible teachers in Christian schools. As the time draws near for Christ's return, peoples' opportunities to respond to the Gospel or obey the Word of God become fewer. We must speak the truth—in love, yes (Ephesians 4:15)—but always the truth.

We Must Refuse to Neglect the Church

This exhortation is for every Christian, not just those who preach or teach the Word: "Not forsaking the assembling of ourselves together, as is the manner of some, but exhorting one another, and so much the more as you see the Day approaching" (Hebrews 10:25).

"The Day" is the day of Christ's coming for His Church. And as things begin to cycle downward in the last days, it will take being an active part of the body of Christ to "stir up love and good works" (verse 24) as things become more and more dark. Church attendance is not just for contributing money and singing worship songs. It is to be encouraged by the Word and the Spirit and by one another! It's not easy to maintain a faithful Christian walk in today's world, and the possibility is good that it is going to get more difficult in the future.

In light of that reality, it is amazing that church attendance is falling. Many Christians think nothing of skipping a Sunday morning service for the slightest of reasons. Don't be one of those. Be found in the midst of a corporate body of believers as often as possible to give and receive encouragement.

We Must Reach the Lost for Jesus Christ

Finally, we must take to heart the words of Jude: "And on some have compassion, making a distinction; but others save with fear, pulling them out of the fire" (verses 22–23).

The end times are nearer today than they were yesterday. That means we have less time than before to extend the saving Gospel of Christ to those who will end up with Satan, the

Antichrist, and the False Prophet in the lake of fire if they don't embrace it. And how will they hear without someone to tell them (Romans 10:14)? May you and I redouble our desire and effort to pull them "out of the fire."

And may our prayer be, with the apostle John, "Even so, come, Lord Jesus!" (Revelation 22:20)

APPLICATION

Personal Questions

1. Describe the setting of Luke 4:16–22. (When was it in Jesus' ministry; to whom was He speaking?)

   a. Compare the text of Isaiah 6:1–2 with Jesus' quotation of it in Luke 4:18–19. Find the key element from Isaiah that Jesus did not quote. (Hint: it's in Isaiah 61:2.)

   b. Why didn't Jesus quote that portion of Isaiah's prophecy?

   c. Separate the elements of Isaiah 61:1–2 into two categories: those pertaining to Christ's first coming and His second coming.

   Christ's First Coming   Christ's Second Coming

   _____   _____

   _____   _____

   _____   _____

   _____   _____

   _____   _____

   _____   _____

   d. How does Revelation 19:11–21 fulfill Isaiah 61:2?

2. Read Isaiah 11:1–10.

    a. Divide the elements of this passage into those pertaining to the first and second comings of Christ (list them by verses).

Christ's First Coming   Christ's Second Coming

    _____   _____

    _____   _____

    _____   _____

    _____   _____

    _____   _____

    _____   _____

    b. How do the prophets' visions parallel the way God sees time? That is, does God see past, present, and future separately or as one vision?

Group Questions

1. Discuss why the instructions in Isaiah 2:4 and Micah 4:3 are not contradictory to the instructions found in Joel 3:10. When were each intended to be fulfilled?

How are Isaiah 2:4 and Micah 4:3 fulfilled in Revelation 20:1–6?

2. What promise is given in Revelation 22:7 concerning the prophecies of the book of Revelation?

    a. What motivation should that provide for studying and teaching these prophecies?

    b. Share with the group how the lessons in this series have changed your own attitude about biblical prophecy and the future.

DID YOU KNOW?

George Frideric Handel's most well-known composition is *Messiah,* written in 1741, of which the most beloved section is the "Hallelujah Chorus." That chorus is based on three Scripture passages from Revelation that describe the Second Coming of Christ: (1) Revelation 11:15— "The kingdoms of this world have become the kingdoms of our Lord and of His Christ, and He shall reign forever and ever!" (2) Revelation 19:6—"Alleluia! For the Lord God Omnipotent reigns!" (3) Revelation 19:16— "And He has on His robe and on His thigh a name written: KING OF KINGS AND LORD OF LORDS."

Millennium

REVELATION 20:1–10

In this lesson we learn about Christ's future thousand-year rule over earth.

Imagine a TV nature show where you see a lion sneaking up on a bale of hay instead of an antelope. During the Millennium, peace will rule the earth—including the animals! Christ's kingdom will be characterized by peace, prosperity, purity, prolonged life, and personal joy.

OUTLINE

I. **Three Perspectives on the Millennium**
   A. Post-Millennialism
   B. A-Millennialism
   C. Pre-Millennialism

II. **Four Purposes of the Millennium**
   A. To Reward the People of God
   B. To Respond to the Prophets' Predictions
   C. To Receive the Answer to the Disciples' Prayer
   D. To Reemphasize Man's Depravity and the Necessity of Christ's Death

III. **Five Profiles of the Millennium**
   A. It Will Be a Time of Peace
   B. It Will Be a Time of Prosperity

C. It Will Be a Time of Purity
D. It Will Be a Time of Prolonged Life
E. It Will Be a Time of Personal Joy

OVERVIEW

Almost everyone knows the lyrics to Isaac Watts' famous hymn, "Joy to the World," but few people realize that it is not really a Christmas hymn. A quick look at the lyrics will explain why:

Joy to the world, the Lord is come!
Let earth receive her King;
Let every heart prepare Him room,
And heaven and nature sing . . . .
[Did mankind receive the King when Jesus was born at Bethlehem?]

Joy to the earth, the Savior reigns!
Let men their songs employ;
While fields and floods, rocks, hills and plains,
Repeat the sounding joy . . . .
[Has nature rejoiced at the coming of Christ?]

No more let sins and sorrows grow,
Nor thorns infest the ground;
He comes to make His blessing flow
Far as the curse is found . . . .
[Has the curse been lifted from the earth?]

He rules the world with truth and grace,
And makes the nations prove
The glories of His righteousness,
And wonders of His love . . . .
[Is Jesus ruling the nations of the world?]

The words of this great hymn more accurately describe the coming Millennium, the time when Christ will rule over the earth at His Second Coming, not His first. The Millennium will be a foretaste of the heavenly state that is to follow. Revelation 20:1–10 is the central passage in the Bible on the Millennium and will be our focus in this lesson.

"Millennium" is a Latin word made up of two words: *mille* means "thousand," and *annum* means "years." Therefore, combining the two yields millennium, or a period of 1,000 years. "Millennium" doesn't occur in our English Bibles, but the reference to a thousand-year period of time does—six times in Revelation 20:1–10. As we will see in this lesson, the Millennium is a period of 1,000 years that begins with Christ's Second Coming to earth. He establishes His kingdom in Jerusalem and brings in a period of peace and justice on the earth.

Christians through the years have viewed the Millennium from three different perspectives.

Three Perspectives on the Millennium

Few topics in Bible interpretation generate as much heat among Christians as does the Millennium because of the way one's view impacts other end-time events.

Post-Millennialism

The word "post," when used as a prefix, means "after." Therefore, Post-Millennialists believe that Christ's Second Coming will occur after the Millennium.

A Unitarian minister named Daniel Whitby originated this view in the mid-seventeenth century. This view suggests that the Church will saturate the world with the Gospel. Its impact on people and culture will be radical, transforming the earth into a place of peace and prosperity where the worship of God is universal. Christ will then return to inherit the peaceable kingdom that His Gospel has brought about.

Post-Millennialism was popular until World War I shattered the notion that mankind could ever bring about universal peace. Then World War II happened, further reinforcing the notion of man's sinfulness, not his goodness. This view has lost credibility ever since, as universal peace has been a rare commodity despite the spread of the Gospel.

A-Millennialism

The prefix "a" on a word acts to negate the meaning of the word (for example, "amoral" means "without morals"). Therefore, A-Millennialism means there will be no literal Millennium, no thousand-year period of time. The "thousand" in Revelation 20:1–10 is purely symbolic according to this view.

Proponents of this view believe the events described in Revelation 20:1–10 are happening now; they have been working themselves out in the Church over the last 2,000 years. The Church is reigning with Christ at present, this view holds. The peace and prosperity assigned to the Millennium is a spiritual peace and prosperity, not a literal one.

The key to this view is to spiritualize certain parts of the Bible—assigning spiritual meaning to literal words. That is, when the Bible says "a thousand years," it doesn't really mean a thousand literal years. There is a deeper spiritual meaning that is assigned to the text. The problems with that method of interpretation are obvious.

Pre-Millennialism

The prefix "pre" means "before." Pre-Millennialism teaches that the return of Jesus Christ to earth will happen before the Millennial period, not after (Post-Millennialism). Christ will defeat the enemies of God (the Battle of Armageddon) and establish a thousand-year reign of peace and justice on earth.

Here's a simple diagram showing where the Millennium fits in God's plan:

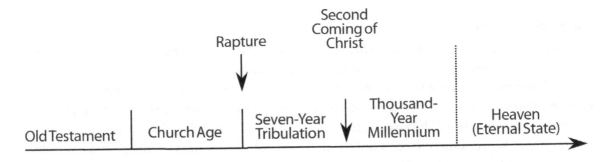

This diagram will be familiar to many as a diagram of Pre-Millennial eschatology (doctrine of the last things). At the Rapture, Christ returns in the air to remove His Church from the earth. Dead believers are resurrected and living believers follow them into the air, where they meet the Lord. The seven-year Tribulation ensues, concluded by the Battle of Armageddon where Christ returns to defeat the enemies of God. The Second Coming of Christ inaugurates the thousand-year reign of Christ, a time of universal peace on earth. At the conclusion of the Millennium, the Great White Throne Judgment consigns the wicked, the devil, and his angels to the lake of fire. The earth is renovated, the New Jerusalem descends upon the earth, and the eternal state begins.

The Pre-Millennial view holds that all the promises made to Israel in the Old Testament are fulfilled, and believing Jews are returned to their homeland in Israel to serve their Messiah, Jesus Christ.

The Pre-Millennial view is the oldest interpretation of Revelation 20:1–10 in Church history and is embraced by more evangelical Christians today than any other view of the Millennium.

Four Purposes of the Millennium

There are four purposes for the thousand-year period of time on earth, each supporting the necessity for a literal thousand-year period of time on earth.

To Reward the People of God

There are many promises in the Bible about rewards that are to be given to the people of God for their faithful service (Isaiah 40:10; Matthew 16:27; 25:34; Colossians 3:24; Revelation 22:12). A kingdom has been prepared, Jesus said, for those blessed of the Father as an inheritance (Matthew 25:34), and Paul said that Christians will receive the "reward of the inheritance" (Colossians 3:24).

This reward is different from the reward of the crowns we discussed in a previous lesson. The Millennial Kingdom is a reward by which we will reign and rule with Christ over the earth for 1,000 years (Matthew 19:28; 1 Corinthians 6:2; Revelation 20:4). When Christ returns to earth, He will bring with Him the saints who have believed in Him. The twelve apostles will sit on twelve thrones "judging the twelve tribes of Israel" (Matthew 19:28). Our responsibilities in the Millennium will be based on our faithfulness in this life (Matthew 25:14–30).

Randy Alcorn has written these helpful words on this subject: "Service is a reward, not a punishment. This idea is foreign to a lot of people who dislike their work and only put up with it until retirement. But God offers us something very different: more work, more responsibilities, increased opportunities, along with greater abilities, resources, wisdom, and empowerment. We will have sharp minds, strong bodies, clear purpose, and unabated joy."[1]

To Respond to the Prophets' Predictions

The second purpose of the Millennium is to fulfill the words of the Old Testament prophets. Without the Millennium, the Old Testament Scriptures are left open-ended and unfulfilled. Here are just a few that are yet to be fulfilled:

- Psalm 72:11: Kings and nations must worship Christ.
- Isaiah 9:7: The Messiah's government must be established on David's throne.
- Isaiah 60:21: Israel must turn to righteousness and inherit her land forever.
- Zechariah 9:10: The nations must live in peace under the Messiah's rule.
- Luke 1:32–33: Christ must rule over Israel as her Messiah in an unbroken rule.

Without the Millennium, these and many other prophecies would go unfulfilled. The focus of God's promises to Israel was that she was and is His chosen nation to be ruled over by the Prince of Peace. That has not happened yet, so it must happen in the future. Christ was rejected once by Israel (John 1:11), but He will ultimately be received by her (Zechariah 12:10). The kingdom that the apostles were looking for (Acts 1:6) will indeed come to pass for 1,000 years in the Millennium.

To Receive the Answer to the Disciples' Prayer

Jesus taught His disciples to pray, "Your kingdom come. Your will be done on earth as it is in heaven" (Matthew 6:10). That prayer, prayed innumerable times through the centuries of Church history, remains unanswered. With the Millennium will come the kingdom of God on earth—and the answer to the disciples' prayer.

To Reemphasize Man's Depravity and the Necessity of Christ's Death

Satan will be bound during the Millennium (Revelation 20:2–3). But the last phrase of Revelation 20:3 says he will be released for a "little while" at the end of the 1,000 years, at which time he will lead a rebellion against Christ, the King (Revelation 20:7–9).

People forget that during the 1,000 years on earth, the righteous believers who enter the kingdom will bear children, but righteousness is not inherited. The sin nature of man will still be alive and well, and some will not submit to the rule of King Jesus then any more than they do now—though with Satan being out of the picture for 1,000 years, the sin nature of man will not be enticed as it is now. But when Satan is released, he will stir up rebellion against God just as he did in the Garden of Eden.

This experience will demonstrate that sin is man's fundamental problem—not the environment, training, education, influences, or genetics. At the end of the Millennium, at the Great White Throne Judgment, no one will be able to blame their environment. Even with Christ on the throne in a righteous world, some will still choose to rebel.

Five Profiles of the Millennium

Following are five characteristics of the Millennium—what life will be like during the 1,000 years.

It Will Be a Time of Peace

It will take more than the United Nations to bring "peace on earth and goodwill toward men." Indeed, it will take God Himself. The Scriptures are full of predictions concerning the peace that one day will characterize planet earth. The famous words of Micah 4:3 are a well-known example:

> He shall judge between many peoples,
> And rebuke strong nations afar off;
> They shall beat their swords into plowshares,
> And their spears into pruning hooks;
> Nation shall not lift up sword against nation,
> Neither shall they learn war anymore.

Isaiah 11:6–9 is another well-known passage that indicates there will be peace even in the animal kingdom and between man and the beasts of the field. There will be no armies, no military budgets, and no wars. What the United Nations has tried to do, Jesus will bring to pass.

It Will Be a Time of Prosperity

Everyone is seeking prosperity in this world, but the Millennium will be a time of prosperity like nothing ever seen before. Most of the promises given to Israel concerning future prosperity were given in agricultural terms because that was common in that day. But the same environment that will allow agriculture to abound will also support prosperity in other endeavors as well.

Consider the words of Ezekiel 34:26–27 as an example:

> I will make them and the places all around My hill a blessing; and I will cause showers to come down in their season; there shall be showers of blessing. Then the trees of the field shall yield their fruit, and the earth shall yield her increase. They shall be safe in their land; and they shall know that I am the LORD, when I have broken the bands of their yoke and delivered them from the hand of those who enslaved them.

Amos 9:13 says, "The plowman shall overtake the reaper," and Isaiah 35:1 says, "The desert shall rejoice and blossom as the rose."

Prosperity will cover the earth like the morning dew.

It Will Be a Time of Purity

Sin will be kept in check, and disobedience will be dealt with efficiently. Christ's rule will be righteous, and His kingdom will be holy.

Isaiah 11:9 says, "The earth shall be full of the knowledge of the LORD as the waters cover the sea." And Zechariah 13:2 says, "I will cut off the names of the idols from the land, and they shall no longer be remembered. I will also cause the prophets and the unclean spirit to depart from the land."

An amazing thing will happen during the Millennium: "In those days ten men from every language of the nations shall grasp the sleeve of a Jewish man, saying, 'Let us go with you, for we have heard that God is with you'" (Zechariah 8:23). Christ's presence will be known and felt all over the earth, and many will willingly respond to His rule in submission.

It Will Be a Time of Prolonged Life

We know that life spans were hundreds of years long before the Flood in Genesis and declined steadily thereafter. But in the Millennium, people will once again live long lives. In fact, a 100-year-old person will be considered to be still a child (Isaiah 65:20). If a person 100 years old is viewed as a child, then it appears life spans will revert to pre-Flood lengths: 700, 800, and 900 years long. Science has failed to produce a "Fountain of Youth," but the Millennium will restore longevity to all inhabitants of planet earth.

It Will Be a Time of Personal Joy

Because of the rule of a righteous King whose justice will keep life in balance around the world, many of the causes of heartache will be removed. The Millennium will be a time of unprecedented joy as a natural by-product of peace. Isaiah 14:7 says, "The whole earth is at rest and quiet; they break forth into singing." When was the last time you heard people at a shopping mall break into singing because of their joy?

The day is coming, as Paul wrote, when every knee will bow and every tongue will confess that Christ is Lord (Philippians 2:10–11)—and it is called the Millennium. If you want to live to see that day, you must begin today by bowing and confessing that Jesus is Lord.

APPLICATION

Personal Questions

1. Read Isaiah 9:7.

   a. From whose throne would the coming Messiah rule over His kingdom?

   b. Of what would there be no end in His kingdom?

   c. By what two standards would the Messiah's kingdom be ordered and established?

d. When would the kingdom end once the coming Messiah took the throne?

e. Identify several traits of the Millennial Kingdom of Christ that are consistent with Isaiah's vision (Revelation 20:1–10).

2. What will those who have believed in Christ receive when He returns (Colossians 3:24)?

What will those rewards (responsibilities) be based on (Matthew 25:14–30; see verse 21)?

3. What did the disciples ask Christ before His ascension (Acts 1:6)?

a. What did Jesus teach His disciples to pray for while anticipating His return at the Millennium (Matthew 6:10)?

b. Which aspect of the Millennial Kingdom of Christ do you most anticipate (based on the reversal of the current conditions on earth)?

4. During the Millennium, where will Satan be (Revelation 20:2–3)?

a. Though he will initially be bound, what will occur at the end of the Millennium (Revelation 20:7–9)?

b. Despite sin being man's fundamental problem, in what ways can you prepare for the Millennial Kingdom today? (How can you practice righteousness on earth?)

Group Questions

1. Discuss the three perspectives on the Millennium as mentioned in this lesson:

a. Post-Millennialism:

b. A-Millennialism:

c. Pre-Millennialism:

2. Which view is the oldest interpretation of the Millennium (as found in Revelation 20:1–10)?

   a. According to this view of the Millennium, what event will occur directly before the thousand-year reign of Christ?

   b. What will occur directly after Christ's reign?

   c. During the Millennium, in what way will the living (animals and humans) dwell together (Isaiah 11:6–9)?

   d. How long will people live during the thousand-year reign of Christ? At what age will a "child" die (Isaiah 65:20)?

   e. The whole earth will be at _____ and _____ and will break forth into _____ at the Millennium (Isaiah 14:7).

3. What major event at the Millennium does Paul say will occur in the name of Jesus (Philippians 2:10–11)?

4. What do the following Old Testament Scriptures proclaim about Christ's reign?

   a. Psalm 72:11:

   b. Isaiah 9:7:

   c. Isaiah 60:21:

   d. Zechariah 9:10:

   e. Luke 1:32–33:

5. Discuss the connection you see in Paul's efforts on behalf of the Gentiles in Acts 15:19 and the prophet's anticipation of Gentiles entering the future kingdom of God (Isaiah 11:10; Amos 9:12).

DID YOU KNOW?

As mentioned in this lesson, the English word "millennium" is derived from two Latin words: *mille* (thousand) and *annum* (year). Within the Christian tradition, three schools of interpretation have developed about the Millennium or thousand-year rule of Christ mentioned in Revelation 20:1–6. Pre-Millennialists take this reign literally, the "pre" referring to Christ's return being before the Millennium as taught in this study guide. A-Millennialists believe the thousand years should be taken figuratively, not literally; that it refers to the present period in which Christ's victorious rule over Satan and death is experienced. And Post-Millennialists believe the Church creates a righteous reign on earth for 1,000 years, following which Christ returns.

Note
1. Warren W. Wiersbe, *Ephesians Through Revelation*, The Bible Exposition Commentary, vol. 2 (Colorado Springs, CO: David C. Cook, 2001), 621.

Great White Throne Judgment

REVELATION 20:11-15

*In this lesson we learn about the judgment awaiting those
who have not responded to God's Gospel of grace.*

Every human being who has not responded by faith to God's grace throughout human history will stand before Christ the Judge at the Great White Throne Judgment. There the books will be opened, and all will be found guilty and sentenced to eternal condemnation.

OUTLINE

I. **The Place of the Great White Throne**

II. **The Person on the Great White Throne**

III. **The People Before the Great White Throne**

IV. **The Purpose of the Great White Throne**
  A. The Book of Law
  B. The Book of Works
  C. The Book of Secrets
  D. The Book of Words
  E. The Book of Conscience
  F. The Book of Life

V. **The Punishment at the Great White Throne**

OVERVIEW

Most people are correct in believing a day of judgment is coming: "And as it is appointed for men to die once, but after this the judgment" (Hebrews 9:27). But beyond that fact, there is much misunderstanding. The final judgment of the human race has a number of variables, the most important being one's relationship with Jesus Christ.

For Christians, judgment takes place at the Judgment Seat of Christ immediately after the Rapture of the Church (Romans 14:10; 2 Corinthians 5:10). This judgment will take place in heaven, its purpose being to evaluate the quality of a believer's life—whether one's life has been lived by faith and obedience or not (1 Corinthians 3:12). The result of that judgment will determine the rewards a believer receives.

For non-Christians, their judgment will come at the Great White Throne, upon which Christ will sit as Judge (Revelation 20:11–15). Those who have rejected Christ and been unwilling to submit to Him as Lord will discover their eternal fate. Warren Wiersbe has described it this way: "At the White Throne, there will be a Judge but no jury, a prosecution but no defense, a sentence but no appeal. No one will be able to defend himself or accuse God of unrighteousness."[1]

These two judgments are based on the two resurrections mentioned in the Bible—the resurrection to life and the resurrection to condemnation (Daniel 12:2; John 5:28–29). Christians are resurrected at the Rapture of the Church, while nonbelievers are resurrected at the end of the Millennium for the Great White Throne Judgment. Everyone is resurrected, contrary to the teaching of some groups and individuals that only believers will be resurrected and that nonbelievers are annihilated at death and never resurrected. But that is not what the Bible teaches.

The resurrection of believers is called "the first resurrection" (Revelation 20:5–6). Included in it are Christians who are resurrected at the Rapture, martyred Tribulation believers, and Old Testament believers (Daniel 12:1–2; Isaiah 26:19) at the end of the Tribulation when Christ returns to establish his Millennial Kingdom. When Christ returns, all believers from all ages will have been resurrected—this is the first resurrection.

In Revelation 20, we learn about the second resurrection—the resurrection unto condemnation or judgment (verses 5, 12–15): "And I saw the dead, small and great, standing before God, and books were opened. . . . And the dead were judged according to their works, by the things which were written in the books" (verse 12). This resurrection takes place at the end of the Millennium, 1,000 years after the first resurrection. All the unsaved dead from Creation to the end of the Millennium will be included. After this resurrection, there will be no human bodies left in graves anywhere on earth.

It is on the Great White Throne Judgment that we focus in this lesson: the place, person, people, purpose, and punishment of that judgment.

The Place of the Great White Throne

We are not told exactly where this judgment will take place, but we can suggest where it will not take place: neither in heaven nor on earth. Both flee from the sight of Christ, the Judge (Revelation 20:11). And no sinner can enter the holy realm of heaven. Some scholars have suggested it will take place somewhere beyond our universe—somewhere between heaven and earth. More important than the location is the gravity of its description: Great (infinite, divine), White (holiness, purity, justice), and Throne (majesty of the Judge).

The Person on the Great White Throne

The Judge is none other than Christ Jesus Himself: "For the Father . . . has committed all judgment to the Son" (John 5:22, 27). Paul writes that God will "judge the secrets of men by *Jesus Christ*" (Romans 2:16, emphasis added). Peter declared that Christ was "ordained by God to be Judge of the living [the righteous] and the dead [the unrighteous]" (Acts 10:42). Christ will judge the spiritually living at the Judgment Seat of Christ and the spiritually dead at the Great White Throne Judgment.

The People Before the Great White Throne

As John viewed the Great White Throne, he saw the dead—all who died without a relationship with Jesus Christ. John says that this group will be made up of both "small and great"—an expression found often in the Old Testament and occurring five times in the book of Revelation (11:18; 13:16; 19:5, 18; 20:12). Everyone who stands before the Great White Throne Judgment, regardless of their status on this earth, will have this one thing in common: they died without Christ and they have no hope.

The Purpose of the Great White Throne

Revelation 20:12 says "books were opened . . . and the dead were judged according to their works, by the things which were written in the books." That is the purpose of the Great White Throne Judgment—to judge the unsaved on the basis of their works which are found recorded in the "books." We are told the name of only one of the books—"the Book of Life"

(Revelation 20:15)—but based on other parts of Scripture, we can surmise what the others might be.

The Book of Law

The Jewish leaders of Jesus' day thought they could merit salvation through obedience to the Law, and many Christians today make the same mistake. People cannot earn salvation through the Law unless they keep it perfectly, which we fallen humans cannot do. In Romans, Paul points out that salvation comes only through submitting to Christ and claiming His grace. As a result, there is "no condemnation to those who are in Christ Jesus" (Romans 8:1). Anyone who stands before the Judge claiming to be justified by the Law will be condemned by the Law—only those who are in Christ will be found not guilty before the Law.

The Book of Works

John saw in his vision that the unsaved were "judged, each one according to his works" (Revelation 20:13; see also Paul's words in 2 Corinthians 11:15 and Jesus' words in Matthew 16:27 on the same subject).

God will have a complete record of every moment of every person's life, everything done publicly and privately—that is, his or her works. This will be the ultimate test for those who believe their good works will get them into heaven. Because no one has lived a perfect or sinless life, no one's works will be sufficient. Becoming a Christian means we no longer gain salvation by our works but by the grace of God (Ephesians 2:8–10). Yes, Christians are expected to do good works, but they are the *result of*, not the *reason for*, salvation. The only way to pass from death to life—to bypass the Great White Throne Judgment—is through faith in Christ (John 5:24; Romans 8:1; Revelation 3:5).

The Book of Secrets

Jesus also said, "For nothing is secret that will not be revealed, nor anything hidden that will not be known and come to light" (Luke 8:17). Both Paul (Romans 2:16) and King Solomon (Ecclesiastes 12:14) made similar statements. No one would like the darkest secrets of his heart revealed, but the secrets of the unsaved will be made known at the Great White Throne Judgment.

The Book of Words

Jesus said men will give account of their words in the day of judgment: "By your words you will be justified, and by your words you will be condemned" (Matthew 12:36–37). No spoken word is ever lost. Those words will be brought back as a source of condemnation at the final judgment.

The Book of Conscience

In Romans 2:15, the apostle Paul talks about the human conscience and its role in guiding behavior. This suggests that one day the human conscience may play a role in judging human behavior. The conscience is not an infallible guide for life by any means. But when someone brazenly violates the terms of their own conscience, it shows a blatant disregard for the difference between right and wrong and may be used as condemning evidence at the final judgment.

The Book of Life

The only one of the "books" named is "the Book of Life" (Revelation 20:15), a book mentioned often in Scripture (Exodus 32:32–33; Psalm 69:28; Daniel 12:1; Philippians 4:3; Revelation 3:5; 13:8; 17:8; 21:27; 22:19).

Cities in John's day had a register that contained the name of every citizen. If a person committed a serious offense, he could be called before the town tribunal to witness the blotting out of his name from the register. That meant he was no longer considered a citizen of the town and would be forced to move elsewhere.

I believe this is a fair representation of the Book of Life—a "register" containing the name of every person born into this world but are subject to being removed. Revelation 3:5 has Christ stating that He "will not blot out [the name of the righteous] from the Book of Life; but I will confess his name before My Father and before His angels." Presumably, at the Great White Throne Judgment, a "blot" instead of a name in the Book of Life means that person will have no access to heaven.

The Punishment at the Great White Throne

John clearly saw what happens when a person's name is not found in the Book of Life: "And anyone not found written in the Book of Life was cast into the lake of fire" (Revelation 20:15). "Death and Hades" were also consigned to the lake of fire: "This is the second death" (Revelation 20:14).

The first death is experienced by humans (except those alive at the Rapture) when we die and our soul is separated from the body. In the second death, the physical body and spiritual soul, having been reunited, are cast into the lake of fire forever. The unsaved person, raised from the dead, is judged at the Great White Throne Judgment, found wanting, and is consigned to eternal separation from God. At the first death, the soul and body are separated for a time. At the second death, both body and soul are separated from God for eternity.

Both here, and in 2 Thessalonians 1:9 and Matthew 25:41, 46, the doctrine of eternal punishment is taught. It is not a pleasant or popular topic, but it is a biblical truth. The most graphic description of the fate of the unsaved is found in Revelation 14:9–11—the description of the fate of those who willingly receive the mark of the Beast, the Antichrist:

> Then a third angel followed them, saying with a loud voice, "If anyone worships the beast and his image, and receives his mark on his forehead or on his hand, he himself shall also drink of the wine of the wrath of God, which is poured out full strength into the cup of His indignation. He shall be tormented with fire and brimstone in the presence of the holy angels and in the presence of the Lamb. And the smoke of their torment ascends forever and ever; and they have no rest day or night, who worship the beast and his image, and whoever receives the mark of his name."

Scripture offers a grim picture of hell. It is a place of "torment and flames" (see Luke 16:24–28), a place of "wailing and gnashing of teeth" (Matthew 13:42), a place where the "worm does not die and the fire is not quenched" (Mark 9:48), and a place of "fire and brimstone" (Revelation 14:10, 11; 21:8). It is also the final abode of the Antichrist and the False Prophet (Revelation 19:20; 20:10). At the end of the Millennium, Satan is cast into the lake of fire to join the Antichrist and False Prophet, to be "tormented day and night forever and ever" (Revelation 20:10). Finally, after the Great White Throne Judgment, the unsaved are also cast into the lake of fire (Revelation 20:15).

Just as the believer at the Judgment Seat of Christ receives rewards based upon his or her good works, likewise, the unbelievers will receive degrees of punishment in the lake of fire on the basis of their sinful works. Jesus illustrated this principle with the cities of Chorazin, Bethsaida, and Capernaum. Because He spent lots of time there, and those cities had every opportunity to receive Him, their unbelief will be punished more severely than the cities of Tyre and Sidon (Matthew 11:20–24). So the degree of punishment is dependent on the degree of light available and how one responded to that light.

Think of Western nations where the Gospel has been available—through the local church, radio, television, the Internet, and in print—for many years. Our punishment will be far greater if we do not repent and receive God's forgiveness and grace. We have been given much! Because of that, we are more responsible before God than those who have not been given as many opportunities.

In Revelation 21, John tells us what kind of people end up in the lake of fire: "But the cowardly, unbelieving, abominable, murderers, sexually immoral, sorcerers, idolaters, and all liars shall have their part in the lake which burns with fire and brimstone, which is the second death" (Revelation 21:8). The "unbelieving" are listed among all the morally evil people in God's sight. One does not have to be the worst sinner in the world to land in the lake of fire;

one just has to be an unbelieving sinner. There are only two choices: accept Him now as Lord and Savior, or face Him as Judge at the end of the Millennium.

The book of Revelation is like all prophecy: It is an accurate foretelling of future events to provide an opportunity to prepare for and respond to that which will unfold. Those who hear and believe God's Word will not "come into judgment, but [will pass] from death into life" (John 5:24).

APPLICATION

Personal Questions

1. When and where will Christians be judged? And when and where will unbelievers be judged?

   a. What is the basis for these two judgments?

   b. How is the judgment of non-Christians described?

   c. Who is the Judge who presides at these judgments?

   d. What about unbelievers' lives will not matter when they are judged?

2. Describe the first and second deaths.

   a. Who experiences the first death?

   b. Who experiences the second death?

3. Where will the Antichrist, the False Prophet, Satan, and unbelievers spend eternity?

4. How do the following Scriptures describe hell?

    a. Luke 16:28:

    b. Matthew 13:42:

    c. Mark 9:48:

    d. Revelation 14:9–11:

    e. Revelation 21:8:

5. What is the degree of punishment for unbelievers in hell based upon?

6. What is the only way to bypass the Great White Throne Judgment?

7. How does the reality of the Great White Throne Judgment convict you to share the Gospel with unsaved family and friends?

Group Questions

1. Discuss the two resurrections which are the basis for the two judgments.

    a. Who is included in each resurrection?

    b. Those resurrected in the second resurrection are resurrected to what?

2. Describe the books mentioned in Revelation 20:12.

   a. What book is specifically named in Revelation 20:15?

   b. Whose names will be blotted out of this book?

   c. Based on Scripture, what can we surmise the other books may be?

   d. Why is it impossible to earn salvation by obeying the Law?

   e. Why are good works not enough to gain entrance into heaven?

3. Share how this lesson compels you to share the Gospel with others.

   a. What are some avenues you can use to share Christ with those around you?

   b. What steps can you take this week to be a witness for Christ?

   c. How can you as a group encourage and help each other share Christ with others?

DID YOU KNOW?

The image of the "judgment seat of Christ" (Romans 14:10; 2 Corinthians 5:10) is taken from first-century culture. The judgment seat (*bema* in Greek) was used in trial and judicial settings where an authority would sit while rendering judgment. It is referred to during the trials of Christ (Matthew 27:19; John 19:13) and the trials of Paul (Acts 18:12; 25:6). Paul used that familiar image when referring to the meeting between Christians and Jesus Christ where believers' works (not their salvation) will be evaluated. The purpose of this judgment is to separate works done in the flesh for self from works done by faith for Christ (1 Corinthians 3:11–15).

Note

1. Warren Wiersbe, *Be Victorious: In Christ You Are an Overcomer* (Colorado Springs, CO: David C. Cook, 2010) 176.

New Heaven and New Earth

2 PETER 3:10-13;
REVELATION 21:1, 5; 22:3

In this lesson we learn that planet earth is our eternal home.

There has been much confusion about the fate of planet earth. Some have read the Bible's words about fire and burning to mean that the earth will be obliterated at the end of the age. Not so. There will be fire, but it will be restorative instead of destructive. The earth is our home forever.

OUTLINE

I. **The Promise of a New Heaven and a New Earth**

II. **The Purification of the New Heaven and New Earth**
   A. The Information (2 Peter 3:10, 12)
   B. The Interpretation
   C. The Illustration (2 Peter 3:5–7)

III. **The Principles of the New Heaven and New Earth**
   A. The Removal of the Sea (Revelation 21:1)
   B. The Reversal of the Curse (Revelation 22:3)
   C. The Restoration of All Things (Ephesians 1:10)

OVERVIEW

History is filled with man's efforts to establish some kind of heaven on earth. It even shows up in the efforts of politicians when they make promises to make things better, or different, to right the wrongs of the past and create an environment where man can reach his true potential. President Roosevelt offered "The New Deal" and President Johnson proposed "The Great Society." Intellectuals like Leo Tolstoy in Russia and Henry David Thoreau in New England made efforts to create utopian living conditions. Even Lenin's Communism was an effort to create a workers' paradise where greed would be outlawed and all would prosper equally.

Of course, none of these efforts achieved what their proponents envisioned. But it was not because they longed for something unattainable. In the heart of every person is a longing for something perfect based on the eternity that God has put in every human heart (Ecclesiastes 3:11). Indeed, the idea is a godly one—and it takes God to achieve it. That is exactly why the God-Man, Jesus Christ, taught His disciples to pray, "Your kingdom come. Your will be done on earth as it is in heaven."

This prayer will be answered, but not during earth's current economy. There's no way, when sin and death are rampant on earth, that utopia will be achieved. But the hope for a "golden age" is legitimate and in the heart of every human being. Indeed, it is that hope that allowed many saints of old to endure suffering in their lives while on this earth (Hebrews 11:14–16).

The human race is homesick for the Garden of Eden. In this lesson, we will look at the Scriptures that point to the new heaven and new earth that God will one day bring to pass.

The Promise of a New Heaven and a New Earth

The prophets of the Old Testament saw a new heaven and new earth coming that would last forever—one so wonderful that the former earth would not even be remembered (Isaiah 66:22; 65:17). The apostle Peter also wrote, "We . . . look for new heavens and a new earth in which righteousness dwells" (2 Peter 3:13).

The writer to the Hebrews quotes Psalm 102, which talks about the heavens and the earth perishing and growing old. Then he writes, "Like a cloak You will fold them up, and they will be changed . . ." (Hebrews 1:12; see also Psalm 102:25–27). The writer to the Hebrews says God is going to one day take this world and, like a coat, fold it up and put it away and make everything new. And, as you might expect, John saw a new heaven and new earth in his vision on Patmos: "Now I saw a new heaven and a new earth, for the first heaven and the first earth had passed away" (Revelation 21:1; see also verse 5).

So the idea of a new heaven and a new earth, ones better than our current ones, is biblical.

The Purification of the New Heaven and New Earth

Next, we must consider how the transformation takes place. How do the new heaven and earth come to be?

The Information (2 Peter 3:10, 12)

There is not room in this lesson to go into all the relevant Scriptures, but here is the basic timeline for when the new heaven and new earth will come to pass. First, there will be a seven-year period of tribulation on the earth terminated by the Battle of Armageddon and brought to an end with the return of Christ to the earth. Christ then rules over all the earth for 1,000 years (the Millennium). At the end of the Millennium, Satan leads a final rebellion that is put down by Christ, after which Satan is cast into the lake of fire. The Great White Throne Judgment will then consign all who have rejected Christ to the lake of fire as well.

After all of this, the last thing that happens on this earth—or to this earth—is described by Peter: "The heavens will pass away with a great noise, and the elements will melt with fervent heat; both the earth and the works that are in it will be burned up. . . . The heavens will be dissolved, being on fire, and the elements will melt with fervent heat" (2 Peter 3:10, 12).

The Interpretation

That's the information—now, what does it all mean? Many have heard this event described as something like a nuclear conflagration—the earth dissolving in an indescribable ball of fire. Randy Alcorn has verbalized his own change of thinking on this subject, which parallels my own: "For many years as a Bible student and later as a pastor, I didn't think in terms of renewal or restoration. Instead, I believed God was going to destroy the earth, abandon His original design and plan, and start over by implementing a new plan in an unearthly heaven. Only in the past fifteen years have my eyes been open to what Scripture has said all along."[1]

Peter's words about burning and fire certainly sound like . . . well, burning and fire. But the original Greek does not suggest that interpretation. The New International Version has a more accurate rendering: "The earth and everything done in it will be laid bare." The idea is that of being uncovered, not destroyed; purified, not burned up. The material elements of the current earth will disintegrate and fall apart, and out of what remains, God will create something new.

There are two words for "new" in the Greek language. The one Peter uses (2 Peter 3:13) is the word that means new in terms of quality, not new in terms of never existing before. That means the new earth is not something that is brand new but a new version of the original. It is the original earth, but in a renovated and refreshed form. At the end of the Millennium, after all the judgments and prior to the beginning of the eternal state, all the decay and corruption of the earth is going to be taken away. All evidence of disease and destruction and depravity, insofar as it impacted the physical earth, will be eliminated; the present earth will be cleansed, purified, and made new.

Commentator William Hendriksen describes the change this way: "The first heavens and the first earth have passed away. . . . The very foundations of the earth have been subjected to purifying fire. Every stain of sin, every trace of death has been removed. Out of the great conflagration, a new universe has been born. The word used in the original implies that it was new, but not 'other.' It is a new world, but not another world. It is the same heaven and [the same earth,] but gloriously rejuvenated."[2]

God's original declaration that the earth was "very good" (Genesis 1:31) has not been rescinded. He is not going to destroy His original creation—just make it pure once again as it was in the beginning.

Again, Randy Alcorn says: "God doesn't throw away His handiwork and start from scratch—instead, He uses the same canvas to repair and make more beautiful the painting marred by the vandal. The vandal doesn't get the satisfaction of destroying his rival's masterpiece. On the contrary, God makes an even greater masterpiece out of what His enemy sought to destroy."[3]

The Illustration (2 Peter 3:5–7)

Fortunately, Peter gives us an illustration to help us picture the renovation that is to come upon the earth: the Flood in Noah's day. The Flood in Genesis did not annihilate the earth. In fact, the water that covered the earth is a good picture of "cleansing." Indeed, the earth remained in order for Noah and his family to inhabit it after the Flood receded. Likewise, the fire that comes upon the earth at the end of the age will not destroy the earth but renovate it.

The Principles of the New Heaven and New Earth

We now look at what the new heaven and new earth are going to be like. What kind of home will a renovated earth be?

The Removal of the Sea (Revelation 21:1)

One of the most surprising things we learn from Revelation 21:1 is that there will be no more sea—the oceans are gone! Three-fourths of our present world is covered by oceans, so this will certainly be something new.

Here is the explanation by world-renowned scientist, the late Dr. Henry Morris:

> There will be, in fact, no need for a sea on the new earth. The present sea is needed for a reservoir for the maintenance of the hydrologic cycle.... In the new earth, all men and women who live there will have their glorified bodies with no more need of water. Their resurrected bodies will be composed, like that of the Lord Jesus, of flesh and bone but apparently with no need of blood to serve as a cleanser and restorer of the body's flesh as it is at present. This, in turn, eliminates the major need for water on earth (blood is 90 percent water, and present-day human flesh is about 65 percent water).[4]

In other words, the ecology of the new earth will be completely different from that of the present earth. The New Jerusalem will have a fresh water river flowing from the throne of God, watering the trees of life growing on its shores. But there will be no salt-water oceans. Since salt is a preservative, and there will be no decay, no salt will be needed.

The Reversal of the Curse (Revelation 22:3)

If you recall, the curse in Genesis 3 is what created our present earth environment. When Adam and Eve disobeyed God in the Garden of Eden, it resulted in God cursing the earth. The ground was cursed, causing it to produce thistles and thorns and making it difficult to grow food. Only by the sweat of his brow would Adam and his descendants be able to eke out a living. The most important part of the curse was death: Adam and Eve and their descendants would not live forever. Death became a part of the culture of planet earth.

In the new heaven and new earth, the curse will be reversed—there will be no more death. Thorns and thistles—and tombstones—will disappear from the ground. The redemption accomplished by Christ not only delivers man from death but also the earth from the effects of sin as well.

The Restoration of All Things (Ephesians 1:10)

We read Ephesians 1:10 without noticing an important point: In "the fullness of the times" God is going to "gather together in one all things in Christ, *both which are in heaven and which are on earth*—in Him" (emphasis added).

Today there is a great division between heaven and earth—God is in heaven, and man is on earth. But God is going to bring all things together under one head: Christ. Heaven and earth will be united into one new universe, ruled by the Lord Jesus Christ. The wall that divides heaven and earth today will be torn down.

We have said previously that the New Jerusalem will be our domicile as the capital city of heaven. But the New Jerusalem will be on the renovated earth. After all, what purpose would there be at the end of the Millennium for God to renovate the earth if no one was going to live on it? Some Christians are disappointed when they find out they're going to be living on earth instead of "in heaven." But it's at this point that "heaven on earth" will finally become a reality.

This is a bit of a paradigm shift for many believers, but it can lead to two new appreciations for those who embrace it.

1. A New Appreciation for the World in Which We Now Live

Christians have a reputation for not being very good ecologists. Our mentality of being taken off the earth and spending eternity in heaven has caused us not to give the attention this earth deserves. And that violates our commission to be good stewards of the earth (Genesis 1:26).

But that changes when we realize that this earth is going to be our eternal home. Yes, it will be a new earth, but the same earth nonetheless. That fact should cause us to look at this earth with a new set of eyes and view it differently.

The apostle John wrote that we should not love this world (1 John 2:15), but he didn't mean the physical world. He meant the spiritual systems of this world, empowered by Satan. But we should love and care for this planet that God has given us as a home. The fact that it is going to be our refurbished home for eternity should give us a new appreciation for it today.

2. A New Anticipation of the World to Which We Are Going

We think the starry heavens are beautiful now—and they are! But the beauty of the heavens now is nothing compared to the beauty we will one day experience. It will be a place characterized by laughter without tears and life without death and singing without mourning and contentment without crying and pleasure without pain. And our Lord and Savior, Jesus Christ, will be there as well as our loving heavenly Father and the blessed Holy Spirit. And there will be a resplendent, brilliant, and sparkling city called the New Jerusalem that will be our heavenly home.

When I think of what awaits me in heaven—and specifically, the new heaven and the new earth—I can hardly contain my excitement.

I hope you feel the same way and that you will remember the way to get there. Jesus Christ said, "I am the way, the truth, and the life. No one comes to the Father except through Me" (John 14:6). If you want to be there—and I hope you do—you can only get there through Him.

APPLICATION

Personal Questions

1. Read 2 Peter 3:1–14.

   a. What is Peter's purpose in writing to the believers in his letters (verses 1–2)?

   b. What is his first warning to them (verse 3)?

   c. What claim will end-time scoffers make (verse 4)?

   d. What key events in history do they fail to remember (verses 5–6)?

   e. How are those events tied to what will happen in the future (verse 7)?

   f. What do you imagine scoffers might have said to Noah in his day as he built the ark?

   g. What are the "heavens and the earth" being reserved for at the present time (verse 7)?

   h. Why is time never the issue when it comes to the fulfillment of God's plans (verses 8–9)?

   i. What will happen to the earth we now live on (verses 10, 12)?

   j. What are Christ followers looking for as a "replacement" for the current heavens and earth (verse 13)?

   k. What will be the distinguishing characteristic of the new heaven and new earth (verse 13)?

   l. What should characterize your life as you wait for God's refurbishing of the earth (verse 14)?

2. What part of the new heaven and new earth do you most anticipate enjoying?

Group Questions

1. Discuss why the heavens and earth need to be renovated (made righteous; 2 Peter 3:13) before the New Jerusalem descends to the earth (Revelation 21:1–2).

   How will the current heavens and earth pass away (Hebrews 1:12; Psalm 102:25–27)?

2. Read Isaiah 65:17–25 and answer the following questions:

   a. What did Isaiah's messianic vision of the future entail (verse 17)?

   b. How does Isaiah's vision of Jerusalem correspond to what you have learned about the coming New Jerusalem in Revelation 21 (verses 18–19)?

   c. List the various "idyllic" signs of God's blessing on Jerusalem and the new heaven and new earth in verses 20–25.

3. Turn to Ephesians 1:10 and answer the following questions:

   a. Currently, though there is a division between heaven and earth, what is God going to do "in the fullness of times"?

   b. Under whom will these things be brought together?

   c. What are we to do on earth until that time (see Genesis 1:26)?

   d. According to the apostle John, what are we not to do (1 John 2:15)? What part of this world did he reference?

4. Share some ways in which you can care for this earth while anticipating the new heaven and new earth that are to come.

DID YOU KNOW?

The end of the age and the appearing of the new heaven and new earth will happen in the "dispensation [or administration, NASB] of the fullness of the times" (Ephesians 1:10). The word "dispensation" (or administration) translates the Greek *oikonomia*, from which we get our English word "economy." Just as modern governments put together economic plans for sustaining their nations, so God has an "economy," or plan, for the sustaining of His kingdom on planet earth. That plan calls for God to "gather together in one all things in Christ, both which are in heaven and which are on earth" (Ephesians 1:10).

Notes

1. Randy Alcorn, *Heaven* (Wheaton, IL: Tyndale House Publishers, 2004), 89.
2. William Hendriksen, *More Than Conquerors* (Grand Rapids. MI: Baker, 1982), 198.
3. Alcorn, *Heaven,* 100.
4. Henry Morris, *The Revelation Record* (Wheaton, IL: Tyndale House Publishers, 1983), 436.

Holy City

REVELATION 21–22

In this lesson we discover the glory of the New Jerusalem, our heavenly home.

Parts of heaven are like folklore—"streets of gold," "pearly gates," and the like. But the city called the New Jerusalem is not fable or fancy; it is a literal city that will be the eternal capital of heaven. Believers who intend to live there should become familiar with their future home.

OUTLINE

   I. The Dimensions of the City

  II. The Description of the City
    A. The Holy City
    B. The Pearly Gates
    C. The Foundations of Precious Stones
    D. The Streets of Gold
    E. The Lamb That Is the Light
    F. The Tree of Life
    G. The River of Life

 III. The Denial to the City

My wife and I have had the privilege of traveling to many of the world's most beautiful cities. After growing up in a small town in Ohio called Cedarville, I went away to seminary in Dallas, Texas, and became a confirmed big-city person.

There are a lot of big cities in the United States. Sitka, Alaska, is the largest geographically (4,811 square miles—larger than Delaware!), and Jacksonville, Florida, is the largest geographically in the lower forty-eight states (885 square miles). New York City, of course, is the largest in terms of population in the United States, but there are a few cities in the world that have larger populations than New York. In terms of greater metropolitan areas, Tokyo has nearly thirty-eight million people, New York City has close to twenty-one million, and Mexico City has about twenty million.

To put all that in perspective, the largest city in AD 100 was Rome, with a population of only 400,000. Today there are more than 100 cities in China with more than a million people, more than forty-five in the Americas, at least thirty-six in Europe, and about fifteen in Africa. By the year 2030, more than sixty percent of the world's inhabitants will be living in cities.

As great as the cities of our world are, they cannot compare with the city God is building for His children to inhabit for eternity. This city is mentioned almost a dozen times in Revelation 21–22, and not metaphorically—it is an actual physical city where God and His people will live together forever. This city has been mentioned numerous times throughout Scripture as the eventual destination of man's pilgrimage (Hebrews 11:10; 12:22; Galatians 4:26; Revelation 3:12). Not surprisingly, this city is called the New Jerusalem.

The New Jerusalem is not synonymous with heaven. Rather, it is a city in the third heaven. John said he saw the New Jerusalem coming down *out of heaven* (Revelation 21:2, emphasis added). We can assume from Scripture that God is preparing the New Jerusalem to become the capital, so to speak, of heaven in the future. Jesus called the New Jerusalem "the city of My God" (Revelation 3:12). This is the city Jesus referred to in John 14:3 when He told His disciples He was going to prepare a place for them. According to some Bible scholars, during the Millennium, the thousand-year reign of Christ on earth, the New Jerusalem will hover over the earth. Then, after the Millennium, in the eternal state, it will rest on the renovated earth and serve as the focal point of life in eternity.

Its dimensions and description certainly qualify it to be a focal point!

The Dimensions of the City

People often wonder how all the believers from history are going to fit into heaven and, specifically, the New Jerusalem. The basic dimensions of the city are given in Revelation 21:15–16. It is actually a cube 1,500 miles in length, height, and width. That means it covers more than two million square miles of land area. That makes the city, in terms of land area, twenty times larger than New Zealand, ten times larger than Germany, ten times larger than France, and forty times larger than England. It is even larger than India.[1]

J. B. Smith has compared the New Jerusalem to the United States this way: "If you compare the New Jerusalem to the United States, you would measure from the Atlantic Ocean coastal line and westward, it would mean a city from the furthest Maine to the furthest Florida, and from the shore of the Atlantic to Colorado. And from the United States' Pacific coast eastward, it would cover the United States as far as the Mississippi River, with the line extending north through Chicago and continuing on the west coast of Lake Michigan, up to the Canadian border."[2]

A single city that large—and remember, it is a cube, so it extends upward as far as it does outward—is difficult to comprehend. But the same God who spoke the planets into existence will have no trouble building and deploying a city that large onto planet earth. If you're wondering about transportation inside such a structure, remember that our glorified bodies will be different, that the Lord Jesus simply appeared in a room with the disciples after His resurrection, unhindered by physical barriers.

The cubic design of the New Jerusalem should come as no surprise—the Holy of Holies inside the temple in Jerusalem was a cube: 20 x 20 x 20 cubits. And Revelation 21:3 refers to the New Jerusalem as the "tabernacle of God." So just as God's dwelling place on earth was a cube, so will the New Jerusalem, His eternal "tabernacle," be a cube as well.

The Description of the City

In reading the following seven descriptions of the New Jerusalem, be aware that many people allegorize, or spiritualize, these elements of the city. They simply can't imagine that anything like what John describes in Revelation could possibly exist one day. I choose to submit my human reason and understanding to the Word of God and view these descriptions literally. I can't imagine how God could have created the heavens and the earth either, but I choose to believe that He did. Likewise, I choose to believe the amazing descriptions of the New Jerusalem we are given in Scripture.

The Holy City

First, we read in Revelation 21:2 that the New Jerusalem is a "holy city." I've seen some big cities in the world, but I've never seen a holy one. Here's how the *Wycliffe Bible Commentary* describes the holy city: "A holy city will be one in which no lie will be uttered in one hundred million years, no evil word will ever be spoken. No shady business deals will ever be discussed, no unclean picture will ever be seen, no corruption of life will ever be manifest. It will be holy because everyone in it will be holy."[3]

Only those who have been cleansed of their sins by the blood of Christ will be able to enter the holy city.

The Pearly Gates

The "pearly gates" of heaven have assumed the status of folklore, but they are real (see Revelation 21:2, 17–18). Revelation 21:21 says, "The twelve gates were twelve pearls: each individual gate was of one pearl." The gates have the names of the twelve tribes of Israel on them and are part of a city that glimmers and shines like a sparkling jewel, given the gold and precious jewels of which it is made.

W. A. Criswell has pointed out that pearls are formed in oysters as a result of a wound, and that we'll be reminded as we go in and out of the gates of pearl that we are there only because of the wounds of Christ.[4]

The Foundations of Precious Stones

A twelve-layer foundation of the city is built from twelve precious stones: emeralds, sapphires, topaz, and the like (see Revelation 21:19–20). Looking at these layers of beautiful stones will be like looking at a shimmering rainbow with light reflecting off of and through them into the city.

The Streets of Gold

Heaven's streets of gold are also part of folklore to many, but they couldn't be more real: "The street of the city was pure gold, like transparent glass" (Revelation 21:21). Gold as we know it is not transparent. Perhaps this refers more to translucence than transparency due to the purity of the gold. It's hard to say how we will see and perceive things in our glorified bodies compared to how we perceive them today. But one way or another, what John saw was streets of transparent gold. And I believe they will look that same way to us when we see them.

The Lamb That Is the Light

There will be no lights in the New Jerusalem: "The Lamb is its light" (Revelation 21:23). The glory of God will illuminate the entire city (Isaiah 60:19).

Imagine approaching the city from a distance—a city of gold, a twelve-layer foundation, gates of pearl, streets of gold, fully illuminated from within by the glow of the glory of God. No wonder Paul wrote, "Eye has not seen, nor ear heard, nor have entered into the heart of man the things which God has prepared for those who love Him" (1 Corinthians 2:9).

You've heard it said that some people are "so heavenly minded they're no earthly good." I believe we should all be more heavenly minded, not less. God has prepared an unbelievable place in which we will live for eternity, yet we rarely talk about it, and most Christians know little about it at all. We might be more earthly good if we were more heavenly minded!

The Tree of Life

There is a river flowing through the middle of the New Jerusalem, and on either side are growing the trees of life ("trees" is plural in the original). There are twelve trees of life "which bore twelve fruits, each tree yielding its fruit every month" (Revelation 22:2). We will eat from these trees freely—which raises the issue of eating in heaven. I believe we will eat as much as we want, without any of the negative ramifications of our earthly appetites. Our appetites in heaven will be redeemed along with the rest of us, so our perspective on food will be different.

The leaves of the trees are for "the healing of the nations." "Healing" is the Greek word for therapy; so this healing is not the healing of diseases, but healing in a therapeutic sense: growing in our sense of fulfillment, pleasure, and joy at being in the presence of God.

The River of Life

The last thing we'll highlight is the "pure river of water of life, clear as crystal, proceeding from the throne of God and of the Lamb" (Revelation 22:1–2). This sounds like Psalm 46:4: "There is a river whose streams shall make glad the city of God." It also calls to mind the "living water" Jesus said would flow from the heart of those who believe in Him (John 7:38).

The New Jerusalem will be something impossible to comprehend in its glory while we are on earth. But it will be the future home of every person who has been a believer, children who have died without the chance to believe, and those not mentally capable of believing the Gospel. The cube-city will be large enough to sustain all those millions of people at a level of glory and satisfaction far beyond anything ever experienced on earth. It will be beautiful and radiant—words fail to describe its glory.

There is an island-city in Greece called Santorini that is built on the top of an ancient volcano. It sits high on a cliff and is a fascinating place to visit—all the houses and shops are painted white. When you approach Santorini from the sea, you look up and see this gleaming white city that appears to be suspended in the air above the sea. It is an amazing sight! When I saw it on one occasion, I said to myself that even such a place as beautiful as Santorini cannot compare to the beauty of the New Jerusalem. One day when we enter the holy city of God, our mouths will fall open at the beauty that God has prepared for us as evidence of His love.

The Denial to the City

It is unfortunate, but not every person that has lived on earth will gain entrance to the heavenly city. In Revelation 21:8 we read, "But the cowardly, unbelieving, abominable, murderers, sexually immoral, sorcerers, idolaters, and all liars shall have their part in the lake which burns with fire and brimstone, which is the second death."

Verse 27 also says, "But there shall by no means enter it anything that defiles, or causes an abomination or a lie, but only those who are written in the Lamb's Book of Life."

The Bible doesn't say that people who have ever committed any of these sins will not enter the New Jerusalem. It refers to these sins as lifestyles. And those people who have practiced those sins willingly and have never repented and received the forgiveness of their sins through Christ. Every person who enters the New Jerusalem will be a person who has sinned, and in many cases the sins will be some of those listed above. But they will be sins that have been repented of and forgiven and that no longer characterize the life of the one who once committed them.

Our calling as Christians today is to go throughout the world as Christ's ambassadors, telling people of the place God has prepared for them and inviting them to accept Christ's invitation to come to Him to be made ready for the city of God. We get that message out every way we can: in person, in print, on television and radio, the Internet—whatever is available, we will use. After reading the glorious description of the city God has prepared for us, doesn't it break your heart to know that some may not get to enjoy it? They at least need to know of the opportunity. If they reject Christ's invitation, that is one thing. But if they die without having heard of the opportunity, that is another. And we are accountable for their failure to hear the Good News that is for them.

Don't let "pearly gates" and "streets of gold" lull you into a false security about some pie-in-the-sky place that doesn't exist. Heaven is real, and so is the New Jerusalem. But it is only for those who have received the forgiveness of sins Christ offers that makes them pure enough to enter the holy city of God. Make sure that you are one of those who has made a reservation to stay in the New Jerusalem for all eternity. If you wait until the city appears, it will be too late.

APPLICATION

Personal Questions

1. What did the apostle John see descending out of heaven in his vision in Revelation 21 (verse 2)?

a. What is the meaning of the "bride" metaphor (Revelation 21:2; see Ephesians 5:25–27)?

b. Contrast the words in Revelation 21:3 with John 1:11, 14 in terms of God coming to dwell among men.

c. How will the New Jerusalem be different from the old Jerusalem (Revelation 21:4)?

d. What is the primary difference between the old and new Jerusalems mentioned in Revelation 21:22?

e. Why will there be no need for a temple (Revelation 21:3; compare Exodus 25:8)?

f. Where is the New Jerusalem to be located (Revelation 21:24; compare 2 Peter 3:13)?

2. Turn to "The Denial to the City." Will every person gain entrance into the heavenly city?

a. Only who will dwell in the New Jerusalem (Revelation 21:27)?

b. Who will not dwell there (Revelation 21:8, 27)?

c. Does the Bible say that in order to dwell in the New Jerusalem, you can't ever commit a sin?

Group Questions

1. Under what circumstances might someone's place in the New Jerusalem be removed (Revelation 22:19)?

2. Read Revelation 21:15–17.

a. How many furlongs will the New Jerusalem be (verse 16)?

b. How many cubits will its walls be (verse 17)?

3. Discuss the different elements of the New Jerusalem found in Revelation below:

   a. The Holy City (21:2):

   b. The Pearly Gates (21:12, 17–18, 21):

   c. The Foundations of Precious Stones (21:19–20):

   d. The Streets of Gold (21:18–21):

   e. The Lamb That Is the Light (21:11, 23):

   f. The Tree of Life (22:2):

   g. The River of Life (22:1–2):

DID YOU KNOW?

The New Jerusalem seen by John in his revelation had twelve gates with twelve angels at the gates, and the names of the twelve tribes of Israel written on them (Revelation 21:12). The walls had twelve foundation stones, each of which had the name of one of the twelve "apostles of the Lamb" (Revelation 21:14). The tree of life, in the midst of the city, bore twelve crops of fruit, a new crop each month (Revelation 22:2). The number twelve appears twenty-two times in the book of Revelation, a continual reference to the people of God in the Old (twelve tribes of Israel) and New (twelve apostles) Testaments.

Notes
1. F. W. Boreham, *Wisps of Wildfire* (London, UK: Epworth Press, 1924), 202–203.
2. J. B. Smith, *A Revelation of Jesus Christ* (Harrisonburg, VA: Herald Press, 1961), 289.
3. Charles F. Pfeiffer and Everett F. Harrison, eds., *The Wycliffe Bible Commentary* (Chicago, IL: Moody Press, 1962), 1522.
4. W. A. Criswell, *Expository Sermons on Revelation* (Grand Rapids, MI: Zondervan Publishing House, 1969), 130.

Leader's Guide

Thank you for your commitment to lead a group through *The Book of Signs*. Being a leader has its own rewards. You may discover that your walk with the Lord deepens through this experience. Throughout the study guide, your group will explore new topics and review study questions that encourage thought-provoking group discussion.

The lessons in this study guide are suitable for Sunday school classes, small-group studies, elective Bible studies, or home Bible study groups. Each lesson is structured to provoke thought and help you grow in your knowledge and understanding of God. There are multiple components in this section that can help you structure your lessons and discussion time, so make sure you read and consider each one.

Before You Begin

Before you begin each meeting, make sure you and your group are well-versed with the content of the lesson. Group members should have their own study guide so they can follow along and write in the study guide if need be. You may wish to assign the study guide lesson as homework prior to the meeting of the group and then use the meeting time to discuss the lesson.

To ensure that everyone has a chance to participate in the discussion, the ideal size for a group is around eight to ten people. If there are more than ten people, try to break up the bigger group into smaller subgroups. Make sure the members are committed to participating each week, as this will help create stability and help you better prepare the structure of the meeting.

At the beginning of the study each week, start the session with a question to challenge group members to think about the issues you will be discussing. The members can answer briefly, but the goal is to have an idea in their mind as you go over the lesson. This allows the group members to become engaged and ready to interact with the group.

After reviewing the lesson, try to initiate a free-flowing discussion. Invite group members to bring questions and insights they may have discovered to the next meeting, especially if they were unsure of the meaning of some parts of the lesson. Be prepared to discuss how biblical truth applies to the world we live in today.

Weekly Preparation

As the group leader, here are a few things you can do to prepare for each meeting:

- *Make sure you are thoroughly familiar with the material in the lesson.* Make sure you understand the content of the lesson so you know how to structure group time and are prepared to lead group discussion.

- *Decide, ahead of time, which questions you want to discuss.* Depending on how much time you have each week, you may not be able to reflect on every question. Select specific questions that you feel will evoke the best discussion.

- *Take prayer requests.* At the end of your discussion, take prayer requests from your group members and pray for each other.

Structuring the Discussion Time

If you need help in organizing your time when planning your group Bible study, the following schedule, for sixty minutes and ninety minutes, can give you a structure for the lesson:

Section	60 Minutes	90 Minutes
WELCOME: Members arrive and get settled	5 minutes	10 minutes
GETTING STARTED QUESTION: Prepares the group for interacting with one another	10 minutes	10 minutes
MESSAGE: Review the lesson	15 minutes	25 minutes
DISCUSSION: Discuss group study questions	25 minutes	35 minutes
PRAYER AND APPLICATION: Final application for the week and prayer before dismissal	5 minutes	10 minutes

As the group leader, it is up to you to keep track of the time and keep things moving along according to your schedule. If your group is having a good discussion, don't feel the need to stop and move on to the next question. Remember, the purpose is to pull together ideas and share unique insights on the lesson. Make time each week to discuss how to apply these truths to living for Christ today.

The purpose of discussion is for everyone to participate, but don't be concerned if certain group members are more quiet—they may be internally reflecting on the questions and need time to process their ideas before they can share them.

Group Dynamics

Leading a group study can be a rewarding experience for you and your group members—but that doesn't mean there won't be challenges. Certain members may feel uncomfortable discussing topics that they consider very personal and might be afraid of being called on. Some members might have disagreements on specific issues. To help prevent these scenarios, consider the following ground rules:

- If someone has a question that may seem off topic, suggest that it is discussed at another time, or ask the group if they are okay with addressing that topic.

- If someone asks a question you don't know the answer to, confess that you don't know and move on. If you feel comfortable, invite other group members to give their opinions or share their comments based on personal experience.

- If you feel like a couple of people are talking much more than others, direct questions to people who may not have shared yet. You could even ask the more dominating members to help draw out the quiet ones.

- When there is a disagreement, encourage the group members to process the matter in love. Invite members from opposing sides to evaluate their opinions and consider the ideas of the other members. Lead the group through Scripture that addresses the topic, and look for common ground.

When issues arise, encourage your group to think of Scripture: "Love one another" (John 13:34), "If it is possible, as far as it depends on you, live at peace with everyone" (Romans 12:18 NIV), and "Be quick to listen, slow to speak and slow to become angry" (James 1:19 NIV).

About
Dr. David Jeremiah and Turning Point

Dr. David Jeremiah is the founder of Turning Point, a ministry committed to providing Christians with sound Bible teaching relevant to today's changing times through radio and television broadcasts, audio series, books, and live events. Dr. Jeremiah's common-sense teaching on topics such as family, prayer, worship, angels, and biblical prophecy forms the foundation of Turning Point.

David and his wife, Donna, reside in El Cajon, California, where he serves as the senior pastor of Shadow Mountain Community Church. David and Donna have four children and twelve grandchildren.

In 1982, Dr. Jeremiah brought the same solid teaching to San Diego television that he shares weekly with his congregation. Shortly thereafter, Turning Point expanded its ministry to radio. Dr. Jeremiah's inspiring messages can now be heard worldwide on radio, television, and the Internet.

Because Dr. Jeremiah desires to know his listening audience, he travels nationwide holding ministry rallies and spiritual enrichment conferences that touch the hearts and lives of many people. According to Dr. Jeremiah, "At some point in time, everyone reaches a turning point; and for every person, that moment is unique, an experience to hold onto forever. There's so much changing in today's world that sometimes it's difficult to choose the right path. Turning Point offers people an understanding of God's Word as well as the opportunity to make a difference in their lives."

Dr. Jeremiah has authored numerous books, including *Escape the Coming Night* (Revelation), *The Handwriting on the Wall* (Daniel), *Overcoming Loneliness*, *Prayer—The Great Adventure*, *God in You* (Holy Spirit), *When Your World Falls Apart*, *Slaying the Giants in Your Life*, *My Heart's Desire*, *Hope for Today*, *Captured by Grace*, *Signs of Life*, *What in the World Is Going On?*, *The Coming Economic Armageddon*, *I Never Thought I'd See the Day!*, *God Loves You: He Always Has—He Always Will*, *Agents of the Apocalypse*, *Agents of Babylon*, *Revealing the Mysteries of Heaven*, *People Are Asking . . . Is This the End?*, *A Life Beyond Amazing*, and *Overcomer*.

STAY CONNECTED TO
DR. DAVID JEREMIAH

Take advantage of two great ways to let Dr. David Jeremiah give you spiritual direction every day! Both are absolutely FREE.

Turning Points Magazine and Devotional

Receive Dr. David Jeremiah's magazine, *Turning Points*, each month:

- Thematic study focus
- 48 pages of life-changing reading
- Relevant articles
- Special features
- Daily devotional readings
- Bible study resource offers
- Live event schedule
- Radio & television information

Daily Turning Point E-Devotional

Start your day off right! Find words of inspiration and spiritual motivation waiting for you on your computer every morning! Receive a daily e-devotion communication from David Jeremiah that will strengthen your walk with God and encourage you to live the authentic Christian life.

There are two easy ways to sign up for these free resources from Turning Point. Visit us online at www.DavidJeremiah.org and select "Subscribe to Daily Devotional by Email" or visit the home page and find Daily Devotional to subscribe to your monthly copy of *Turning Points*.

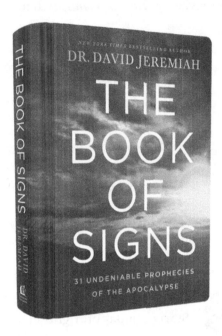